To Shana,
Carol Bengle Gilbert

en route to
Knockaderry

Carol Bengle Gilbert

En Route to Knockaderry is a geneaological memoir, reliant in part upon the memories of people who often didn't share common experience. I have done my utmost to record events acccurately. Compiling a genealogy involves educated judgments. Representations of ancestral relationships and life stories should not be taken as irrefutable fact; rather they should be understood as good-faith depictions of the genealogist's current state of understanding, using her available tools and experience.

ISBN 979-8-988105-60-2

9 798988 105602

52199 >

Title page photograph: Mary Daly Corcoran (1868-1938).

"Both justice and decency require that we should bestow upon our forefathers an honorable remembrance."
- Thucydides

To Nanny for telling me the stories that would pique my curiosity and for instilling in me a devotion to my Irish ancestry. To all of my forebears, especially those who struggled, with little to sustain them— you earned my deepest respect and admiration by book's end. To my children Andrew, Cynthia, and Amy Gilbert, for whom I wrote this book.

MUST READ!

AN IMPORTANT NOTE ABOUT THIS BOOK'S GENEALOGICAL FOUNDATION

Piecing together a family history is an art. The most important skill required for this endeavor is flexibility. The stories our grandparents told us may turn out to be kernels of what was, stirred into a soup of assumptions. It's hard to let go of stories we've believed since childhood, but unless we're willing, we can't faithfully document our ancestry.

The thrill of accomplishment sounds another warning bell. Just as we need to adapt "truths" we've been told to realities before our eyes, we can't let our excitement at illusory successes stand in the way of accuracy. We easily attach to antics of the ancestors we find and when the occasional presumptive forebear turns out not to be related after all, we have to relinquish him to his rightful family, even if we temporarily lose a tree limb or two in the process.

This book reflects the changing reality experienced as a genealogical history is uncovered. The human mind is prone to fill gaps with reason, but history and reason are not always compatible, and our story changes as we fill in actual facts to replace conjecture that slipped in unnoticed. This story also exposes the fallibility of bringing too much of our contemporary experience into the lives of those who lived in times when knowing one's birth year wasn't useful and the spelling of one's name was of little consequence. You'll notice that the spellings of family names in this book will vary depending on who's using them and where, just as they did in life.

For the reader's convenience, all dates in this book correspond with the calendar currently in use, and geo-political designations are described using present-day boundaries. Like some people you will read about herein, sourcing got the boot, in this case into the index— don't you hate the distraction of in-text sourcing? The one exception is direct quotes, in which case there's a footnote identifying the source number for ease of reference.

CHAPTER 1

NANNY'S STORIES

I set out for Knockaderry without the slightest inkling that Knockaderry existed. And who would know about such a place? A one-street townland an ocean away from home. A townland whose name Knockaderry, meaning Hill of the Oak Wood, is about as unique as the name O'Brien or Daly. The particular Knockaderry awaiting my arrival sits in Molahiffe Parish in County Kerry on the west coast of Ireland. County Kerry, an Atlantic-facing collection of peninsulas and inlets with stunning vistas, incongruously one of the most mountainous regions in Ireland. Home to the Daly clan, with their Mamies and Julias, Daniels and Timothys, multitude of Elizabeths and the occasional Patrick or Norah.

My route to Knockaderry was neither direct nor obvious. It wound through diverse countries and peoples and wove through centuries of soldier-adventurers, colonists and revolutionaries, millhands, detectives, royalty and protectorates, and a lone pushcart vendor. They lived in ramshackle cottages, convents, castles, and tenements. When times became hard, one of my forebears might appear suddenly on a sibling's doorstep, suitcase in hand, announcing their intent to move in. Or they would return north or head south or west or cross an ocean in steerage seasarching for what they didn't have. For some, times were always hard. Others were dealt a fair hand.

You could say my journey began in my elementary years when an odd collection of relatives I mostly never met joined us for supper or teatime. Nanny brought them, and the only way to keep track of which were alive and which dead was to attend to the supplication glued to the names of those departed as if they had always been called Baby-Ella-May-God-Rest-Her-Soul or Daniel-Francis-May-God-Rest-His-Soul. Who was yet living and who long passed seemed a mere technicality as the quotidian experience of those with beating hearts was so blanketed with Secrecy, and conducted at such a distance from the kitchen with the red and gray formica table where we gathered for supper and tea time, that my chances of encountering members of either group appeared about equal. Nanny's stories gave me a sense we were connected to someone, somewhere, but as I mulled those connections, Suspicion summoned up Shame, countering my efforts at mustering Pride.

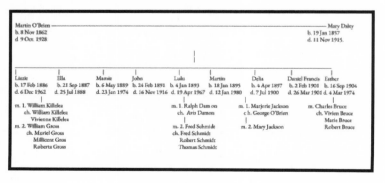

What did I know of the lives of my great these and those?

- There was the time one of Nanny's older sisters— I think it was Lulu, née Julia-the-umpteenth— dropped their mother's rosary beads in the sewer on the way home from school. The O'Brien girls scrambled to fetch a sanitation worker, beseeching him to dig them out, with Mama-May-God-Rest-Her-Soul none the wiser. This was probably sometime between the 1890's and the early aughts.
- Nanny's sister Lizzie had a husband who poked himself with a pencil and died of blood poisoning. Nanny never forgot the danger a simple pencil might pose, nor dared her pencil-leery grandchildren lose sight of it.
- One night, Nanny and her other sisters shook their sister Mamie awake, yelling "Wake up! The house is on fire!" Because it was. But Mamie wasn't interested. "Let it burn," she told them, and rolled over to go back to sleep.
- Twenty-five-year-old John-May-God-Rest-His-Soul was so close to his mother, his heart broke altogether a year after she passed in the Spanish Flu Epidemic of 1918. As we sipped our tea and aimed our forks at "just a taste" of pie circa 1967, Nanny lamented this brother's death as if it were yesterday, and with the same intensity as she mourned her sister Baby-Delia-May-God-Rest-Her-Soul, who succumbed to whooping cough— or maybe it was

diphtheria— in 1900, four years before Nanny herself came into the world.

In point of fact, Mary Daley O'Brien's death certificate is dated November 11, 1915. Cause of death: heart disease. John died a year later, but in an inexplicable twist for a man dead of a broken heart, spent his final days in a tuberculosis sanatorium. The influenza pandemic was two years on the horizon. I didn't know these facts then. The stories Nanny told me were Gospel. Unraveling the yarn of reality from the strands of fiction braided throughout occurred years later on the long, long road to Knockaderry.

At the beginning: I descended from destitute farmers digging among the rocks and tenement dwellers living hand-to-mouth, ne'er-do-wells, and impoverished mill workers. The whole lot of them dropouts. On my mother's side, there was the potato famine as the impetus for migration. On my father's, the lure of menial jobs sent my ancestors yo-yoing up and down the Eastern seaboard from Québec to Indian Orchard, Palmer, Massachusetts and back. In my immediate family, Nanny had an eighth grade education, while my father dropped out of tenth grade, and my mother finished tenth grade but didn't make it to eleventh. Our statistics did not hint at greatness. Yet, maybe there was someone, somewhere in my lineage, worthy of admiration for their social standing, someone with enough gumption to have overcome obstacles of birth and chosen a life path peppered with accomplishments? I kept a lookout but saw no encouraging signs. My forebears were the objects in sentences, not the subjects.

When anyone in Nanny's extended family lacked for work, lost a spouse, or suffered any other calamity, they packed up their kids and clothes and showed up on another family member's stoop, never doubting obligation or welcome. In autumn 1928, the Hungry Hill home in Springfield, Massachusetts of Nanny's eldest sister Lizzie became the refuge of choice for O'Briens down on their luck, filling the place to overflow capacity. Their widowed Pa, Martin O'Brien, had moved in with twice-widowed Lizzie and her five young children two years earlier upon his retirement from the Linden Paper mill where he'd eked out a living, but not a retirement nest egg, in those pre-Social Security times. Nanny, pregnant with my mother, joined the flock while her husband Charlie (or "Brucie" as he was sometimes called) took an extended trip to New York in search of work. Her sister Lulu, toting children Avis and Freddie, accompanied Nanny from Hartford while Lulu's second husband Fred ("Schmidty") stayed behind to work. Prior to the migration, Nanny and Charlie had been living with Lulu and Fred, and they would return to that arrangement sometime after my mother's birth. What was remarkable about this particular confluence, beyond its size, was the unfortunate timing. As Nanny's pregnancy progressed through its eighth month, her young nieces Millicent, Muriel, and Roberta returned home from elementary school one day to discover their grandfather dead in his chair, felled by a heart attack. Nanny's sisters Lizzie and Lulu, worried about grief's effect on her pregnancy, conspired to hide their father's death from her for the ensuing seven weeks. But for her seven-year-old niece Avis breaking the code of silence, there's no telling how or when Nanny might have learned of her father's death despite sharing the same household.

With this history, it was disconcerting, but not surprising, when Nanny expected us to house her grown son, my Uncle Bobby or, in later years, her sister Mamie. Bobby lasted the better part of a year— during which time Nanny slept in my bed and I slept on the floor— until he drank my father's aftershave. My mother gave Mamie the bum's rush almost as soon as she stepped out of the taxi, dispatching her and her single suitcase back to her one room flat with a hot plate and communal bathroom to await nursing home arrangements. My poor teenage sister Jan was collected and deposited in the same place, expected without any preparation whatsoever to oversee for an indeterminate time the needs of a great-aunt she barely knew and whose mind and body had seen better days. They shared their time with school children gathered outside the window, visible to no one but Mamie. She seemed to enjoy chatting with them, Jan recalled, but intermittently shushed them or chided that Sister would be angry at them for going outdoors. In her working years, Mamie had had a soft spot for children though she had none of her own.[1] After Nanny's regular visits, Mamie would send her home with 50 cents to buy cupcakes for the grandchildren. This long-past history, only vaguely remembered, did not ease Jan's stay in Mamie's dimly lit, sparse room in a malodorous building populated with leering

---

[1] Devoutly religious, Mamie (aka Mary, Mary Ellen, Nellie) had aspired to become a nun, but without the means to contribute to a convent dowry, she was unable to do so.

and stumbling men, and women holding on to life by a thread.

Our relatives did not come with warning labels, instructions, or even advance greetings. So it happened one night in 1966 when I was eight years old, just after the 11 o'clock news ended, someone started banging nonstop on the window to our kitchen door as we prepared for bed upstairs. Nanny sent me to see who it was. I stepped far enough into the kitchen to determine that I didn't recognize whoever it was and scuttled back upstairs to report my findings. Nanny went downstairs then with me trailing her, and when she saw the stranger still banging away, she exclaimed, "What's the matter with you? Why didn't you open the door for your Uncle Bobby?" as she dashed across the kitchen to welcome him into our home and her embrace. Uncle Bobby was only a name to me. He'd been away in the Army thirteen years and up until that moment, I had no reason to believe he was anywhere other than Vietnam, let alone on our back porch. And that's when I learned he'd be taking Nanny's bedroom and Nanny would be in my bed until whenever. Whenever might have been forever, but for my father's aftershave.

Despite his official ban from our house by my father, Uncle Bobby got many a free ride back in a police car. It was possible to avoid spending time in a lockup if an address could be provided, and on those mornings and afternoons, while Dad was away at work, Nanny's will dominated. Bobby slept in our house, with the understanding he'd be roused, fed, and shuffled out of sight by 5 p.m. All the while, Nanny's faith in Bobby's caliber never wavered. She encouraged him to get another job and to find a way to bring home the woman he'd dated in Vietnam, assuring him, "If you love her, we'll love her."

Now if you're intent on pursuing the springboard to my genealogical quest, you might take note of the fledgling hop-steps taken in the pre-internet days to discover an ancestor with any hint of competency in their history, anyone whose existence would bolster the untested notion that I was a person of substance. I looked scattershot and often not in the right places. I pursued realities that turned out to be fictional and bypassed truths I found preposterous. I sometimes refused to believe my ancestors capable of bearing particular characteristics on insubstantial grounds, captured in scenarios like this one: Many men shared my maternal grandfather's common name, Charles Bruce, and I didn't have his death year or city. This complicated finding his records in the Social Security Death Index. The unmanageable list had to be pruned; some of those Charlies had to go. While I had no idea what my grandfather's middle name was, surely it was not Otis! So Charles Otis Bruce got the heave-ho without a second glance, along with Charles Bruce who died on a Caribbean island, because my Charlie no doubt couldn't afford such luxury and besides who would he know there? Charles Otis and Caribbean Charlie disappeared in the company of tens of other Charles Bruces suffering a variety of real or imagined quality control deficits, substantially delaying my discovery of maternal grandfather Charles o. Bruce's date and place of death.

I wrote letters, mailed in requests for birth, marriage, and death certificates, forced to guess a five year time frame for each search. Weeks, sometimes months, elapsed before return correspondence arrived. Dead end piled upon dead end, alongside occasional successes. My devotion to my by then long-deceased Nanny (May God Rest Her Soul) with her constant profession of loyalty to an Ireland she never visited made finding my 100% Irish history on my maternal side— with a suspected touch of British blood contributed by Charlie (who was 100% Irish himself)— my highest priority. But the direct path was buried in brambles, burned out for miles, sunk in a swamp, trampled, with signposts mismarked, and obscured by relentless gray skies. So I took the roundabout course. And decades later, here I am, close, but still en route to Knockaderry.

CHAPTER 2

BUT HE'S A ROGUE!

Uncovering "Otis" was the least of the indignities I would encounter when it came to names. There were the direct assaults, names so odd and unpleasant they blighted the leaves of my family tree: Egnizose, Arethusa, Verelia, Urania, Superan, Elphege, Alcide, Ovila, and Deodatus. There were the sneak attacks, name variants that hid among the records defying detection with their artful ruses: Jeremiah disguised as Darby, Diarmud, Dermot or Demetrius; while Delia might be lurking under the pretenses of Bridget or Bridie. The peculiar names and the sneaky names were entirely outdone by the names that didn't belong to their owner at all, instead adopted willy-nilly as if to thwart my search. Narcisse moonlighted as Nelson. His second wife Célina, who wasn't a Célina but an Archange, apparently traded her real moniker for that of Nelson-Narcisse's first wife, putting the notion in my head that he was unable to adapt to a new companion with an unfamiliar name. And there was my own mother, whose informal name change at age twelve from Charlene to Marie posed sufficient challenges without the discovery of a birth certificate in the never-used name of Beverly. Finally, there were the outlandish traditions that obscured even the most respectable of names, the Québecois creating an indistinct mass of Josephs in the records offices by adding that honorarium to the beginning of every boy's name while doing the same with Marie for the girls. This custom may have produced minimal consternation in its familiar Québec environment, but it was responsible for serious wreckage in the records offices here in the United States where the quaint practice was generally unknown.

Date discrepancies were rampant, with some conflicts oozing a motivation trail and others defying explanation. The mixing and matching of records with variant names, spellings, and ages made for a complex web of uncertainty about many of my results. Thus, it was a relief to connect with Jacques Bengle, an elderly, third cousin who had spent years researching my father's family from the Canadian side and persuaded me to allow that my Bengle collection might include Bingels, Bangals, and Bingks. While meeting Jacques wasn't the beginning of my journey, it was the propulsion that transformed much of my early research from vague possibilities into meaningful results. And despite this preliminary emphasis on my paternal line, for lack of information about my maternal one, these discoveries provided the roadmap that would eventually lead to Knockaderry.

My first major achievement, naturally, given my skepticism that anyone dangling from the branches of my tree might be respectable, was discovery of the family rogue. Now we had our rummies and ne'er-do-wells, we had a real-life mystery in the dubious comings and goings (voluntary and otherwise) of my mother's estranged sister Vivien, we had enough eccentrics to populate our own side show. We even had a murder victim and an unconfirmed international smuggler. But a rogue? That role was open, and who better to fill those jackboots than my fourth great-grandfather Count Philipp II Ernst zu Schaumburg-Lippe?

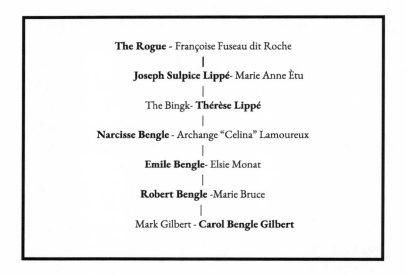

The Rogue - Françoise Fuseau dit Roche
|
Joseph Sulpice Lippé- Marie Anne Ètu
|
The Bingk- **Thérèse Lippé**
|
Narcisse Bengle - Archange "Celina" Lamoureux
|
Emile Bengle- Elsie Monat
|
Robert Bengle -Marie Bruce
|
Mark Gilbert - **Carol Bengle Gilbert**

Accustomed to ancestors who toiled in the mills or mopped floors, I perceived in Philipp II Ernst an astonishing upgrade at first blush. While not a king or prince, by God, he had a title! A title! Philipp II Ernst generated excitement for another reason; he was the first traceable link between Europe and North America, the founder of a North American branch of the family. In 1975, while I was occupied seeking my first life upgrade by filling out college and scholarship applications, Pierre Beaudin, the industrious husband of an unknown 5th cousin in Montréal, published a thousand year history of La Famille Lippé. Jacques alerted me to Bengles creeping into the Lippe lineage in the early 1800s with the marriage of Thérèse Lippé to Wilhelm Bingk. By dusting off my French literary skills, I might net myself some royal underpinnings.

The history started out promising enough, with Arminius foiling an attempted invasion by the Roman Legions of Varus into the Lippe territory in 9 B.C. thereby changing the course of European history. I'm no devotee of European history, but ancestral lands sounded tantalizing so I kept reading. I ran into the epitome of name-terror, a man with neither a first nor a last name. Wittekind, it turns out, is a kenning, or metaphor, meaning "child of the wood." He wasn't going to be easy to research, this no-name-described-only-by-metaphor, so it was inevitable *he'd* turn out to be the founder of the House of Lippe. On the plus side, his mug made its way into a painting at the Palace of Versailles, depicting him as he submitted to Charlemagne, unfortunately undoing the life's work of Arminius.[2]

Skimming through the names in the Lippe history, I landed on Simon V Lippe, protector of Martin Luther, a startling development in a family staunchly and forever

---

[2] Arminius fought off Roman legions attempting to subject the territory to Rome's rule so effectively that the survival of the Roman Empire was at stake.

Catholic on both sides with the single exception of Protestant Charlie. Reading further, I bumped into Sofie, the daughter of Simon VI— a Lippe-Biesterfeld, a distinct line of Lippes— who married a reigning prince by the name of Ludwig d'Anhalt-Kothen. Sofie and Ludwig, along with my own Counts of Schaumberg-Lippe and the Dukes of Saxe-Weimar-Eisenach, became protectors of composer Johann Sebastian Bach and his family.

Something was amiss. How could it be that these Lippes laid claim to ancestral lands, fancy titles, and enough spare cash to support Martin Luther and the whole family of Johann Sebastian Bach? That guy had 20 kids! When I was in kindergarten, Mrs. Danio, the crossing guard, brought me shoes after weeks of seeing my toes poking out. Not infrequently, we rummaged for pennies, then slunk over to Finast to pick out the cheapest mound of hamburger in the display case to accompany the worst mashed potatoes history has ever known, inflicted upon us by my culinarily-challenged mother. What forces determined some in the Lippe line should have castles and live symphonies while my lot gets decrepit footwear, cut-rate hamburger, and dastardly mashed potatoes? There was a grave injustice here, and my next mission was finding out who was responsible.

Like many noble-born of his generation, Philipp II Ernst spoke French fluently. In case he's listening from beyond the grave, let me share some delightful French words. "Espiègle!" is a favorite when encountering a rogue of historical proportions.[3] In a pinch, shouting "Quel voyou!"

[3] Espiègle!: Rogue!

will also do the trick.[4] "Sacripant!" requires an infusion of gruffness to achieve its full potency.[5] All of these words precisely describe Philipp II Ernst. Because I hold narrator's privilege in my pocket, I'm captioning his image "La Fripouille Fétide de la Famille Lippé." [6]

Not only did this rogue deprive me of my rightful heritage by sneaking over to the Americas like a common criminal, he committed scoundrelly acts unlike any others who came before or after. I'm not talking about a little pirating or bootlegging here. Philipp II Ernst committed bigamy. Twice. He abandoned his wife, Dutchess Ernestine Albertine, and three of their four children— the eldest died before His Roguishness thought to abandon him— precipitously circa 1762. Despite having attained the rank of Colonel and Adjutant-General in his own army, he did the unthinkable, fleeing the European Continent as an enlisted soldier in the army of his English cousin King George III. Yes, *that* King George, America's favorite. Once relocated to Canada, while still married to the Dutchess, he almost immediately exchanged vows with 22-year-old Françoise Fuseau dit Roche and fathered seven more children he would soon enough abandon. Abandoning two wives and ten children was insufficiently knavish for my ancestral reprobate, so he faked his own death before heading back to Germany to commit bigamy again by marrying Princess Juliane de von

---

[4] Quel Voyou!: What a rogue!
[5] Sacripant!: Rogue!
[6] La Fripouille Fétide de la Famille Lippé: The Stinking Rogue of the Lippé Family.

Hessen-Phillipsthal-Barchfeld with whom he fathered yet four more children.

Upon discovering my long-craved royal ancestor actually existed, but in the form of a rogue, I had to decide, hold my head a little higher or cover my face and run?

CHAPTER 3

WORSE THAN A MERCENARY

Rogue-weary, but reinvigorated by having spotted a Bingk[7] in the Lippe history as foretold, I changed gears. I was going to find that Bingk! Maybe he'd prove to be my first Bengle ancestor in the New World. With Canadian genealogy resources at his disposal, Jacques beat me to the first clue. He mailed me a book, *Les Mercenaires Allemands au Québec*, by Jean-Pierre Wilhelmy. The title made my nerves tingle. This wasn't going to find me a humanitarian or philanthropist ancestor, a statesman, or even a zookeeper. Not with the title *German Mercenaries in Québec*.

---

[7] The Bingk, it turns out, after years of our knowing him as such, was never a Bingk at all. Using a magnifying glass, Jacques one day discovered that what appeared to be a "K" was actually an "l" and "e" superimposed, making him just another Bingle.

For some reason, it concerned Monsieur Wilhemy that Canada might forget the 30,000 mercenaries Canadians had theretofore omitted from their history, and he felt compelled to come up with a fix. It didn't take long to uncover why. The Suspect admits his ulterior motive on page 11: one of these mercenaries was his own ancestor. The entry "Bengle" is on page 13. I don't know what was more grating, that this Bengle, a mercenary, was not the kind of ancestor needed to shore up my rogue-tarnished family tree or that he was paid by King George III— that pesky King George, again— to help stave off the American Revolution.

In the same way that the Québecois have a Joseph problem in their records offices, the Germans are overrun with Johannes-somebody-or-others. So, learning that the Bengle referenced in the mercenary list was identified in an update as "Bengle/Bingle/Beingle/Pingle, Johannes" gave me indigestion, not guidance. The search was on for any shred of exculpatory evidence. It took years to find Adam Bangle's will, but the investigation resulting from discovery of that document provided the key to establishing that the wretched mercenary Johannes was not my ancestor.

Adam Bangle was the grandfather of the Bingk. Tagged Johann Adam Bingle by his Johann-obsessed culture, he came to be known as Adam Bangle once in the New World. He emigrated from Dirmstein, Germany to Philadelphia on the ship Jeneffer in 1764, upending the family immigration narrative depicting our "American" arrivals as occurring in the late 19th century. Adam was naturalized in 1768. He made his home in upstate New York in the Palatine district on the banks of Mohawk River before the war began. *Not* a mercenary! His wife and daughter immigrated with him, as did son Johann Adam, called John. Also *not* a mercenary! His younger son Wilhem, born after their arrival, would one day become the Bingk's father. Not a mercenary bone in his body. Momentarily, I was relieved.

Finding out your ancestor isn't a mercenary should be cause for celebration. It was for a short time. Then I discovered the events preceding Lampman's Battle, undoubtedly the most perplexing battle precursor in world history. And a very bad sign for my poor, struggling family tree which was already sagging under the weight of a rogue.

Adam and his family were Loyalists, disinclined to commit to the Patriot cause when the American Revolution loomed. He and his four sons, including my third great-grandfather Wilhem, joined the King's Royal Regiment of New York under Captain Alexander McDonnell. Fighting for the British. Against American independence. A relative or five fighting on the wrong side of the war might be cause for alarm in some circumstances, but to someone overcome with relief at escaping an ancestral mercenary their indiscretion in choosing sides barely registered. Yet there was a whisper of unquiet about these ancestors, starting with Adam's will. Written during his final illness in 1799, that will excluded only John, among his surviving children, as a residual beneficiary of his estate upon his wife's death. Although a previous distribution of assets to John as the eldest son was one likely reason, the exclusion aroused my suspicions. Maybe it was the evasive language, disinheriting John for unstated "reasons known to him." The specification that John was outside the province also hinted at possible estrangement. So I kept digging and at the bottom of a miserable genealogical pit discovered the events culminating in Lampman's Battle.

Calling the lead-up to Lampman's Battle confusing is a laughable understatement. People with the same name faced off on opposite sides, and family members prepared for battle against each other. Some of the fighters involved weren't in any military. And some, including a military officer, switched sides. Deciphering the cast of characters sent my brain into convulsions. But in the end, it didn't really matter. The horrifying truth is that Adam and John, with pernicious motives, joined a raiding party intent on attacking their former neighbor, now Patriot, Johannes Bellinger's house.

Raiding parties were common on both sides and often involved starving and bedraggled forces attacking the homes of former neighbors. Typically, these raiding parties plundered the homes for food and other supplies, took able-bodied prisoners, and set the house on fire. With some degree of frequency, they murdered the residents, most often when their attacks were vigorously defended. But this raiding party had worse designs. Had their plan not been impeded, they intended from the outset to murder the Bellinger parents, steal their belongings, and kidnap their six daughters for sexual exploitation.[8] The would-be raiders allegedly had

---

[8] Although the source of this information is virulent in hatred of Loyalists, the account is supported in part by an affidavit from a turncoat military officer establishing that these men were in the area together though it

decided in advance which young man was to take which Bellinger daughter. Adam would not likely have been allocated one of the girls— he was 62 years old and referred to by the others as Old Bangle— but there's no indication that he spoke out against the plan. Did his son's character cause a rift between them, leading to his disinheritance, or were they of the same mind and the disinheritance due to previous gifts? Either way, the boughs of the family tree are bent to the breaking point after the addition of these ancestors.

***

It was only a matter of time until I began to wonder if my variant, unrelated strands of ancestors ever came face to face. While I wouldn't know it for years yet, down in those troublesome Patriot strongholds, one of the aforementioned Charlie's forebears was Benjamin Tucker, Jr. In the dark of night on December 16, 1773, Benjamin, my 5th great-grandfather, and his buddies, some dressed as Native Americans bearing tomahawks, climbed aboard three ships docked at Griffin's Wharf in Boston Harbor. They hatcheted open 342 chests of tea, then tossed them overboard to protest unjust taxation. By guess who? Why, it's that ever-intrusive King George again, hiding everywhere from your broom closet to your underwear drawer, popping out to startle you with his unwelcome initiatives.

---

omits mention of any intended raid. The information about their intent came from a man who was part of the group and had a change of heart and voluntarily abandoned them to issue a warning. He was genuinely attracted to one of the Bellinger sisters and later married her.

Did my miscreant forebears not realize the effect their little skirmishes might have on their progeny? We could have been preempted, all thanks to that boogeyman King George III and a lack of foresight by the likes of Billy and Benny.

CHAPTER 4

THE ROYAL BRUTE

Caught up in the misdeeds of pokes-his-nose-into-everything-King-George-III, perhaps you missed an unnerving calculus. The Rogue is my fourth great-grandfather. King George III is the Rogue's cousin. This gives me highly unfavorable odds of waking up one morning to discover that Royal Brute eating breakfast in my tree.

King George III, The Royal Brute. King George III in Coronation Robes by Allan Ramsay. Public domain.

CHAPTER 5

SECRETS BEGONE!

Forever a book-lover, I'm ecstatic to find my
ancestors' names in print provided the subject isn't
mercenaries or raiding parties. I could not have imagined
growing up that my family was of a kind about which any
book or part thereof would be written, let alone books plural.
My closest whiff of ancestor in the pages of a book followed
my parents' deaths. My mother, the woman who responded
to simple questions about family as if we were trying to wrest
away State Secrets with tongs seasoned in the firepit, had gone
to her grave without cracking. I felt the wind of doors
slamming in my face. I saw slips of life stories float into the
sky, out of reach forever. Fragmented bits of biography,
dreams and disappointments, connections made and missed,
never to be pieced together to answer the questions burning
inside me. I grilled my poor father as if I were a one-woman

interrogation squad extracting those State Secrets my mother hid so determinedly. And then, through causes unrelated, my father died. My mother's past was lost... unless it could be captured up in Gill.

Up in Gill. Words I'd heard without grasping their significance. Were it up to my mother, I'd be lucky to know her name, let alone disquieting personal details like where she'd lived or who she'd known. I knew from Nanny's stories they'd lived up in Gill for a time. Never "in" Gill, always "up in Gill." When Nanny spoke about their days up in Gill, Gill seemed mythical and impossibly distant. Until my father died, it never occurred to me to look it up. Surprise! It was in our backyard, a 45 minute drive from home, a hill community settled on old Nipmuc territory, barely inside the Massachusetts-Vermont boundary. Forty-five minutes, yet almost three-quarters of a century away.

During World War II, Nanny and Charlie forgot one night to draw the blackout shades. In the morning, the Bruces were the talk of the town of Gill by those who'd seen the lone light up on the hill and apparently lacked for exciting conversation. For a sociology class once, I read about social stratification and hills. People with status on top, the bottom dwellers mired in poverty. Everything I'd absorbed about my family growing up pointed to our place at rock bottom. In a gully if there was one. Revisiting the blackout shade story gave me pause. Their light was up atop the hill. But when I arrived in Gill, there wasn't a trace of the family Bruce, or anyone who remembered them, up the hills or down. So I trudged through the snow into a nearby graveyard. It wasn't large. I found the Bruce grave without much effort. It was among the ones with the bigger headstones.

Gill presents the image of the stereotypical New England community with a whitewashed town square. In 2001, the shingled gray face of the Gill Store on the side of that square looked to be unchanged since World War II. The proprietor was a woman probably in her forties, and she had not heard of the Bruce family. Moving across the street, I found a small goldmine in the Town Hall. A resident had compiled the town history. In that compilation, I found a notation about my mother earning her Second Class badge as a teenage Girl Scout in May 1943. Even though I had been a Girl Scout, my mother never had shared her own experience in that organization. But the book revealed more. Charlie's father, also Charles Otis Bruce, a painter at the Mt. Hermon School, had been a Town Selectman for 22 years and a founding member of the Gill Community Club. Apparently, he died not long before Charlie and Nanny moved to town. My mother's Secrets were shaking loose. And Charlie's reputation as a ne'er-do-well from a no-account family was up for reconsideration.

The biggest Secrets enshrouding my mother's family swirled around Vivien (aka Charlotte), her estranged sister. Bruised by decades of curiosity crashing into

CLASSIFIED TOP SECRET

rebuffs, I considered my uncovering any scant detail about Vivien's life a shining accomplishment, unleashing untold emotional satisfaction. Like digging buried treasure. Secrets are the amateur genealogist's nemesis, and I came at this one with the force of a hundred Antigones.

Nanny never spoke of or to Vivien during my lifetime, except to weave a yarn so preposterous as to attract immediate disbelief even in gullible grandchildren. Who lets their neighbor move away with their baby daughter? What illness could have infected Nanny, Charlie, and newborn Vivien that would have stretched on for two years in the adults, making them unable to care for the ill-but-recovered baby? Suspicion prowled the perimeter of those rare mentions of Vivien, with Shame on its heels.

Long-gone Vivien returned to her birth family precipitously just before her sixteenth birthday with nary a word of warning but in time to be included as a one-liner in Gill's town history. And for reasons wedged into the bottom of the family vault, she and Nanny never spoke again once Nanny and Charlie separated a few years later, and Vivien moved to New York with her father. As Nanny and Charlie, though separated, never divorced and had adult children in common, there were occasions when they had reason to speak on the phone. Nanny would insist that my mother place the call and get her father on the line, rather than risk Vivien picking up the receiver.

Vivien was ~~four years~~ 22 months older than my mother, who was born in ~~1929~~ 1928. By the time I acquired my grandparents' marriage record, showing a 1924 marriage, I knew my mother's correct birth year. That four year span between her and Vivien fed Suspicion's innuendo about the truth of Vivien's birth circumstances only until Vivien's birth certificate with a 1927 birthdate surfaced. My father, Bob Bengle, hadn't known why Vivien was brought to live elsewhere as an infant. Nanny's niece (Lizzie's daughter) Roberta Gasteyer believed Vivien was taken to her grandmother because she was sickly and stood a better chance of survival in the country. Roberta's elder half-sister, Sr. Julia Frances Killelea, had a similar understanding about the illness, except in her telling, it was Charlie's father who took in the baby. The difference could be significant, since Charlie's mother died when Vivien was seven months old. With no immediate relatives left to hound, I zeroed in on finding Charlie's deceased sister's progeny. When that mission smoldered, defeat seemed inescapable.

Except... it was possible Vivien was still alive. I understood from my father that Vivien had stopped working after a bout of mental illness in adulthood and was supported by Charlie. Charlie's last known occupation was janitor, his savings potential dim. Assuming Vivien outlived Charlie, with no means of financial support upon his death, would Vivien have turned to public assistance? And would those records lead me to her? How could I break through the red tape to find out?

I can't reveal how— some Secrets need to be kept— but with red tape tattered at my ankles, I learned Vivien was deceased. With my next efforts, the slashed red tape piled up to my knees. Some of the information I would unearth came from Charlie's own mouth. Decades earlier, he'd said Nanny didn't want baby Vivien, so he brought her to his father. Charles, Sr. was too old and sick, at 58, to care for a baby and boarded her with a New York foster family, my source indicated. But Charlie also had leaked some intriguing new details. Vivien wasn't completely estranged from her family all those years. Charlie, whether by himself or with Nanny is not clear, had visited her in her foster home a few times. At 15, she quit school, ran away, and showed up on her parents' doorstep, a doorstep she apparently knew where to find. A runaway! That space in the family tree is ~~unoccupied~~ now filled.

Census research showed Vivien's foster home was not in New York, but in Leverett, Massachusetts. Since Leverett is on the doorstep of Gill where Charlie grew up, it's inconceivable he mistook Leverett for New York. His motive for misstating the location, if he did, is a mystery. I suspect he said nothing about New York at all and perhaps the listener, who was in New York, mistook Leverett Town, as the locale is often called, for the familiar-sounding Levittown, which is in New York.

At about the time of Vivien's relocation, the senior Charles Bruce suffered the death of his wife after losing his mother a year earlier. It's not surprising he didn't have the energy to single-handedly care for an infant and made other arrangements. As a longtime resident and Town Selectman in Gill, Charles, Sr. would have known most of the people in the small town, and that likely included members of the extended Graves and Williams families who lived there. Through his Selectman duties, he was also acquainted with Selectmen from the nearby towns including Leverett's S.M. Graves. It must have been through one of these links that he found Minnie "Effie" Hunt Williams Graves, the woman who became Vivien's foster mother.

Vivien lived with Effie Graves and her grown son Earl Williams. Earl married Evelyn Jackson in the early 1930s, and they started their own family, living together with his mother and Vivien. Their three daughters, Joyce, Rita, and Earla, completed the household. Effie supported herself by doing laundry out of her home, so any money provided her to care for Vivien undoubtedly came in handy.

Like the other children of Leverett, Vivien attended one-room schoolhouses, the North Leverett School for grades 1 to 4 and Moore's Corner Schoolhouse for grades 5 to 8. *10 to 1: Interviews with Leverett Scholars Who Attended One-Room Schoolhouses* is a compilation of interviews of town elders conducted by sixth graders in conjunction with the Leverett Historical Society in 2018. That publication contains a wealth of information about the schools at the time Vivien attended them. The primitive schoolhouses were heated only by a woodstove in the center of the room. They lacked plumbing, so the students retreated to outhouses when nature called. Moore's Corner Schoolhouse had a "two-seater" outhouse, with one side designated for girls, the other for boys. It stands to this day in the yard of the Leverett Historical Society which now owns the building that was once Moore's Corner Schoolhouse. In the early years, the school had only oil lamps for lighting; electricity arrived during the administration of Franklin Delano Roosevelt.

Every morning, the teacher would send two boys to a neighbor's house with pails to bring back drinking water while another student would be sent to the brook to fill a pail with washing water. Everyone drank from the same dipper and sometimes the brook water and well water became intermingled. In their rural community, the children played unsupervised in the road for recess until the teacher rang a cow bell or banged a ruler on the window to draw them back to the classroom. Dodgeball was a favorite game, and the children also played baseball with a taped-up ball or kickball or jacks. The lack of a swingset was no problem for the inventive children of North Leverett attending the Moore's Corner Schoolhouse. They used a grapevine as a substitute-—at least they did until some Nervous Nelly appeared with pruning shears and ruined their fun. It wasn't uncommon for the children to sneak down to the nearby brook, and the teacher would dispatch a reliable student to fetch the offenders. The children crossed the four-way intersection to leave notes for one another tucked into the crevices of an old chimney ruin adjacent to the grist mill kitty-corner across the road. When it snowed, the children of North Leverett sometimes traveled to school by sled.

In 1940, as Vivien entered adolescence, two people who'd played significant roles in her life died, Earl and her grandfather Charles O. Bruce, Sr. Two years later, in December 1942, Vivien dropped out of Amherst High School, which she professed to hate, telling the school officials she was going to work; other students from Leverett who attended Amherst about the same time described feeling uncomfortable among the Amherst students as well, due to bias against their rural background. Once Vivien quit school, she ran away from her Leverett foster home. Why she ran, we'll likely never know, but it was a troubled and insecure teenager who moved in with her birth family which was by then living in nearby Gill. She could never shake the feelings of disapproval not only by Nanny but also by her siblings, Marie and Bobby. From the time of her arrival, arguments dominated the Bruce household.

Apparently, Nanny liked Vivien no better the second time around. In Charlie's words, she tolerated her. Tolerated her, despite the risk of my mother and her younger brother Bobby being seduced into ruffianship. Once, only once, my mother slipped when I squeezed her for details about Vivien. I was about twelve and infatuated with the idea of a mystery sister dropping out of nowhere. My mother acknowledged hoping for a close relationship and having her hopes dashed. She and Vivien were very different, she said in a measured tone, lamenting that Vivien lacked the benefits of her own moral upbringing.[9] This left me the impression Vivien must have been stealing bubble gum or telling lies. What 15-year-old Vivien was actually doing was drinking heavily, and so was Charlie. At the telling of this story, he regretted his judgment. But those many years earlier, he had thought she'd

---

[9] Vivien's foster mother was a religious woman, and Vivien was active in the Graves family's church, the Moore's Corner Church. The Moore's Corner Church was non-denominational. It was established by a protégé of D.L. Moody, a friend of Vivien's grandfather you will learn more about later. From what can be ascertained looking back, it doesn't seem that Vivien lacked moral grounding, despite my mother's feelings about the subject.

be safer drinking in a bar alongside him than drinking on her own, so off they went together.

Before long, Vivien took up with a man and became pregnant, Charlie disclosed, her baby boy, my cousin, given up for adoption.[10] Funny thing about Suspicion— wait long enough and you can pin its fruits on somebody! A few years later, Charlie left Nanny, and Vivien went with him first to Queens and then to Newark, New Jersey, later to be followed by Bobby.

Five-foot-two, brown-haired and blue-eyed, Vivien preferred men's clothes to women's clothes and loved the outdoors. She had already sworn off drinking at 18, and was by this time devoting herself to making a home for her and Charlie, and for a time, Bobby. Though she took a full-time job on the assembly line in a zipper factory in Queens, where Charlie also worked, Charlie said she found it difficult to maintain focus indoors, no surprise given her childhood in the wooded hills of Massachusetts. She longed to live in the country and set her sights on upstate New York where Charlie bought her a house.

Some details are so personal, they belong in history's dustbins out of respect for their owners. Such are the particulars of Vivien's illness which appeared in the mid-late

---

[10] Without the adoption records to show the baby's birthdate, it's impossible to confirm whether Vivien perhaps ran away *because* she was pregnant or became pregnant once in Gill. Charlie said she was 15 when she became pregnant; she turned 16 only six weeks after withdrawing from Amherst High School. That leaves little time for her to have gotten to Gill and become pregnant, though it's certainly possible.

1950s soon after her move to her own house in Richford. In Richford, Vivien grew plants in her large greenhouse and cared for her old dog which had become blind. Before long, Charlie quit his job in Newark and moved in with her, concerned she was developing confusion and other signs of mental instability. She continued to struggle with her mental health, which may have kept her from returning to a formal job, despite her strong work ethic, though it's equally possible that her plan to run a greenhouse was her only intended employment. According to my father, Viven openly expressed her experiences in her mental health struggle, counter to the prevailing social winds of contempt and fear that kept most details of such illness in the shadows. Dad's observations dovetail with Charlie's description of Vivien as an unquestioning person content to accept life as it happened.

While Charlie's account may contain some errors, omissions, or rationalizations, and leaves gaping holes concerning the genesis of Nanny's feelings toward Vivien, overall it rings true. My uncloaking of a considerable portion of the Vivien secret bolstered my research bona fides. Knockaderry was getting closer even though I still had no idea it existed.

CHAPTER 6

ERRONEOUS, HERETICAL, *AND*

OBSTINATE

After some minor, preliminary friction, Nancy Waterman Joyce, one of my third great-grandmothers, proved a refreshing respite from my exposure to the Rogue and Adam Bangle's family. Nancy and Ira Joyce were parents to Isabel Joyce Bruce, Charlie's grandmother and wife of Charles O. Bascom Bruce. Nancys are a troublesome lot. The name Nancy was originally a diminutive-form of Ann. Not only is Ann ubiquitous, Ann infiltrates a wide variety of stand-alone names to create fusion names with endless options for nicknames, any of which could become a Nancy. Finding a Nancy at my latest genealogical wall promised delay and confusion.

It required perserverance to contend with Nancy, but she graciously forgave my frustrations and pointed me to one of my favorite ancestors, Richard Waterman. The road to Richard passed through Superan, Gideon, Abraham, Charles, Benjamin, and Nathaniel, a long road for sure, but I found a short-cut in New England's historical records, packaged in a book helpfully titled, *The Waterman Family, Vol III.*

Richard Waterman dealt the first blow to Charlie's professed ~~100% Irish~~ heritage, as reimagined by Nanny. Born in Nayland, Suffolk, England circa 1590, this Brit arrived in Salem, Massachusetts a mere nine years after the Mayflower docked for the first time at Plymouth Rock. Having accrued accolades for his marksmanship, Richard was recommended to the colony for venison procurement and wolf counter-offensives. But Richard soon expanded his repertoire. He took up canoe inspection, a vital service to forestall drownings in a society dependent on canoe-travel.

Richard Waterman (1590 -1673) - Bethiah ? (? -1680)

Nathaniel Waterman (1637-1711) - Susanna Carder (?)

Capt. Benjamin Waterman (?-1762) - ?

Charles Waterman (1705-1760) - Jemima Hawkins (1708-1781)

Abraham Waterman (1733-1818) - Anne Brown (1732-1817)

Gideon Waterman (1764-1848) - Sally Lee (1768-1852)

Superan Waterman (1800-1859) - Polly Smith (1799-?)

Ira Joyce (1810-1895) - Nancy Waterman (1825-1910)

Samuel O.B. Bruce (1842-1918) - Isabel Joyce (1850-1926)

Charles O. Bruce (1869-1940) - Blanche Whiteman (1882-1927)

Charles O. Bruce, Jr. (1905-1983) - Esther O'Brien (1904-1975)

Robert Bengle (1931-2001) - Marie Bruce Bengle (1928-1995)

Mark Gilbert (1952-2013) - Carol Bengle (1957-)

While admiring of Richard's marksmanship and canoe inspections, Salem's leaders were less fond of Richard's opinions. His certitude put them over the edge. The General Court of Massachusetts banished him and his family to Providence in March 1638 to join his friend and fellow free-thinker Roger Williams. Williams had bought land from the Narragansetts after his own banishment two years earlier for "spreading newe and dangerous opinions."

Digging deeper, I found nothing to alarm me in those shared opinions, not even at my most squeamish moments. Those banishment-inducing opinions held by Williams and Waterman read like a recitation of the United States Constitution. Equal protection of the laws. Freedom of religious belief for all, including Quakers, Jews, and Native Americans. Williams and Waterman acknowledged Native Americans as the true owners of America's land and advocated paying them the same value given the English in real estate transactions. They respected the Native tribes' rights to determine their own spiritual beliefs and practices, free from conversion by Puritan zealots. And for this they were shunned, kicked out of the colony, and forced to start their own society off in the hinterlands today known as Rhode Island.

Rhode Island was soon filling up with similar Massachusetts rejects. Waterman might have lived among them trouble free, but for a trespassing cow. It wasn't his cow. Not his land or cow-controversy, either. The cow trespass didn't even happen in Providence, where he was living. It was a Portsmouth cow, and it meandered onto land owned by a man named Samuel Gorton. Gorton had likewise been chased out of Massachusetts for letting his thoughts form words and flow out of his mouth instead of swallowing them whole.

In response to the bovine transgression, Gorton's maid assaulted the cow's owner. When the court summoned her to defend her behavior, Gorton appeared in her stead. In calling the maid to appear before them, the Magistrates were asserting control over events in a town outside their jurisdictional boundary. This was not Gorton's first run-in with overreaching Magistrates, and his frustration boiled over. He taunted the Magistrates, calling them "asses" and referring to one freeman in town as a "Jack-an-Ape" and others as "saucy boys." He challenged the honesty of the Deputy Governor, proclaiming he'd not touch him with a pair of tongs and suggested the man's failure to respond favorably to Gorton's views might be for lack of ears to hear them with.

Gorton's disenchantment with the colonial courts stemmed from their refusal to recognize rights Englishmen enjoyed under the Crown. The colonial Magistrates claimed for themselves extensive powers unheard of in England. They fined people for missing church, denied them freeman status for attending any religious service other than that favored by the Magistrates, disenfranchised four-fifths of the citizenry which kept them from not only from voting but also from owning land, and imposed a representative rather than popular form of government. The Magistrates punished anyone who entertained a stranger. They held the power to determine who could settle in the colony and to banish anyone found to be in violation.

Two years earlier, in Plymouth, Gorton had feuded with Magistrates when they invoked their rule about strangers against Gorton's servant Ellen Aldridge after a rumor spread that she had smiled in church. The Magistrates had decided that she and anyone who brought her to Plymouth should be deported as vagabonds (this would include Gorton, who was actually quite wealthy and settled in his home). For defending her character in court, Gorton had been charged with contempt for allegedly attempting to delude the court. At that time, Gorton was considered to be quiet, peaceable, and agreeable by his neighbors, and the people had generally supported him in that dispute. In a quiet form of protest, the sixteen men called to the trial as Elders had refused to attend court time and again, despite being fined for their absence each time. The Magistrates had acted as both prosecutors bringing the charges and as decision makers in that, as in every case. Sick of listening to Gorton's arguments in his and his servant's defense, the Jury Foreman had moved that Gorton be forbidden to speak to the court any further. For defending Aldridge, Gorton had been found guilty of and fined for "seditious conduct" and ordered to be out of Plymouth in fourteen days, in blizzard conditions.

Gorton complained that the colonial courts not only failed to apply English law, but they also did not derive their authority from the governed, instead enforcing the Magistrates' personal interpretations of their Bible. The trial in the cow case broke down into hand-to-hand combat with torn clothing and people fleeing. As a result of the unfavorable resolution of the cow case, with Gorton sentenced to be whipped, he decided to move to Providence, but that bastion of free thinking wouldn't have the man who was coming to be viewed as a troublemaker.

Waterman was one of a group of men who came to share Gorton's religious and civic views,[11] including the notions that women deserve rights equal to those of men and that no one needs church leaders to guide their spiritual journeys. For 144 fathoms of wampum, the group members bought land from the Narragansetts in Shawomet.[12] To their great misfortune, one of their most prominent neighbors was Benedict Arnold, great-grandfather of the famous treasonist of the same name from the Revolutionary era, both Benedicts sharing what must have been hereditary poison degrading their souls.

Arnold, his son, son-in-law, and a man named Robert Cole embarked on a scheme to separate the Gortonites from their property. These men were shining examples of good citizenship. Previously, Arnold had publicly supported the right of a man who beat his wife almost to death to continue beating her. Cole had been convicted of public drunkenness and ordered to wear a scarlet "D" on his clothing for a year. This time, they declared their allegiance to Massachusetts in a scheme to sic its militia on the newcomers. To accomplish their ends, they forged deeds and, upon failing to align Narragansett Chief Miantonomi, who was friendly with the

---

[11] The two became good friends, and some of his and Gorton's progeny later intermarried.

[12] These lands comprise the current-day jurisdictions of Warwick, West Warwick, and Coventry, Rhode Island.

Gortonites, to their cause, sought out two of Miantonomi's sachems named Ponham and Soconomo and bribed them with powder and shot. Both were known thieves and were willing to falsely swear they signed the land deed for the Gortonites under duress, that duress being fear of Miantonomi. Their claimed fear of Miantonomi led to them being removed as his subjects and placed under Massachusetts' jurisdiction.

At Arnold's prodding, the sachems then submitted a dispute regarding the land deed's legitimacy to the Massachusetts court which eagerly stretched out its jurisdictional arm, sending 40 weapons-bearing soldiers to enforce its demand that the Gortonites present themselves before its Magistrates. Attempts at discussion proved futile, and the Gortonites chose to flee once told to renounce their views or face death. Shortly thereafter, the soldiers captured them. Waterman was not actually living on his Shawomet property but in Providence. He and a few other stray group members surrendered on the promise they would be allowed to remain free pending trial if they voluntarily accompanied the soldiers to Boston. On their arrival, they were promptly jailed.

As the dispute continued, the Massachusetts government committed despicable offenses against humanity, taking four Narragansett children hostage to ensure the tribe complied with a new peace treaty concerning English jurisdiction over disputes and allying itself with the Mohegans, whom they allowed to murder the much-respected Miantonomi. That murder occurred between Windsor and Hartford in 1643.

Once in court, the pretext of a land complaint against the Gortonites vaporized. Instead, the Magistrates blasted their writings which had been seized by its soldiers and by then examined in detail. The Magistrates grossly distorted the meaning of the Gortonites' words to portray them as haters of God, civilization, and education. Most of the Magistrates favored execution, but the deputies nixed that, so for their humanitarian opinions, the Gortonites were sentenced to jail as "blasphemous enemies of the Lord Jesus." In May 1644, upon Richard's release from jail, an exasperated General Court of Massachusetts had had enough of Richard Waterman, labeling him "erroneous, hereticall, and obstinate."

The people of Boston supported Gorton, Waterman and friends, inviting them into their homes now that they were freed, infuriating the unpopular Magistrates. So the Magistrates obtained a warrant from the Governor requiring the Gortonites to be out of Boston within two hours and out of the colony altogether within 14 days. Typical of the colony's overreach, the order also forbade them from going anywhere near Providence, including their own properties.

The General Court having ordered him to leave Massachusetts— a place he was present only because its soldiers took jurisdiction over his community in Rhode Island and forcefully escorted him to that location— further admonished Richard Waterman never to return to Massachusetts "upon paine of death."

Erroneous, heretical, and obstinate— now that's the kind of color my family tree needs!

CHAPTER 7

AGNES STREET

What defined my early childhood life on Agnes Street was neither relationships nor experiences but what was lacking. The other kids had adventures and stories to tell. Occasionally, I had near misses, but usually I had nothing. My family "almost" went on vaction one time. But we didn't. The Blue Laws, dictating a day of rest on Sunday, sentenced me to a weekly bout of loneliness while friends visited grandparents or played games with parents, siblings, or cousins or took country drives.

As much as I adored Nanny, she was a live-in grandmother, no different on Sunday than any other day of the week. She couldn't fulfill that ache for the missing three grandparents I never got to meet (two deceased and one estranged). I felt shortchanged walking into my own living room or climbing my own stairs to see my one grandmother instead of making a special journey to a magical place called

"Grandma's house." I yearned for the appreciation showered on the kids whose grandparents saw them once a week or a few times a month. For when Monday came, those visits were the talk of the elementary school, and I didn't have a word to contribute. I had 27 cousins on my father's side, most local, yet there were no cousin confidences or even rumpuses to report because I almost never saw any of them. No one outside our household came to our table for Sunday dinner, and we ate at no table but our own. We ate the same sparse meals we ate every other day. Were it not for Nanny's stories, most of our sorry repasts might have been endured in silence. Even with Nanny on hand, meals were eaten with alarming speed and the family dispersed to solitary endeavors. My only sibling Jan glanced down with disinterest from her perch five rungs higher on the age scale, when she bothered to look my way at all.

With positive experiences in scarce supply, the few that crept into my life, however meager they might be, assumed exaggerated importance. They may not have been much, but they were all I had. The times when They weren't around (you'll meet Them mometarily), doing the newspaper crossword became a family affair for the female family members, entertwined with washing the supper dishes. These are among my fondest childhood memories being as they count among few family activities. Whoever sat at the table with the crossword would read out clues and numbers of letters so those washing and drying could assist in solving them. Nanny and Mom may have had limited formal education, but they were both champions at crosswords. I clung to these scant interactions as proof of normalcy in the same way I treasured those rare summer evenings when my parents sat on the screened porch together in awe of nature's lightning spectacle.

Alone in my bed at night, though, I couldn't prevent the chipped veneer that cloaked my dismal existence from falling away. That's when I invented long lost relatives to come and claim me, some of them ordinary, others royalty, but none bearing even a soupçon of resemblance to the Rogue. My royal relatives would never have abandoned a single wife or child, let alone two wives and ten children. My royal relatives snubbed the likes of King George III, instead carefully preserving their status to ensure the world recognized me as royal, not ragamuffin. In their care, I wore gowns and velvet robes in lieu of threadbare dresses and broken down shoes. In this alternate world, I thrived in the nurture absent from my day life and never missed out on experiences that set everyone else's world apart from mine. My imaginary families, royal and regular, gave me what my family did not, a sense of connection and belonging, a place of my own in the world, a hint of respectability.

Most kids went home from school for lunch in those days, and on one day in one of those years, I poured my heart out to my mother at lunch about being the only kid in class who never went anywhere and couldn't fathom what to write in the perennial back-to-school "What Did You Do for Summer Vacation?" essay when I had no vacation story to share.

"Make something up," she told me.

Make something up? That would be lying, and worse it would mean faking my own life.

Although I engaged in near-constant make-believe by this time, I drew a firm line between that enterprise and reality. I had to. I was not willing to pull the shades to hide from the men I could not see looking in our windows.

There was another force that came to define life on Agnes Street, the repugnant visitors who came and went without invitations and without regard to our wishes, visitors so loathesome, They made my Uncle Bobby look like a vaunted houseguest. They were the bane of my existence, although I never met Them. I couldn't pinpoint Their identities, because They weren't called by names or referenced by any of those familiar attributes that distinguished one grown-up from another, like familial relationships, occupations, or addresses. They put Wittekind to shame with Their anonymity.

They made rules, exerting as much control over my life as if They were sitting in my father's rocker watching our television. When my mother would say, "They said we're not allowed to go there," I would ask who They were.

"You know!" she would insist, anger in her voice.

But I didn't know. And They changed their minds retroactively. If I was warned off King's and took care to avoid it, then I should have known it was Bradlee's I wasn't allowed to step foot in.

Permission was untrustworthy. I'd either be given permission or face no objection to wearing a certain outfit or going out with a particular friend, only to be trapped under a lava flow of rage in the days following, with my mother insisting I knew They did not want me to wear "that" or see "her." When They were around, my mother refused to use proper nouns. So at times when I was bombarded with accusations that I knew I wasn't supposed to do "that," go "there," or play with "her" after days stuck in the house doing nothing and seeing no one outside of family, I'd struggle to identify which that, what there, and whatever who might be the source of the fury raining down on me. She would never tell me. She would spit out, "You know!" with an intensity that shut down further inquiry.

There inevitably would come a long stretch of hot summer days when at Their insistence I'd be closed up in the sweltering house with its doors locked, windows closed-and-not-to-be-opened, and curtains drawn. These were uneasy times when my body tingled with instinctive recognition of unseen perils that might leap so suddenly from unexpected places, I'd have no opportunity to steel myself. And then, just as unpredictably as They arrived, They would slip out the door, certain to return at some indefinite, future time, though I always mustered a bit of hope They were gone for good.

CHAPTER 8

SHAME AND SUSPICION, A VEXATIOUS

PAIR

It wasn't only my parents, sister and Nanny who lived with me on Agnes Street. Shame lived there, too. Shame hid in the closets and crept onto the half-vacant shelves in the refrigerator. It lorded over the broken vinyl floor tile that would never be fixed and spread out on the sagging porch. In the torn backs and seats of the padded kitchen chairs, in the jagged patterns on the walls created by painting over chipped layers beneath, Shame waited. Shame spilled out into the patches of dirt that passed for a backyard and popped up among the rank weeds along the chainlink fence separating that yard from the store parking lot. I could escape the house but never Shame as it followed me out the door, keeping pace as I tried to outrun it.

Shame confronted me with regularity on its terms, not mine. My parents struggled to pay the bills, always. When I was five and my sister ten, my parents had one of their many arguments about money. Money arguments stemmed from shortfalls which in turn resulted from unpredictability. If the winter was especially cold and the bill for heating oil was higher than expected or the car's engine up and quit at the most inconvenient of times, the makings of a money argument were in place. My forward-looking father's boyish eagerness to buy something newer and prettier to replace the car he couldn't himself fix, however impractical, was often pit against my mother's suffocating fear of losing what little we had, namely her dingy and tattered security blanket, the house. The argument that day was no different than so many others and would scarcely be memorable but for the interjection of Shame. With bills piling up, irate creditors calling, and nothing but a wish and prayer to pay most of them, my father broached a subject so verboten in my mother's orbit that Shame spied its opportunity and grabbed the reins.

The argument became louder and louder, and then without warning it was quiet. My mother called Jan and me into their bedroom. We hesitated, after all the yelling, but she reassured us they just wanted to ask us a question. We should have run for the hills, any hills, and if we couldn't find hills, highways, or patches of wood. What we should not have done is enter that bedroom to be battered by Shame.

"Do you think we should declare bankruptcy?" my mother asked us children, as casually as if she were inquiring about which color bedspread to buy. Having no idea what bankruptcy was, one of us, probably my sister as she was so much older, asked. That's when Shame, hijacking my mother's voice, barely let an explanation pass her lips before sneering that everyone would know our family was bankrupt. Every time we walked down the street, people would point at us and say, "There go the Bengles. They're *bankrupt*."

Is this what we, the children, wanted? That was the question. Shame not only gave us the answer, it put us on notice that if we dropped our guard, this reputation-destroying monster called bankruptcy might thrust itself upon us at any time and forever after everyone would point, jeer, and label us with that ugly word. Shame informed us we must hide the truth of our existence from the outside world.

Shame turned our lives upside down. We bought brand-name foods and household products, even though generics cost less, to fool Shame and the world at large into thinking we weren't poor, just *temporarily* down on our luck. As if we'd stumbled into the wrong end of some faerie tale bargain and were forced to endure poverty, Shame, and humiliation before we'd be restored to our rightful station. We thumbed our noses at Shame when charities sent collectors door-to-door, putting our dollars in the envelope just like all of our neighbors. When it was time to tip the milkman or mailman for the holidays, they got the going rate. It wasn't a choice but a necessity to preserve the illusion we weren't less than the others. We could be counted on to do our part. We were always last to put in our money for field trips at school, but somehow we got it in, even when my father had to borrow from co-workers until payday. Despite our valiant efforts, Shame reminded me constantly that we'd barely gotten by and might not make it next time. And the money could only stretch so far, leaving the beat up clothes, shoes, and furniture, and the periodic utility turnoffs, to tattle on us and Shame to revel in our failures.

I was ready to take on Shame and win, if only I could find the means. When I was a pre-teen, I was sure I'd discovered the tools I needed but my mother stubbornly refused to assume her part in my master plan. No, she would not stop buying "tin foil"[13] with the groceries each week. She needed it, she insisted, to cover meat in the oven and to wrap around those rare leftovers headed for the refrigerator. Her arbitrary attraction to tin foil infuriated me. If she would give up this unnecessary vice, we could save 29 cents each week and in time we'd have the makings of a weapon to beat back Shame for once and for all. With the nest egg saved from crossing tin foil off the grocery list, we'd be able to plan rather than react to whatever circumstances life tossed our way. For weeks, I carried on about the irrationality of buying tin foil and nurtured resentment that my plot to decimate Shame was being undermined by someone who ought to have been my partner in the effort, but eventually I saw the futility of trying to change her mind and abandoned the Tin Foil Eradication Project.

---

[13] Although aluminum foil replaced tin foil in the American marketplace as far back as 1926, my family, probably due to Nanny's influence, always called that stuff we had in our cupboard tin foil.

Suspicion and Shame worked hand in hand. Agnes Street. Who lived in such a place? The address embarrassed me, and I cringed writing it on school forms. Bengle, what kind of name was that? It didn't help that everyone always asked me that as if I came from an alien planet. Suspicion drilled into me that whatever I had, it was probably Shameful. Suspicion pummeled my every choice, my every association.

The police pulling up with Uncle Bobby in the backseat and those erratic visits from Them melded into a grim shadow that threatened to push everyone away. The shadow took the shape of Shame. The constant trips to the grocery store I was forced to make, asking the butcher for a cheaper package of hamburger if the pennies I counted didn't add up to the price printed on the smallest plastic-wrapped tray in the refrigerated case, weaved Shame into my daily existence. But it wasn't just the penny counting that made those grocery trips agonizing. My mother would send me to the store for one item and immediately send me back for something else on my return, sometimes three or four times in a row, relishing her power over me as I begged her to send me for everything at once. Cashiers glared at me and made pointed comments about my competency. When I got older and They wed my mother to one ragged housedress whose hem and front placket had worn through, she took it off just before the dry cleaner closed every day and demanded I rush its decaying carcass there and request overnight service. The next morning, I'd be sent to retrieve it. Shame left me no room to breathe.

Shame laughed in the face of the child who thought she might outwit it, leaving her to eventually seek respite in her ancestry in the hopes something buried deep within would reveal the Pride she dared hope might be her birthright.

CHAPTER 9

BOOTED OUT X 2

My ancestors on both sides of the family had a knack for getting the boot. Two-and-a-half centuries after Massachusetts dispatched Richard Waterman without a hint of deference to his near-decade-long service to the colony, it was the Monat family's turn. And, after being exiled from Three Rivers, Massachusetts, and relocating in Detroit, the Monats faced another abrupt and forced goodbye as the U.S. government kicked one of our family out of the country altogether.

Frank and Agnes Monat were my paternal grandmother's parents. Frank, president of the carpenter's union, was a civic-minded and well-respected member of the business community in the small village of Three Rivers, Massachusetts. One news report from May 1919 credits Frank with organizing a well-attended meeting at the Empire Theater to protest impending Prohibition. Besides his work as a carpenter, Frank owned a confectionery and fruit store and held ownership in Crystal Lake. He was treasurer of the Three Rivers Volunteer Fire Department where his son-in-law Emile Bengle, my grandfather, was a volunteer firefighter. He was nominated to run for the town planning board in early 1927 but withdrew his name from consideration for reasons unknown but likely linked to controversy surrounding that election, months before the events that would drive him from Three Rivers.

Frank and Agnes' feisty teenage daughters Rose and Elenor? Not so well respected. Solicitation was not popular in Three Rivers even in the promiscuous Roaring '20's. Whether the offense they were informally accused of in 1927 was literally solicitation, as understood by one of Frank and Agnes' granddaughters who passed the story to me, or something equally unsavory, the police gave the family a choice, relocate far away or the sixteen–and–seventeen–year–old daughters were getting locked up. So the Monats skedaddled, selling off their household goods and taking up residence in Detroit where their grown son Frank, Jr. and his wife Jeannette lived. Contemporaneous news reports, while omitting any mention of the hushed-up scandal, support the sudden and unplanned nature of the move. On May 24, a news article announced that Frank had moved his confectionery and fruit business from one building to another within Three Rivers. By October 4, Frank had left with his daughters Rose and Elenor to live in Detroit. Agnes had gone ahead to establish a home for them.

Within months of arriving in Detroit, Elenor became pregnant and crossed over into Windsor, Ontario, living with her boyfriend Robert McAlear. Their son, also named Robert McAlear but called Robert Monat during his childhood years, was born in September. When baby Robert was eight days old, Frank and Agnes whisked him to Detroit. Family accounts explain the necessity of this move, noting Eleanor's boyfriend had been arrested, allegedly for smuggling drugs across the U.S-Canadian border. Unfortunately, the Monats did not seek government permission for the baby to immigrate.

It was 1928, and the notorious criminal enterprise of Al Capone at once terrified and captivated the public. News items about "Scarface" Al Capone and his gang were legion. The friends of Robert McAlear no doubt drew inspiration from the famed criminal, calling their gang, which reassembled from the ashes of the notorious local Corktown Mob after police crushed it, the Scarface Gang. The Scarface Gang was identified as the perpetrator of numerous armed robberies. After robbing a gas station at Five Mile Road and Blackstone Avenue in Detroit one September night, they high-tailed it to Windsor, where Ontario police caught up with them. Shortly thereafter, they were deported to Detroit to face charges. Numerous attestations of good character failed to sway the judge toward leniency.

"You may have been good boys once, but you certainly have gone wrong," Judge Arthur W. Kilpatrick said. "If I show clemency to you, it will be a direct invitation to other youths who are so minded to go out and hold people up."[14]

He sentenced McAlear to two-and-a-half to 15 years in the Ionia, Michigan reformatory. So far as I have been able to ascertain, drug smuggling was not involved, but his arrest and imprisonment did lead to the relocation of infant Robert to his grandparents' home.

Elenor and Robert-the-robber married in August 1931 and remained in Canada. Young Robert continued to reside with his grandparents. For 12 years, he went to school like the other kids and afterwards played with neighborhood friends. At some point, his grandparents realized they needed a visa for him because he was Canadian; the exact trigger for their visa application on his behalf is unknown. But their request was denied on the grounds they hadn't adopted him. So two years later, they filed an adoption petition, this time being turned down because they didn't have a visa for Robert. When they refiled the adoption petition, the Immigation and Naturalization Service swooped in and seized Robert from his grandparents, branding him a deportable alien.

The treacherous Elenor orchestrated this; family accounts suggest her motivation was a recent venture into farming and the need for an extra farm hand, with Robert representing free labor. For weeks, Robert lived in a juvenile detention center awaiting deportation or a reprieve. He was shuffled between Federal Court, the Probate Count and

---

[14] Source 44.

Immigration offices, bombarded by incoherent sounds like "habeas corpus." He watched his grandpa plead, his fate hanging in the balance. His grandpa secured his release, but days later Judge Ernest A. O'Brien sent him right back to detention, as if his mere presence in his grandparents' house were a crime he'd committed, as though it were his decision where to live when his father chose crime and his unmarried teenage mother was unable or unwilling to care for their newborn son alone. A contemporaneous news account described Robert as "bewildered and a little frightened," noting his desire to take his new bicycle with him if a compulsory relocation to Canada proved inevitable. On November 27, 1940, the United States of America deported Robert, forcing him to abandon the only home he'd ever known and take up residence in a country foreign to him in every way, with parents whose chief interest in him was said to be exploiting his labors.

Learning that one of my ancestors got banned from Massachusetts by Puritans in the 1600s amused me, and I cheered on Richard Waterman for his outspokenness. This banning was quaint, and *singular*. But finding out another group of my ancestors, from the other side of the family no less, was brusquely ordered to leave, brought out different feelings entirely. Feelings of rejection. What was it about my family that drew so much ire that they couldn't simply be those unpopular folks over yonder but would be ordered by town authorities to go away and never come back? With the passage of 300 years, these prickly little Massachusetts towns couldn't have found a means to accommodate us?

According to the Miriam Webster online dictionary, "pile on" is an informal phrasal verb meaning "to join other people in criticizing something or someone in usually an unfair way." Piling on is what it feels like town leaders in Massachusetts were doing when they decided to ban my ancestors for a second time. The good news is, if they stick to their timetable, we probably have another couple hundred years before we have to contend with that again.

CHAPTER 10

TREE DESPOILERS

While anticipating ne'er do wells of every ilk to have found their way into my family tree, I started my journey with confidence that whatever Shame could find to throw my way, it would not include a slaveholding history. Not only were my family northerners, and poor ones at that, our immigration story began after slavery ended. And then those would-be-rapist-murderer-thieves showed up to wreak havoc with my timeline, and Richard Waterman sauntered in, pushing it back almost to the Mayflower. And these guys weren't as poor as I'd been led to believe our entire lot was. Suddenly, I had a possible new source of chagrin staring me down.

"What's more disgraceful than a rogue?"

"Who gives off a worse stench than a mercenary?"

"With those Revolutionary raiders up there on their rotting limb, would it be a surprise to find a slaveholder lounging alongside them?"

Cringing at every step, I investigated. My research into the strong links between early colonial slavery and Rhode Island increased my dread. More than a thousand slaving voyages set sail from the state, exceeding half of the total slaving voyages ever launched from what would become the United States of America. Now those Puritans who expelled Richard Waterman, I could see them justifying ownership of other human beings. But Richard himself? It was almost unthinkable. But not impossible and not entirely unlikely. He lived in Rhode Island, the center of the New England slave trade. And believing in equality in an unequal world was no insurance against unjust acts, especially acts that were taken for granted by many in their time and intended to ensure a family's prosperity or safety.

The original Rhode Island slaves seized by colonists were Native Americans captured in various warlike encounters. Sometimes they were traded for African slaves from the West Indies or sold outright in Barbados. With respect to captives coming directly from Africa, Rhode Island slavers initially engaged primarily in triangular trade, setting off with rum to be traded for slaves on the African coast, trading the slaves for sugar and molasses in the West Indies, and returning home to Rhode Island to make more rum with the molasses. With the number of slaves in the state approximating 175 in the late 17th century, surely Richard

Waterman– my venerable ancestor, Richard Waterman-wasn't one of those slave holders? Slaveholding in those years would make him an anomaly. The math didn't exonerate him but offered reason for optimism.

By the early to mid-1700s, slaveholding exploded, with the southern region of the state almost one-third black, almost all black residents enslaved. Rhode Island didn't effectively ban slavery until 1843.[15] That left a century and a half's worth of ancestors getting the stink eye until further notice. I checked my list of Waterman ancestors predating the Emancipation Proclamation— Richard, Nathaniel, Benjamin, Charles, and Abraham were tentative perps. Gideon moved the family to Connecticut and then Vermont where slavery had been outlawed earlier, so he and Superan got marked safe.

With trepidation, I pored through censuses and genealogies. Richard shared common political views with Roger Williams, an abolitionist. Surely not him. Richard soon joined the safe list. Before long, Benjamin, Charles, and Abraham hopped aboard. But in the process of clearing them, I spotted something heinous. And there it was again, and again. Richard Waterman descendants who had been involved in the slave trade.

Richard's son, Nathaniel Waterman, was my one ancestor in the group. His home was used as a garrison for two months toward the end of King Philip's War. Various

---

[15] Officially, Rhode Island banned slavery in 1642 but the law was commonly circumvented.

prominent citizens, including him, were directed to arrange for the sale of a group of Native American prisoners of war, including women and children, after the war ended. In the same meeting that the town officials directed the sale at prevailing prices and allocated the designated sellers shares of the proceeds, they explained why the law nominally prohibiting slavery didn't bar these transactions. The former prisoners would not be outright enslaved, their convoluted reasoning went, instead serving a term of years dependent on their age, after which they would be freed. Children under 5, presumably the least culpable in any warfare, faced the most stringent conditions, servitude until age 30; children 5–10 until age 28; 10–15 until age 27; 15–20 until age 26; 20–30, eight years; and above age 30, seven years. The terms were based on perceived future risk, not blameworthy conduct. Although lifelong slavery had been banished, term slavery imposed for a crime or participation in war was not viewed in the same light. Nor, apparently, was visiting the sins of the parents upon the children. The justification for this treatment of former prisoners was self-defense.

The going price for one of those slaves was 32 shillings cash. Many were bartered. Among the deals struck, there were slaves valued, respectively, at 12 bushels of Indian corn, silver amounting to 2 pounds and ten shillings, 100 pounds of wool, and three fat sheep. In the end, the sellers received slightly more than 16 shillings per share.

Here's where the history gets messy. Slavery worked in both directions. Native Americans also enslaved the colonists they captured in this and other wars. The Native

American slaveholding practice didn't begin with those invasive colonists but was practiced by tribes vis-a-vis each other before the colonists arrived.

My own history makes it messier, yet: I have both colonial and Abenaki bloodlines. One relative described to me growing up with a father proud of his Abenaki ancestry and speaking with family elders who recalled their Abenaki kin smoking corncob pipes in the kitchen in the early 1900s. The Abenaki, "people of the dawn," so called because they lived on the east coast where they were first to see the sun rise, lived in loosely organized bands. My ancestors hail from the eastern Abanaki living in New Brunswick and in Maine east of the White Mountains.

Roger Williams was a vocal opponent of slavery, yet his general objections to enslaving fellow humans apparently didn't extend to term slavery for particular humans who chose to participate in wars against his community or commit crimes, or their innocent family members. Along with Nathaniel, he was granted a share of the proceeds from selling those prisoners from King Philip's War. This made me wonder if Richard Waterman would have acted likewise had he not died before then.

With my tree polluted by a slave-holder ancestor, albeit one with asterisks, spouting a litany of excuses for his searing human rights violations, I wondered whether my tree's outlying twigs were in danger of breaking off with the burden of so many distant slave-holder relatives. I still didn't know whether their transgressions were war related like

Nathaniel's or products of the vigorous Atlantic slave trade. The breadth of Waterman genealogy is dizzying, and it was a laborious task to measure my distance from these slavers. I was sick knowing that, even momentarily disregarding Nathaniel, no amount of distance between us was sufficient.

The closest of those tree poisoners, it turns out, are two second cousins, eight times removed, Rufus and Captain Elisha. What this means is their line branched off after Nathaniel– I descended from Nathaniel's son Benjamin, while they descended from one of Benjamin's siblings. Rufus and Captain Elisha weren't the only heritage despoilers I was trying to shove down the trunk. Four others are second cousins, nine times removed (Thomas, Col. John, Benoni, and 4th Generation Resolved), and one a third cousin, eight times removed (Capt. John), with Richard our only common ancestor.

Uncovering the identity of people once held as slaves poses name issues whose abtrusity is matched only by the tribulations of Wittekind. My accomplishments here are slim. Censuses provide a number of people held as slaves but not names. Personal records sometimes identify individuals as black or "Indian" without specifying whether they were free or enslaved. There also was a hierarchy within households such that a testator identifies by name in a last will and testament certain people held as slaves to be passed to an heir and others only by quantity.

Benoni Waterman's papers demonstrate that the answer to the Atlantic slave trade question is an appalling yes.

Cudgo, a black boy about 13 years old, is listed on a bill of sale— just writing this turns my stomach inside out— between Benoni and a Captain Page. Historians who have studied Benoni's papers believe the man he called Old Miah was an enslaved African. The Spyman family may have been enslaved Native American. Cuff, Flora, and Philes were people listed in Benoni's will, people he gifted to his relatives. But the horror doesn't stop there. Benoni's widow later willed Prince, a man who used the surname Waterman, and Claro to their sons Resolved and John, and four unnamed people they held as slaves to their son Caleb. Later records show Cuff and Cola, a married couple, to be "property" of Col. John. Cola lived to age 90, never freed. Vilet, Jack, and the aforementioned Prince were enslaved men who were passed through 4th-generation-Resolved's will to his sons 5th-generation-Resolved, Andrew, and John. Parmalie and Colie are listed on a monument to the Waterman family slaves belatedly placed by a Waterman descendant in the graveyard in which they are buried.

Seeing people identified in a will as property to be passed from one generation to the next in my own extended family had an internally wrenching effect. And the ads— Benoni Waterman placed ads in Boston newspapers offering people he brought back from the West Indies for sale, listing them alongside rum and sugar like just another product acquired on his travels, to my utter horror. Seeing this personalized documentation was radically different from obtaining common knowledge of these historical practices in books. It wasn't only the surprise, for I surely never expected this in my family, who wasn't even supposed to be here before the Emancipation Proclamation, but the regularity, the unquestioned acceptance of denying autonomy to other humans without the slightest hesitation, let alone guilt. Seeing close friends and associates of people I'd come to admire in my ancestry linked to the slave trade gave me new and not entirely welcome insight into our nation's history.

Before slavery was finally banned, several other people were enslaved by Col. John Waterman, his daughter Dorcas Gardner, Thomas Waterman, and William Waterman: Bess, Pedro, and Cato Sweet are among them. Others in those records who may have been enslaved include Amos Budlong, Pero Cheese, Ruben Roberts, Boston Talbury, Sam Lockwood, Lucy Waterman, "Sampson Indian" and "Margaret Indian." It's impossible for these people whose lives were controlled by others to fully achieve their rightful niche in history when their contemporaries so often refused to acknowledge their proper full names and shrunk their life stories to the single word "slave."

Hope for the Waterman progeny appears in one of the Waterman lines with the introduction of a famous abolitionist. Phebe Waterman, who is a 5th generation descendant of Richard through his son Resolved, married Moses Brown. It was a second marriage for her and a third for him. In his young adult years, Brown enslaved people. He also had a history of slave running, albeit a short one. Growing up in his uncle's household, he worked for his uncle's shipping firm which ran one verified slave voyage. When his uncle died, he and his brothers renamed the firm Nicholas Brown & Co. Their entry into the slaving business consisted of one venture only, due to disaster. Most of the men forced into servitude and loaded onto the ship *Sally* died on the return voyage, some due to disease and others as a result of revolts.

After Brown's first wife died, he freed the people he had enslaved and became a Quaker. From this point forward, he spoke forcefully against slavery, engaging in public relations efforts and unsuccessfully lobbying for years before the legislature finally passed a 1787 state law prohibiting slave trading. He worked through organizations to ensure enforcement of the new law and sought to have a national law passed to forbid foreign ships with slaves aboard from getting assistance in American ports. Brown's commitment to end slavery also moved him to provide financial assistance to individualpeople who were enslaved and to free blacks. Most of Brown's important anti-slavery work occurred before he married into the Waterman family. So, while the Waterman family deserves no credit for Brown's work, the marriage hints that a commitment to abolition may have blossomed belatedly in one of the lines of descendancy containing slave holders.

CHAPTER 11

THE NIGHT THE DANCING STOPPED

When I was very young, my parents used to go out square dancing on Friday nights, sometimes with my Aunt Jeannette and Uncle Pete, other times with couples they'd befriended at the Russell Ridge Runners Square Dance Club, or the Russell Club for short. There was an energy in the room when my mother dressed up in her flared skirts and put on lipstick. She had one bright red skirt I especially liked. It would swirl outward as she practiced her Allemande Lefts and Promenades with an imaginary partner on the dining room tile. On a big reel-to-reel tape recorder of my father's, she played the music they would later dance to with other couples, including one song I partially remember to this day, an adaptation of Just Because, a song recorded by the Shelton Brothers that Elvis had covered on his first album. The lyrics, of course, were switched out for square dance calls, "Do-si-do your partner, do-si-do your friend, do-si-do your partner once again... and we all promenade, because, just because."

After "that night" the dancing stopped. It stopped as mail bringing the Christmas cards she taped above the knick knack shelves annually slowed to a trickle. It stopped in the face of well-meaning overtures meeting brusque rebuffs. It stopped when she no longer went to Lerner's to sell clothes and instead took to sitting upright on her bed staring at the wall for most of the day, some days at first and eventually most days. After it stopped, those men looking in the windows came so often, she insisted on keeping the curtains drawn.

The questions were posed as if they were innocent inquiries. Why my mother didn't, why my mother did, where my mother was, where my mother wasn't? It was their fixation that gave them away. They weren't asking casual questions out of politeness, the kind that might flutter by the wayside in the face of distraction. They were gathering gossip material, satisfying morbid curiosity, indulging their fascination with the aberrant, and I was their pawn. I wasn't a very useful pawn. Despite keeping so many Secrets from me, my mother and Nanny bred into me the imperative of guarding the vault containing the family Secrets. Suspicion attached to anyone in the vicinity carrying any tool that might function as a crowbar to pry that vault open. So usually I just shrugged and said I didn't know, regardless of the question and even if I did know. When they pushed, I became more convinced than ever they were pumping me for information and closed my shell up tighter than a bivalve with clenched adductors.

"That night," you may be asking, what was "that night" she mentioned? You may be disappointed to learn that I have no knowledge of anything that may have happened that night. What I know is that one Thursday in early November 1964, I scampered off to bed unaware that when I awoke the next morning, the mother I knew would be gone, forever. It was as if a faerie crossed our threshold in the midnight hours with such stealth as to remain undiscovered as she carried away my mother, leaving a changeling in her place. And everyone pretended it hadn't happened even as the *locum tenens* chewed up every remaining morsel of normalcy in our lives.

CHAPTER 12

TERROR ON THE FRONTIER

Shame's most frightening companion was aptly named Terror. Terror encroached into intimate spaces, like the depths of my hippocampus, strewing the imagery that would form into persistent nightmares. In some of these nightmares, I'd flee at breakneck speed, certain death was at hand if I couldn't outrun the unseen forces in pursuit. To know my pursuer was to embrace Terror, so I never looked back. When I didn't run, I hid, often in the attic, crouched under the eaves, willing my breathing to still. It was that changeling coming for me with a ferocity unseen in the natural world. I'd sink deeper into the corner, my acute sensitivities attuned to her every footfall. Occasionally, I'd find relief as the sound portended movement away from my hiding spot, but more often thoughts of suffocation (from my efforts to keep my breathing from betraying me) consumed me when the telltale squeak of the door opening or the creak of human weight on the stairs foretold my impending end. The certainty of imminent discovery cloaked me in dread that persisted beyond my inevitable awakening.

When I learned how Terror also chased down my ancestors, I nearly abandoned hope that my genealogical exploration could bring me any comfort. Three hundred and four years to the day before my generation froze in horror as televised images and somber commentary depicted passenger jets crashing into the Twin Towers and the Pentagon on September 11, 2001, Terror delivered to my 8th great-grandmother and her family their own 9/11. For most of them, it proved deadly.

Hannah Prescott, daughter of John Prescott and Mary Gawkroger of Platts, was born in 1639, possibly in Barbados, a place John and Mary lived briefly between leaving the Parish of Standish, Lancashire, England and settling in Lancaster, Massachusetts Bay Colony. John Prescott is said to have been the great-grandson of James Prescott of Standish. James Prescott was in the service of Queen Elizabeth, required by an order dated 1564 to keep horsemen and suits of armor at the ready in case she might fancy starting a war. James' wife was a daughter of Roger Standish, Esq. Their eldest son became a Lord, entitling him to be addressed as "Sir," and to bear his own coat of arms; our luck being what it is, we descended from a younger son, Roger, and have to make do with "Hey, you!" and be grateful for a coat of any kind. Well, maybe it's not quite that bad. Our presumptive ancestor Roger Prescott lived in Shevington in the Standish parish. He and his second wife Ellen Shaw were parents to some dude named Ralph who was born approximately 1572.

Ralph married Ellen, last name unknown, and she gave birth to a John, who is thought to be our John, in 1605. This bloodline, if firmly established, would make John a man of some stature before his arrival in the New World.

Whether the royal connection stands up, there is a frightening and inescapable púca hovering about my windpipe, humming as it zeros in to crush. The John Prescott who emigrated to the New World, whomever his forebears might have been, is a forebear himself to the poet Robert Frost (my seventh cousin, thrice removed) and to Samuel Prescott, who completed Paul Revere's famous ride (my third cousin, seven times removed.) But before I could get overly excited about these finds, I learned he's, unfortunately, also a forebear of George W. Bush, my second-to-last choice for kinship among American presidents. Though if historical surprises keep spilling from the spigot, it's possible George'll move up a slot or two.

Considered Lancaster's founder, the John Prescott that I am now forced to share with W left a whirlwind of firsts in his wake. He was the town's first blacksmith, first sawmill operator, first grist mill operator and owner of the first trading post, all in his spare time when he wasn't farming. Prescott was renowned for his cleverness, said on one occasion to have subdued Native Americans attacking him with tomahawks with a demonstration of the strength of his armor, convincing them he was a supernatural being. With the help of his wife Mary, who reloaded his gun for him, he many times defended his house from Native American attacks by running from window to window to shoot, creating the impression that there was a group of shooters inside. With his skill and versatility, is it any wonder he could supply John Rugg with not one wife but two? John Rugg, another of Lancaster's 55 original settlers and a freeman, married John and Mary Prescott's daughter Martha Prescott in 1654. The following year, she died, shortly after giving birth to twins, both of whom also died. Five years later, he married Hannah, Martha's sister and my 8th great-grandmother. Together they raised eight children.

In the 1600's, Lancaster was the frontier. In the early days of the settlement, the English and the Native Americans enjoyed a relatively peaceful relationship. When Metacom, the Wampanoag Chief, who came to be known as King Philip, gained power, everything changed. King Philip engaged in warfare with settlers throughout the New England colonies. Historians suggest that declining Native population and fear of being outnumbered or forced to live under the rule of English law may be what caused King Philip to set his wars in motion. Whatever the cause, the early assaults did not involve Lancaster.

That changed in June 1675, when an English spy living among the Native Americans alerted the town to King Philip's plan to attack, beginning with the destruction of their bridge, which would hinder escape and preclude incoming assistance. Eight months later, King Philip led 1,500 warriors from three different tribes in an attack on Lancaster that killed 50 townspeople. Notably the participants included warriors from the Narragansett tribe, which had long maintained good relations with the settlers.

Women and children were kidnapped for ransom, and homes were burned. Hannah's brother Jonathan Prescott, along with nonrelatives Peeter Gardiner and Daniel Chamney, was entrusted with negotiating the release of several women and child hostages, including a Mrs. Rowlandson who later published a now-famous account of her time in captivity. The negotiation occurred between Groton and Concord, with prompt results, some captives ransomed and some released unconditionally. Many of the townspeople fled Lancaster after this attack and didn't return. King Philip died shortly thereafter.

It took four years for rebuilding to begin in earnest, but in the ensuing decade, the town began to grow again. With King William's war breaking out between England and France in 1689, there was general uneasiness in the New England and Canadian colonies as they were left to their own industry in defending themselves against any real or perceived threats by the colonists aligned with the opposing European power and their Native American allies. In 1692, there was another Native American attack in Lancaster, possibly resulting from disagreeable interactions between a mouthy settler named Mrs. Joslin and some Native Americans who entered her house making demands. Two women and three children were killed, while one hostage was carried off.

In 1697, William's War ended on the Continent, but word didn't reach the colonies in time to prevent a massive attack. At noon on September 11, about 40 Native Americans descended on Lancaster, killing 26 colonists, including elderly people who were burned alive when their houses were set afire. Two residents were wounded, six kidnapped. Two barns and two garrisons were also burned. Eight of the 26 killed, almost one-third of the total, were from the extended Rugg family.

Hannah Prescott Rugg, my eighth great-grandmother, was murdered in this massacre. Hannah is believed to have been living with her adult son Joseph and his wife since her husband John died the previous year. They were murdered with her, as were three of their four children. Two of her sister Rebecca's children were also killed. The invaders took Joseph's fourth child, eight-year-old Hannah Rugg, with them, first to Albany and later to Canada. Her ultimate fate is unknown, but she was determined to be still living in Canada at the age of 23, when the Rugg estate was settled by John Rugg, Jr. Four of the other five kidnap victims were released; the fifth died in captivity. Why the kidnappers treated little Hannah differently remains unanswered. However, Native Americans were known for incorporating some white hostages into their tribes and given Hannah's tender years, it's likely this is what happened.

What unspeakable turn of events kept Hannah Jr.'s Uncle Jonathan from charging to the rescue? He was still alive, he boasted a history of successful hostage negotiation, and no one else was getting the job done. Yet not a word about Uncle Johnathan polishing up his negotiating tools and heading to Albany.

Cotton Mather— famed dispenser of deadly supernatural advice during the Salem witch trials which happened but four years preceding— described the aftermath of the massacre that killed the Ruggs in his *Magnalia Christi Americana*. Capt. Brown took charge of the pursuit of the Native Americans, taking several men with him, he noted. When they stopped to sleep, they heard unfamiliar dogs barking which apparently alarmed the kidnappers, sending them running into the woods in the dark night, but not before first stripping and scalping one of their captives. After two days of "bootless labor," Mather said, the search party gave up in defeat.[16]

The Ruggs killed September 11, 1697 were not the only Ruggs to be murdered by Native Americans. Hannah Sr.'s nephew David, who was Hannah Jr.'s cousin and my own first cousin eight times removed, was randomly murdered and his remains treated most gruesomely 38 years later. When a group of Native Americans and their French allies failed in an attempted attack on a garrison in Putney, Vermont, they captured a man named Nehemiah Howe cutting wood nearby and took him prisoner. But for his capture, there would be no witness to David's Rugg's end and its aftermath. On the move after capturing Howe, three miles up the Connecticut River near Taylor Island, the French and Native Americans spotted David Rugg and Robert Baker crossing the river in a canoe. They fired a volley of 20–30 shots at them, killing David. Baker escaped. Some of the Natives swam to the canoe and brought it to shore where they scalped David, leaving his body behind. With red paint, they made a face on the underside of the scalp which they then affixed to a pole and paraded as a trophy through

---

[16] Source 74.

Charlestown, N.H. and Crown Point, N.Y. en route to Québec.

Terror's savagery, its unrelenting, centuries long stranglehold, thwarted my effort to find solace in my ancestry. But as Terror dredged its horror stories out of my family history, I plowed through records of ancestor after ancestor, determined to confine Terror to its rightful and limited place.

CHAPTER 13

DIVINE RETRIBUTION

I had the feeling Mischief would show herself. She's been a frequent visitor in my life, and I know she and my father were also well-acquainted. The thing about Mischief is she's hard to pin down. You never know when she's about unless she wants you to. So while I suspected at least some of my ancestors rubbed shoulders with her, I couldn't be sure until I read the town history of Royalton, Vermont. Now keep in mind most town histories don't even try to capture all the events that happened there; they aim merely to impart a flavor of what life was like in the period described. So, it's telling that of all the stories the authors could have included, they chose one in which Mischief, while not mentioned by name, was subtly performing as stage director in cahoots with one of my ancestors.

My Uncle Butch, née Donald, my father's younger brother, was not a fan of Mischief thanks to an incident involving fruitcake in 1942 at their home in West Springfield, Massachusetts. Fruitcake, you may know, is an almost-universally-loathed holiday opportunist riding coattails into households adorned with wreaths, garlands and mistletoe. After being snubbed throughout the festivities, untouched fruitcakes are stashed in the way back of pantries until their continuing presence is ultimately remarked upon with disgust. Then, they're removed, not to a garbage disposal which they would surely jam, but to that heavy-duty trash barrel outside. I'm not sure what Butch's feelings about fruitcake were before the incident in 1942, but I'm inclined to think he had little affection for it afterwards. Before we go on, I need to tell you something shocking about my father. He... well... it's embarrassing, but... he loved fruitcake. Not to substitute for a press weight or use as a missile to hurl at his nettlesome siblings. My father *ate* fruitcake. I know this because I saw him eat it, not in 1942, of course, but decades later when he confessed to a lifelong fondness for it.

Possibly because she was Canadian, or maybe because my father was around to eat it, my grandmother Elsie (who died years before my birth)[17] would sometimes bake fruitcake. On that 1942 afternoon, she set her fresh-out-of-the-oven mound on the kitchen table to cool and went about her business. Sometime later, eleven-year-old Bob happened to pass through the kitchen and on spotting the unattended fruitcake spontaneously made off with it, with Mischief nodding approvingly. He gobbled up his fill, then found himself face-to-face with a pan full of tattletale fruitcake

[17] Contrary to your reasonable suspicions, it wasn't fruitcake but heart disease that ended her life.

remnants sure to become his downfall if Elsie were to discover it. So he dashed down into the cellar and dumped the cake crumbs, pan and all, into the coal bin.

When Elsie returned to the kitchen to find an empty table where the fruitcake had been, she demanded all seven of the children still living at home assemble in front of her.

"Who took the fruitcake?"

No one replied. She read them the Riot Act. When that produced no results, she progressed to the Insurrection Act. Still no confession was forthcoming, so she raised the stakes to the penultimate threat level— the Treason Act— but the children remained mum. She closed with a promise of Divine Retribution for the still-unidentified fruitcake thief.

"God knows which one of you did it, and he will make you pay," she told them.

Someone did pay, but it wasn't the fruitcake thief, and it's not likely the Almighty played a role, though certainly Mischief had. Five-year-old Butch got a tummy ache that night, a run-of-the-mill, non-fruitcake-induced upset. He cried for his mommy to come and comfort him but Elsie, seeing the Divine at work, refused.

"You got what you deserved for stealing that fruitcake," she scolded him.

For years afterwards, Elsie shared this story of the wrath of God descending upon the child who stole her fruitcake at Sunday dinners and family get-togethers. Butch vigorously defended himself each time, but, occasion to occasion, year after year, Elsie decried his protests. Only after he was married, safely out of the house and far from Elsie's reprisal, did Bob confess to his role in the fruitcake's disappearance. Mischief slipped away, undetected.

Knowing the role Mischief played in the events leading up to the Divine Retribution of 1942, and familiar with her elusiveness, I made more than a cursory effort to spot evidence of her presence elsewhere in my family history. And sure enough, her imprint was there in Royalton as the 18th century gave berth to the 19th. Gideon Waterman, the ancestor who moved to Connecticut and then Vermont, avoiding the slaving, married Sally Lee, one of my most challenging genealogical puzzles. They settled and raised their nine children in Royalton.

Upon the founding of Royalton in 1769 (a town chartered by the inexhaustibly annoying and omnipresent Royal Brute), one of the first priorities of the townspeople was building a grist mill along the banks of the White River. Most small farming communities had at least one and frequently more grist mills, essential for grinding the farmers' grains into flours. Powered by water, grist mills were found on the banks of streams, often with an accompanying saw mill. Proximity to the grist mill was so important, real estate ads for farmland mentioned it as a selling point. The Royalton grist mill, originally built alongside a saw mill on lot

35 by Elias Curtis in 1776, sold to Daniel Gilbert [no relation] in 1793, and he continued to own it until 1809. For some or perhaps all of Gilbert's ownership, my fifth great-grandfather Gideon was the grist mill operator.

Grist mills brought the neighbors together with the miller known to everyone in town, an ideal occupation for the outgoing Gideon. As the milling process took considerable time, neighbors "milled about," "fed the rumor mill," and "created grist for the mill" with their chit-chat. They got both reliable intelligence and information of more dubious value from their grist mill visits. It shouldn't be surprising, then, that the one surviving story about Gideon and Sally's life is derived from that very gossip at the grist mill where Gideon toiled and where Mischief awaited an opportunity to ply her trade.

Gideon was known as a gifted storyteller. His wife Sally was likewise talkative, but the outstanding characteristic defining her was her cooking which was highly praised by the townspeople. So it happens that these qualities come together to create the story defining their lives for the descendants who will never meet them, preserved in the history published by the town in conjunction with the Royalton's Women's Club in 1911. Through the rumor mill, a story spread that Gideon kept too much of the farmers' flour as a toll for his services. Some aggrieved farmers reported this perceived injustice to mill owner Gilbert who decided to see for himself whether Gideon was stealing flour. Mischief sprang into action. As Gilbert approached Gideon with a load of his own wheat needing milling, he said, "They say you steal. I'm going to watch you. You are welcome to all the flour you can steal from my wheat."

Gideon greeted this challenge with cunning and with the assistance of his new collaborator Mischief. While Gilbert was momentarily distracted, Gideon and Mischief set Sally to the mission of sneaking flour out of the mill. Gideon captured Gilbert's attention with a long story, engaging him so thoroughly that Sally was able to slip past unnoticed with some of Gilbert's flour. When the job was completed, Gideon invited Gilbert for supper, a welcome invitation given Sally's reputation for making delectable meals. Gilbert didn't notice any flour shortage.

The mill owner praised Sally's hot biscuits that evening, creating an opening for Gideon to ask whether he could identify the source of the flour in those biscuits. When he acknowledged he couldn't, Gideon revealed the flour was Gilbert's own. Since Gilbert had told Gideon to "steal" all the flour he could that day, he didn't consider this conversion of his flour into delicious dinner biscuits theft. To the contrary, the balance may have weighted in his favor. He is said to have responded afterwards to those who had complained Gideon was taking too much of their flour, "We may as well stand it. If he doesn't steal it, his wife will."

No one noticed Mischief as she retreated into the woods to bide her time.

CHAPTER 14

MISCHIEF INFILTRATES A POW CAMP

While Mischief was schooling Bob in the art of crumb concealment and Butch was sniffling over his tummy ache, Elsie had more to contend with than missing fruitcake and Divine Retribution. World War II was underway. This isn't hyperbole characterizing everyday happenings in the Bengle household, like Bob's older sister Marie chasing him from room to room with a hot iron, promising to brand him if she caught him. I refer here to the war fought by soldiers with tanks, airplanes, and machine guns. By 1943, Elsie's eldest son Emile had graduated from high school and enlisted in the Army. When his letters stopped coming shortly after he shipped overseas, friends and family gently prepared her for the possibility he wouldn't make it home. But Elsie was resolute. If her son had died, she would feel it in her heart, she insisted. As months went by with no word, Elsie and her husband Emile watched the mailbox and prayed.

Elsie walked to the movie theater every week on Wednesday night. Those rambunctious Bengle children weren't invited; they were the reason she needed a night out. Her husband couldn't accompany her as she watched the movies because he was working in the projection room.[18] So sitting in the theater alone before the movie started, Elsie would see one of the two weekly newsreels released by the major newsreel companies. For eight to ten minutes, the silver screen would flash news and feature stories, which always included updates on the war's progress. Whatever battlefield horrors found their way into those films, Elsie never lost faith that her son would one day return home.

The Bengles' mailman Earl Murray lived one street over from the Bengle residence. You might wonder at the recitation of such detail as the mailman's name. Who would remember it three-quarters of a century later? Perhaps, a

---

[18] My affection for viewing movies in theaters was inbred. As a member of the Motion Picture Operator's Union, my grandfather Emile (who died when I was an infant) worked 35 years as a projectionist beginning in 1923, at one time or another taking up his trade in the projection rooms of most of the major theaters in the Springfield, Massachusetts area, including the Broadway, the Paramount, Poli, Bijou, Garden, Capitol, Arcade, Jefferson, Majestic, Sundown Drive-In, and Park Theater in Westfield. Projectionist proved to be an advantageous occupation when the Great Depression hit, as Emile was never without work and able to support his wife and eight children. He walked from his home in West Springfield across the river to the theater then employing him in Springfield every day up until two days before he died at age 76 in 1958. My father Bob Bengle began working in theater management in the mid-1940s. He met my mother Marie Bruce at the Poli where she worked for him as an usherette, a quaint word since retired along with the whole notion of being escorted to a seat in a movie theater.

person who knows how the story ends, with the younger Emile marrying the mailman's daughter. But we aren't there yet, and now we won't need to go there at all. Getting back to where we left off, each day before making his rounds, Earl organized the mail by house number. He knew the neighbors to whom he delivered mail each day, and he understood the Bengles were desperate for word about their son. So when he spotted the card with its military markings, he dropped his sack and scrambled posthaste to the Bengles' house. That's how Elsie and her husband Emile learned their son was one of the 93,941 American prisoners of war captured by Germany.

Seized by the Germans in a guileful destination once known as Prussia that thought to obscure its identity with some canny rebranding— such that it now answers to Poland, Russia, Belgium, Lithuania, France, Czechia, Denmark, or Germany depending on who's asking— Emile was initially held in a Polish sawmill. In his travels from one location to another, he sometimes endured lengthy forced marches in which the prisoners were almost continuously on the move, frequently without stopping for meals or rest. On other occasions, he traveled by Forty and Eights. The Forty and Eights, small boxcars designed to transport 40 people or eight horses, were so overloaded with prisoners for their travels that lying down to sleep was only possible in shifts, if at all. The men were given as little as a single sandwich or chunk of cheese to sustain them for up to a week of travel. For water, they sometimes reached outside the boxcar and scraped up snow.

The transit camp Stalag XIIA by Limburg-an-der-Lahn was Emile's first official destination as a prisoner of war. Stalag XIIA was structured as a waystation to interrogate and organize the prisoners by rank and service before sending them to a prison camp. They learned the rules of imprisonment, most importantly that escape attempts, including merely touching the barbed wire fence surrounding the grounds, would be met with gunfire. It was here Emile was allowed to contact his parents by postcard to notify them he'd been taken prisoner, modeling his message on the script every prisoner was instructed to use:

> I have been taken prisoner of war in Germany. I am in good health. We will be transported from here to another camp within a few days. Please do not write until I send a new address.[19]

German POW camps were known for treating American "kriegers" well in the hopes of reciprocity for their own POWs. But Emile seems to have drawn the short straw when it came to camp assignments. Stalag XIIA in Limburg was less equipped than other camps because it was a transit camp, not intended to hold prisoners for any longer than it took to log them in and transport them elsewhere. As the war went on, some POWs languished there, including Emile. By the time he left Stalag XIIA, it was crowded with some 20,000 men, straining resources. Breakfast consisted of a fifth of a loaf of bread and margarine. After roll call, there was ersatz coffee created from large grains of something unidentifiable the men hoped was vegetable matter. Lunch

---

[19] Source 82.

and dinner were usually watery soups, sometimes accompanied by a potato and the occasional brot.

In early October 1944, Emile was reassigned and made a five-day march to Stalag IXB near Bad Orb, nicknamed "Little Siberia." This was the most dreadful of the German POW camps. At this late stage of the war, Germany suffered shortages of almost everything, and the large number of men captured at the Battle of the Bulge stressed this camp beyond its capabilities. Men went from slowly starving in Limburg to dying of starvation at Bad Orb. Many slept on straw on the floor in the frigid winter without a blanket, packed against each other for lack of sufficient bunks and bedding. There was heat in the room for but a few hours each day because of the meager fuel supplies. There were insufficient latrines, no toilet paper, and water shortages that curtailed all but fortnightly bathing. Feces contaminated the barracks. Without bowls or tableware, men drank soup from their helmets and picked up the little food they were given with their unclean hands. Toward the end, the prisoners were eating grass soup. The various forms of vermin were so abundant that the innkeeper Monsieur Thénardier would have been a wealthy man had he set up shop in Bad Orb where his mice and lice surcharges would have provided an endless revenue stream.

The International Committee of the Red Cross issued a situation critical cablegram in April 1945 (just after the camp's liberation) summarizing the desperate conditions detected there during a visit the previous month. They cited "...considerable loss of weight, dysentery, diarrhea hemorrhagica, generalized pneumonia, hygiene nonexistent, vermin swarms, danger typhus, clothing in shreds," with accompanying descriptions of the inadequacy of the food, urgent need for critical medicines, and the complete lack of soap and toilet paper.[20]

German POW camps were generally tedious places to live, but two notable events happened at Stalag IXB during Emile's tenure. The first was an accidental strafing by Allied aircraft which left three POWs dead. The second was Master Sergeant Roddie Edmonds famously saving some of the Jewish American soldiers under his watch from deportation to a slave labor camp. After advising all the Jews not to step forward when instructed to do so by the Germans during roll call, Edmonds insisted to the Commandant, "We are all Jews here."

In the midst of the neverending misery, Emile was surprised one day by Mischief who had abandoned her perch at the Bengle residence and fallen into position alongside him as he marched across the German countryside. On that occasion, the POWs arrived at a farm and were instructed to take up residence in the hayloft for the night. Hungry, and prodded by their mysterious guest, some of the men slid down the grain chute in search of neglected produce. They returned, satiated, having met up with a milk cow. The remaining men, including Emile, made a mad dash for the grain chute on hearing this report, eager to get their own milk. But when they got to the cow's stall, they realized none of them knew how to milk a cow. That poor bovine must

---

[20] Source 91.

have suffered immensely as Emile and his fellow prisoners tugged and pulled, and tugged and pulled, and tugged and pulled, for an eternity before finally extracting milk.

Getting back up the grain chute was considerably more difficult than sliding down, and it was nearly dawn by the time the men were settled back into the hayloft. Dawn is when the farmer showed up to milk his cow. His expressions of consternation at finding his cow unexpectedly dry could be heard above in the hayloft, where Mischief and the POWs shared a rare laugh. Then Mischief took her leave to prepare for her next adventure.

The Allies liberated Stalag IXB on April 2, 1945, ending Emile's POW experience. On June 22, he arrived at Boston Harbor on the Admiral Mayo, his repatriation complete. Mischief's drop-in during the bleak days of imprisonment supplied Emile with inspiration needed to help withstand the daily indignities until liberation day came.

CHAPTER 15

A SPRINKLING OF GOODNESS

To my great relief, not all of my ancestors were troublemakers or trouble magnets. While a perfectly respectable shopkeeper or farmer attempting to claim their rightful limb on the family tree may have to elbow away wolf hunters and bigamists preening in the limelight, their ascendance to their proper leafy enclaves offers respite to those around them including hapless descendants down on their ancestral luck. The existence of such tranquil ancestors proved my family was capable of some sort of normalcy, even though normalcy and all of its close associates had steered clear of our household during my growing-up years.

Ira Joyce and Nancy Waterman Joyce are less splashy ancestors perhaps than a Richard Waterman or Rogue but their lives were marked by a quiet and admirable dignity. Contemporaneous accounts of them exude warmth and decency. Ira and Nancy lived in the small town of Sharon, Vermont whose total residents numbered near 1,000. The local newspapers published the everyday comings and goings of the Joyces and their neighbors. Not only do we hear about who was born, married, and died, we hear who was sick, who had relatives visit, who took a trip out of town, and who attended social events. As a result of these enchanting reports, I have a remarkable picture of my 3rd great-grandparents.

Ira was a first generation American, the child of German immigrant parents. Before marrying Nancy, he had married Lucena Winslow in 1842 and with her had a daughter Ellen in June 1843. Six months later, Lucena, only 25 years old, died. Two years after that, Ira and Nancy married. Ira was a farmer, and later took on the additional responsibility of church sexton, aka grave digger, at Pine Hill Cemetery.

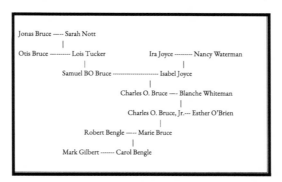

Montpelier's *Argus and Patriot* newspaper teased Ira for his political stances. Days after the presidential election of 1884, when Ira's preferred candidate Democrat Grover Cleveland beat Republican James G. Blaine, the newspaper took jabs at the political split in Ira's family, as his grandson

Charles O. Bruce Sr., Charlie's father, was a longtime Republican delegate:[21]

> The venerable Ira Joyce, grave digger, is feeling well. In case of Cleveland's election some think he will have to bury one entire family of Republican politicians.

Six years later, the publisher chortled:[22]

> "Uncle" Ira Joyce, 82 years old, went on a visiting trip last week seven and one-half miles, on foot, returning in two or three days hale and hearty, probably owing to his being a strong Democrat.

Comments about Ira's industriousness appeared in news reports frequently. The *Landmark* had noted in 1889:[23]

> Ira Joyce of Sharon, aged 81 years, has cut his grass, amounting to several tons; has, unaided, done all the work about his place, including milking, feeding stock, etc.; pitched all of his hay both ways and put it into the barn: driven to the factory and to the store, and he is now ready to work out for a few days.

The Joyces appeared close with their children, and the newspapers dutifully reported on their visits. Through this diligent reporting, we know Ira and Nancy spent Thanksgiving with their daughter Belle and her family in 1891. They visited their son Ed and made another visit to

---

[21] Source 107.
[22] Source 106.
[23] Source 101.

Belle in June the following year. And in February 1893, it was C.H. Joyce's turn for a visit. There are many news items mentioning Nancy's serious illness, but the nature of the illness is never specified. It may have been heart disease since her death at age 85 was attributed to organic disease of the heart and general debility.

Ira was noted for his farm accomplishments. *Spirit of the Age* credited him for his butchering skill in an unusually frigid winter in January 1883:[24]

> Sharon claims a smart old butcher in the person of Ira Joyce, seventy-four years of age, who killed seventy sheep for mutton, in three days, traveled one and one-half miles, took care of a stock of cattle, with the thermometer down to sixteen below zero some of the time.

Not only was he greeted as a smart butcher but an accomplished "veterinary surgeon," albeit one without degrees.[25]

> Dr. Ira Joyce, our veterinary surgeon, demonstrated the physiology of the heart to Edgar Chillson one day recently. He killed one sheep, dressed it all by removing the viscera, and last of all took out the heart and laid it upon bench, so that its pulsations were clearly visible. We did not hear whether the respiratory movements of the thorax were going on at the same time or not.

---

[24] Source 97.
[25] Source 129.

The following summer, the townspeople were in awe when Ira obtained a yield of 40 pounds of white elephant potatoes from just three potatoes he planted.

By the time Ira reached old age, it appears he was a town favorite, with the newspapers remarking frequently on his comings and goings, and particularly on his stamina. When he was 85 years old, the Landmark noted he could still run "like a fox." And when Ira Joyce died at age 86, four generations gathered in the Congregational Church to mourn him. An obituary published in *the Landmark* noted that Ira had been sexton at the Pine Hill Cemetery for 30 years where it said, he'd been "discharging faithfully every duty in storm or sunshine."[26]

---

[26] Source 125.

CHAPTER 16

UNSPEAKABLE LOSS

The pain of illness and death squeezed the hearts of my family as it had done to all other families since the beginning of time. This was none of Shame's business, but Shame had a way of poking its nose into corners, uninvited. When it came to communicable diseases, Shame heaped blame on the already burdened— either those who were sick themselves or their families struggling to care for them. From the Industrial Revolution through the 1970s, where there was illness or death, there was Shame looking over shoulders, waiting for the most opportune time to inflict damage.

One day during the Industrial Revolution, the construction workers were going about their labors when the two-and-a–half-year-old walking by with her mother interrupted them. "Is my 'Lella' down there?" she asked, referring to the massive hole they'd dug. Ella, little Lizzie O'Brien's ten-month old sister, had recently been put in the ground, and this looked to her like a chance to bring her back up. It was cholera infantum, or "summer diarrhea" that stole away Lizzie's baby sister in July 1888. Two more of her siblings would fall prey to disease before she reached adulthood. Lizzie's childhood took place at the end of an era in which twenty percent of the names inscribed on the death rolls were those of infants. Although infant death rates were declining, the incremental progress was slow and inadequate to forestall the tragedies in Lizzie's family, who lived and worked in crowded conditions characteristic of the Industrial Revolution.

Summer diarrhea, marked by not only prolonged diarrhea but also violent vomiting and high fever, had not yet reached its pinnacle when it took baby Ella. Although it was first identified in 1794, its prevalence would not soar until the decades following baby Ella's death. By 1910 to 1930, it was responsible for a full thirty percent of the deaths of babies under two. And then the disease waned for reasons medical experts could not explain. The public health initiatives responsible for reducing diarrhea overall in this age group— water purification, wastewater treatment, and homogenization of milk among them— seemed impotent in addressing the summer variety, according to a 2019 analysis by the IZA Institute of Labor Economics. Even today, researchers can't identify the specific bacterium that produced the cholera infantum epidemics. The pain of losing a child was exacerbated by the very health programs intended to reduce deaths. Shame made sure of it, twisting the public health message into one that cast blame on the sick and their families, attributing disease to their lack of sufficient attention to personal hygiene.

Beloved three-year-old Delia was the second O'Brien sister Lizzie mourned, this time when she was fourteen years old. She and Mamie, 11, John, 9, Lulu, 7, and Marty, 5, were all deeply affected by this loss. Although Nanny wasn't yet born, she came to absorb her parents' and siblings' sadness and spoke of missing Delia as though she too had bounced her on her knee and taught her nursery rhymes. The O'Brien family had barely had time to register Delia's absence when Daniel Francis arrived six months later. And then it was time for another goodbye as Daniel Francis contracted pneumonia after a mere eight weeks and was gone.

Little Delia succumbed to diphtheria and pneumonia. Diphtheria, called the "strangling angel of children" is a particularly ugly disease, causing a thick gray pseudomembrane formed from waste products and proteins to grow over the larynx, nasal tissues, pharynx and/or tonsils. Not only does this growth inhibit breathing, its toxins can travel to the organs and nerves and inflict deadly damage. Fatality rates, normally twenty percent, jumped as high as forty percent during diphtheria epidemics, making it one of the most dreaded childhood diseases. It wasn't until the 1920s that a vaccine was in common use, too late for Delia and her bereaved family. Sixty years later, the O'Brien sisters would still tear up on the frequent occasions when they'd share memories of little Delia.

Thirty years before Delia's death, Lois Tucker and
Otis Bruce, Charlie's great-grandparents, lost two of their
daughters in the space of two weeks to this disease. When
Emma Maryetta Bruce, age 5, and Clara Abbie Anna Bruce,
age 9, died in September 1861, the newspaper reported not
some unthinkable tragedy but a matter-of-fact occurrence, as
diphtheria regularly cut swaths through families. When
examining death records, I could see a slew of other families
similarly affected.

All of the children who didn't have a chance to grow
up are as much a part of my family history as those who did.
Their short lives and wretched endings, meaningful in their
own right, also made a permanent imprint on those who
loved and outlived them.

Survivors of childhood epidemics weren't in the clear
until they dodged yet another disease, this one notorious for
cutting short the lives of young adults and for being one of
Shame's favorites. Known at various times as phthisis, taves,
schachepheth, scofula, the white plague, and consumption,
history finally settled on the name tuberculosis. But Nanny
and her siblings continued to use the old fashioned moniker
"consumption," a name they dared speak only in whispers,
thanks to Shame's unrelenting attacks. Tuberculosis killed
more people in New England than any other disease in the
19th century. While it infected people of all ages, young
adults were its most common victims.

Sidestepping the threat of tuberculosis required
hawk-eyed attention to surroundings and sufficient agility to

leap over damp ground, swerve around long skirts known to be germ-catchers, elude invisible miasmas threatening from the air, and extract oneself from lung-squishing corsets. Of these, only abandoning corsets stood the test of time, and that has nothing to do with tuberculosis. Death did not bring an end to the troubles tuberculosis inflicted on its victims. Its enemies made late night graveyard excursions to hack off the heads of the deceased and hammer stakes through their hearts. Even in the late 1800s, these vampire scares spread through New England occasionally, spurred by the endurance of folkloric beliefs, the prevalence of tuberculosis within families, and the propensity of TB patients to cough up blood.

It might appear that Lizzie and her family had weathered more untimely death than any family should have to bear, but the early years of the 20th century brought more. Nanny's brother John contracted tuberculosis at age 25 in 1916. He passed away five days before the first anniversary of his mother's death. Was it Shame that kept the O'Brien family from telling Nanny the truth? Throughout her life, she believed her brother John died of a broken heart, unable to go on after the loss of their mother, Mary Daley O'Brien. Even John's obituary spread the cover story that he died at his home in Chicopee.

The last two months of John's life were lonely. The brother who would later be described in his obituary as "one of the most popular young men in the city" was sent to the Chicopee Isolation Hospital in Aldenville, Massachusetts. There was little hope of cure, as Chicopee Isolation was dedicated to advanced cases. It had a capacity of 20 patients and charged $10.00 per week. Unfortunately, it was seriously underfunded and lacking modern equipment, more a concern for comfort than survival, since the patients with advanced disease had little to no chance of ever leaving the facility. TB was killing four hundred fifty people per day at that time, and public health authorities were mounting massive campaigns to isolate the sick and teach the public hygiene techniques that would help put an end to its invasions. The use of shared public drinking cups for water was curtailed and public spitting banned.

Despite Jean-Antoine Villemin proving TB's ability to pass from person to person in 1868, many people stubbornly resisted believing it, feeling safer, perhaps, to treat it as a hereditary condition that wouldn't touch their families. For many of those who did accept the scientific advances, the public education efforts backfired as they had with childhood diseases. Understanding the sick could spread the disease to them, they shunned anyone with the telltale cough or pale skin with which TB marked its victims. Job loss and refusal of public accommodation were common. Sadly, many of the sick ended up like our John, alone in targeted facilities to spend their last weeks of life.

Although treatments to slam the door on TB became commonplace in the following generations and outbreaks were almost unheard of in my world, after having killed several of my forebears in past generations, that ghastly disease had not finished with my family. By the time I reached adolescence, Uncle Bobby was years distant from Nanny's

bedroom and rarely came to our house anymore, with or
without a police escort. It was then Nanny got a call from the
hospital informing her Bobby had been admitted and might
not survive. She contacted a priest to administer the Last
Rites. She had my mother dial up Charlie. And she
telephoned the hospital daily to check on Bobby's condition
and ask whether it was yet safe to visit. When Bobby was out
of immediate danger, he was shipped off to a specialized
facility where Nanny was able to take the bus and visit him
each week, following the prescribed precautions.

My mother had always explained illnesses to me as
biological events and discounted associations between illness
and moral deficiency as the product of old-fashioned
superstition, nonsense, something educated people know
better than to believe. When a girl with epilepsy had a seizure
in school one day, Mom and I talked at length when I got
home about the unwarranted prejudices she had seen against
people with illnesses like epilepsy and diabetes when she was
growing up. She remembered them being treated as
unmarriageable by people who didn't want those diseases
brought into their families' genetics. And she talked about
people with fearsome communicable disease being cast aside
as dirty or despicable when they were merely sick. All of this
was wrong. When tuberculous infected Bobby, however,
Shame reproached Mom mercilessly, and her anger boiled
over at Bobby and at Nanny. This disease threatened the
family's reputation. With Shame prodding her, my mother
insisted she didn't want TB or any talk of that dirty disease
brought into her house. Each time Nanny would walk in the
back door after visiting Bobby, Mom's forceful waves of

hostility nearly thrust her back out onto the porch. After some months, Bobby recovered, and the tension abated. Tuberculosis set out for the horizon and was never seen again in our family, one of the few times a nefarious force went away and stayed away. Knock on wood.

CHAPTER 17

A SEASON OF GOODBYES

Before there was Clyde, there was Daffodil. Daffodil was the son of Whiskers, one of her first litter. He was gray with a white bib and paws. In Daffodil's early cathood, he didn't come home one day. We roamed the neighborhood, peering under porches and scouting through patches of woods, calling his name. We phoned Streets and Engineering and the ASPCA but no one had word of him, dead or alive. When Daffodil still hadn't made it home after a week, my mother took me to the pound to look for him ourselves. We checked every cage, but Daffodil wasn't there.

Assuming that Daffodil probably wasn't coming home after all this time, my mother suggested we get a new kitten and steered me to a brown striped male tabby kitten that we named Clyde. Every weekday at lunch time through the remainder of elementary school, Clyde would stand sentry at the intersection of Agnes Street and Island Pond

Road until I came into view, and we'd walk to the house together. Clyde shared peanut butter and bananas on toast when we watched Saturday morning cartoons. He'd sit on the back of the couch waiting for the morsels I offered while Scooby Doo or Archie played on TV. On days I felt sad, I'd bury my face in his fur and cry.

Years later, as the high school French Club set out for Montréal, I boarded the bus in high spirits. As with any social outing, there was a dose of trepidation lurking beneath the excitement. Though my reasons differed from hers, I was as diligent as my mother in protecting her Secrets, for even without knowing what they were, I intuitively understood that their revelation had the power to mow down the measly sprouts of social capital I'd managed to grow. I'd always been cautious in bringing anyone into the Barn, my sister's and my nickname for the dingy house with its slapdash repairs, lumpy couch, and collection of broken appliances neither wishing nor tinkering had succeeded in restoring to working condition. On the occasions I brought anyone in, I was vigilant for signs it was time to get out. My friendships were marked by caution and self-preserving emotional distance. In a group activity, like the trip to Montréal, I clung to the edges of the group, careful not to offend and hoping fervently not to be left behind. Despite this, I was still able to enjoy the trip.

When I returned home at the end of the week, Clyde, my steady companion for the past seven years, was already missing for several days. My parents said they'd shouted his name from the porch repeatedly and telephoned the ASPCA without success. I called again, in case of a late arrival, but

Clyde hadn't been brought in. My new chapter, Life without Clyde, began. It coincided with Life without Nanny who died just before the crocuses bloomed. Nanny had gotten sick in the late summer. Just after Christmas, she went to the hospital, never to return home.

There had always been tension in Mom's relationship with Nanny. It was a studious and ambitious[27] young Mom who was told to drop out of school when Charlie left, to support her mother and younger brother Bobby who was said to need an education more than her. Mom's rational side disdained Nanny's "fantastical" beliefs from Wee Folk and the Banshees[28] to prayers to Jesus turning Lizzie's infant daughter's eyes from blue to brown. For most of her childhood, Mom contended not only with Nanny's magical mindset but those of Nanny's sisters; for Nanny and Lulu and their husbands and kids most often lived in a combined household. With Mamie visiting frequently, and Lizzie often enough, Mom had three or even all four of the sisters insisting she beware of three knocks on the door for it meant death was coming to someone in the house. When a dog howled, her mother and aunts shuddered, for a howling dog was another harbinger of life's end. Though family snapshots were scarce, one fact about them stands out: the entire family is never pictured together. That was taboo, sure to mark one of them for imminent death. Too close to see charm in these harmless old world superstitions, my mother let her emotions

---

[27] She was on the honor roll at Agawam High School where her favorite subject was history.

[28] The O'Briens are one of five Irish families said to be able to hear the keening of the Banshees, along with the O'Neills, O'Connors, O'Gradys, and Kavanaughs. I suspect the Dalys should be added to the list.

slip into Shame's clutches. Yet even as she bristled at the myth clouds enveloping her, Mom didn't tempt fate with her own children. Not a single photograph exists of us together as a family.

Nanny was easily stirred up, and in that state, she was helpless. Mom had most often picked up the slack. But Nanny's biggest sin was Vivien. Duty glued Mom to the party line about Vivien's infancy, and I never knew about Vivien's own son until after both Mom and Nanny were gone, so in retrospect I don't know exactly what she knew or even which baby she was referring to when she blasted Nanny one day with, "You don't give away your baby!" Nanny's reply, "Well, what else could I have done?" likewise is open to interpretation. Irish loyalty and the maternal bond bound them for life but they often lived in a state of uneasy detente. If you've read Fredrik Backman's *My Grandmother Asked Me to Tell You She's Sorry*, you'll understand when I say you couldn't find a more loving grandmother than Nanny, and I'm glad she was my Nanny, but I don't think I'd have wanted her to be my mother.

My mother refused to visit Nanny in the hospital if I was to be there and so she and my father made those trips out to the long-term care facility two towns distant while I stayed home. I thought my mother needed to be there more, even though I wanted to go myself. On one occasion, my mother nervously agreed to our both going. I walked into what I was told was Nanny's hospital room, but unlike my gray-haired Nanny, the woman in the bed had white hair. She gave me a piercing look and said, "Who are you?" I turned to stone, devoid of the savoir faire that might have guided me through this startling development.

That was the last time I saw Nanny. Dad snuck her a cigarette that day as the relatives gathered at her bedside squawked and fluttered, a fellow smoker who knew those cravings and recognized the futility of her quitting. Not long after, I returned from school with my friend Linda, shocked to find no one at home. I feared my mother's absence meant Nanny's condition had worsened. Then, the phone rang. The caller identified herself as a hospital employee and asked me what my parents wanted done with Esther Bruce's body. Nanny had died early that morning.

With Nanny gone, the characteristic grimness of the household grew to become unbearable. And there was no Clyde to absorb my tears.

CHAPTER 18

SURVIVING

Samuel Bascom Otis Bruce wasn't awarded the Purple Heart, the Congressional Medal of Honor, the Distinguished Service Cross, the Silver Star, or the Bronze Star. In my search for ancestors worthy of admiration, he might have been overlooked. I expected my heroes to come in gift-wrap, expertly tagged, and free from misconstruction. As soon as I spotted military overtones in anyone's history, I scanned for awards, for recognition, for famous battles and noted generals. Not finding such accolades or associations, I was inclined to move on. With my military ancestors, that meant erasing them from our history, not necessarily a bad thing I thought. But with Samuel, that would have been a grave mistake.

This ancestor contributes admirable strength and much-needed survivorship to our story. He barely made it out alive from the infamous Civil War prison, popularly referred to as "Andersonville," though it's actual name was Camp Sumpter and its common name derived from its location in Andersonville, Georgia. But he did survive, against frightful odds, and afterwards, he thrived.

Born to Otis Bruce and Lois Tucker Bruce in 1842, Samuel Bascom Otis Bruce's first two names seem to have been a tribute to a recently deceased Congregational Minister in town, Rev. Samuel Bascom. Rev. Bascom's second wife Martha was Lois Tucker Bruce's half-sister. As you can see, the forever Catholic on all sides save Charlie himself was whittled away with each new ancestor added to his side of the tree. I've yet to find a single Catholic in Charlie's ancestry and the Bengle line is also replete with Protestants as well as Catholics.

Samuel enlisted as a Union soldier in August 1862 when he was 20 years old. In enlisting in the military, he was following in the footsteps of his grandfather Jonas who had fought in the American Revolution. Jonas had enlisted as a private in 1775, was promoted to corporal and left the service after spending two years at the rank of sergeant when his service concluded in 1780. This is the same lineage that produced Bobby, of aftershave-guzzling notoriety, so permit me my initial skepticism. In Bobby's defense, he was apparently acclaimed for his skill in electronics when he signed up, against Charlie's advice. Once the ugly truths of war defined his daily repertoire, Bobby found a not-so-temporary relief that would come to define him and prematurely end his life just shy of age 42. But Sam was not Bobby.

Samuel was assigned to the 11th Vermont Regiment, Co. H, working with heavy artillery. This was thought to be a relatively safe assignment; for most of the war, heavy artillery units were assigned to the defense of Washington from fixed locations. This was true of Samuel's unit initially. He mustered in at Brattleboro the first of September and a week later was assigned to the defenses of Washington north of the Potomac. His first post was Ft. Slocum where his unit remained six months until reassigned to Ft. Bunker Hill, a distance of less than three miles. Like many promises of good things, Samuel's military commitment was riddled with exceptions and caveats. When DC seemed secure enough, those crafty military generals scowered the proverbial fine print, then pulled the "heavies" out of their cushy posts and assigned them infantry duty in May 1864. A month later, Samuel was in Richmond at the First Battle of Weldon Road, also known as the Battle of Jerusalem Plank Road, whose purpose was cutting rail supply to the Rebels in Petersburg and expanding westward.

On June 21, a tactical error of disastrous proportions led to the capture of 1800 Union troops at Weldon Road. Samuel was not among them. The next day, the Union forces in Richmond met with some small success in pushing westward. On the 23rd, Samuel's group of Vermonters was sent to tear up the rails to disrupt Confederate supplies and personnel movement. Some 1,000 of the Vermonters were in particularly vulnerable positions, out in front with insufficient protection. When the Confederates arrived, they chased Samuel and his fellow soldiers into the woods and forced a surrender. After his capture, Samuel was taken first to Libby Prison and then transferred to Andersonville where 13,000 of the 45,000 prisoners perished from disease or abuse.[29] Samuel was one of the lucky men who survived Andersonville, but he wasn't able to leave on his own accord; after five months as a prisoner of war, the formerly healthy young man was carried out on a stretcher.

Surviving Andersonville meant surviving living in the elements, digging into the dirt for shelter. It meant having only tattered rags for clothing and so little food that many died of starvation. It also meant enduring constant abuse. The horrors of Andersonville were so extreme compared to other Civil War prisons, the Commandant Henry Wirz was tried on war crimes, sentenced to death, and hanged. First hand accounts of the conditions included this report from a fellow Vermonter held in Andersonville, identified as J.E.H.:

> Captain Wertz (sic) was not content to starve and expose his victims to the inclemencies of the climate, but it pleased him to add insulting and taunting language. Hence it gave him pleasure to kick the dead body of a prisoner, and grinning, (he could not laugh,) say, "Ah, ha, another d----d Yank gone to hell. Hell will soon be so full of them that his Satanic

---

[29] The prisoner parole system had broken down by this point. Up until mid-1863, prisoners were paroled upon promise not to fight again until a prisoner exchange was formalized and then both of the exchanged prisoners could get back to fighting. The system collapsed when the Confederacy refused to treat black soldiers on par with white soldiers.

Majesty will have to annex New England to his dominions for want of room."[30]

He described one act he thought particularly fiendish that occurred on a levee waiting for transport, where no talking was allowed:

> There was a boy of some fifteen or sixteen years old belonging to the 12th Regiment in Iowa infantry. His geniality made him the special favorite of all the prisoners. He was a good singer... His singing was a great irritation to old Wertz , and he tried various modes of punishment to stop it. He would confine him in the dungeon 24 or 48 hours at a time without food or water... The thoughts of home, however, were too strong for young Allen to resist to sing that good old tune, "Home, Sweet Home." A blow from old Wertz's revolver felled him to the ground. He was badly cut on the head... He lived to reach Nashville, Tenn., and there he died beneath that old flag he loved so well, a victim of Capt. Wertz's vindictive hatred of American soldiers.[31]

Mrs. E.M. Warren of Nashville, who served as a nurse in rebel hospitals testified as to her observations during a visit to Andersonville.[32] She described the prisoners as "half-clad human skeletons, devoid of shoes and stockings, standing upon the frosty ground," noting they would "occasionally lift

---

[30] Source 153.
[31] Ibid.
[32] Source 152.

their feet and wrap them in the tattered rags that hung about their person and press their feet close to the body for its warmth to shield them from the frost."

Nurse Warren explained that when prisoners fell from the weight of dead prisoners they were forced to carry to graves, the prison wardens would curse them and prick them with bayonets. "And not infrequently, the bodies of soldiers were carried away for interment before life was extinct." When she rebuked Wirz for these conditions, she said he threatened her life.

When a neighbor of the prison saw the suffering there and carried in some vegetables to nourish the starving prisoners, a soldier under Wirz' command placed poisonous buckeye leaves among the vegetables before serving them to the prisoners of war. At one point, the prisoners were moved to Albany, Georgia due to an advancing Union threat, living half naked in the cold without shelter, with rations barely sufficient to sustain life, and some prisoners became so weak they couldn't walk. When it was time to return to Andersonville, Wirz ordered the camp burned, and those who were not fit to march back to Andersonville and could not otherwise escape the flames were burned alive in the fire.

While the North celebrated the end of the war with bonfires, bell-ringing, and impromptu parades, soldiers like Sam were not necessarily safe. Fifteen hundred of the prisoners of war released from Andersonville, including several from his hometown, were killed when a steam boiler exploded on the ship Sultana as it was carrying them home.

Once he did make it home, Sam convalesced at his parents' house in Sharon, Vermont. After he regained strength, he married Belle Joyce and moved to the nearby village West Hartford (yet one more town chartered in the name of the Royal Brute.) There, they raised two sons. He became a deacon in the Congregational Church, a post he held 27 years, and a member of the vets organization Grand Army of the Republic. The camaraderie of those who shared the war experience was ever important. At a Vermont Veteran Soldiers Reunion in 1882, a Col. Walker mentioned the value of vets having a place where it was acceptable to speak of their war experiences, experiences most of society wanted to relegate to the past and not look back.

Walker described how different the world had become since the war. "As memory flows back to those terrible years," he said, "we begin to realize how trivial and commonplace are the successes of to-day. Now, prosperity abounds throughout our borders, and cheerful faces meet us everywhere. Then, constant and all-pervading anxiety and gloom filled the land. Enquiries for the latest news from the army were in every mouth. Strangers were stopped at every farm house for recital and conjecture."[33]

When Samuel died, the local newspaper noted the large attendance at his funeral and the many floral tributes. It said of him, "He became active in the churchwork and in all that aided the community welfare and was ever-esteemed for

---

[33] Source 158.

his all-round worth by the townspeople and G.A.R. comrades." [34]

[34] Source 181.

CHAPTER 19

INTERMISSION

Step away from the drear and despair, enjoy some momentary entertainment, courtesy of Julien Lippé. My fourth cousin once removed, Julien started his career as a radio actor, later moving on to TV and film. During World War II, when radio broadcasts carried news and entertainment into homes throughout the world, Julien played in at least one program heard in French-speaking Canada and France. The Montreal *Gazette* noted on March 6, 1942 that for only the second time in its history, the Luxe Radio Theater Français prime time programming would be interrupted, the occasion being an address by U.S. President Roosevelt. Even with the war on, or maybe especially with the war on, the importance of escape from everyday worries through the arts was recognized.

For Luxe, Julien played a supporting role in *Madame X*, the story of a shopgirl-married-diplomat whose mother-in-law blackmails her into abandoning her husband and young son after discovering her presence at her lover's accidental death. After a series of degrading life changes, shopgirl encounters con man who unsuccessfully attempts to persuade her to blackmail her husband— so unsuccessfully that she shoots him dead. By this time, her husband is the governor and her abandoned son the public defender charged with representing her as Madame X, the woman who admitted killing the con man but won't reveal her identity. The natural love between mother and child prevails, even though her son never learns Madame X is his mother.

In the 1950s, as the world was transitioning from radio to television, Julien played a recurring role in a popular show aired on both media. *La Famille Plouffe* may have been the most watched broadcast in French Canada due to viewers' ability to identify with the down-to-earth characters who lived like they lived. Indeed, *Macleans* described the fictional Plouffes as "Québec's most famous family." The show aired twice a week on radio and once on television on three channels. It captured so many devotees, merchants closed shops and churches and theatres changed schedules to accommodate Plouffe-watching. Even hockey was postponed. Hockey! In Canada! On Ash Wednesday in 1955, Macleans noted, Rev. J. J. Bradette, of Montreal's Notre Dame de Grâce, cut short the Mass so parishioners could rush home to their televisions.

Julien brought to life Narcisse, the drinking-buddy-friend-confidante of the father character, plumber Theophile Plouffe. The actors performed in both French and English so the show could be enjoyed by the vast majority of Canadians. The series ran 1953-1959, and was revived in the 1980s after Julien's 1978 death. The Audio-Visual Preservation Trust of Canada designated *La Famille Plouffe* a masterwork.

By the 1970s, Julien took his talents to the Big Screen. He played the father of the character Ernest in *La Maudite Galette* (*Dirty Money* in the English-speaking world.) The first full-length feature film directed by Denys Arcand, *La Maudite Galette* satirizes American mid-20th century film noir. The storyline involves a young couple and their tenant Ernest wading into the world of crime. Julien appears near the end of the movie when Ernest retreats to his parents' house to share his spoils.

He also played the role of Auguste in the Gilles Carle film *La Vraie Nature de Bernadette.* That movie screened at Cannes and later went on to win several Canadian Film Awards.It attained the status of masterwork by the Audio-Visual Preservation Trust in 2001. When the Toronto National Film Festival conducted a poll of the top Canadian films of all time in 1984, *La Vraie Nature de Bernadette* placed tenth. Movie-goers in France bought hundreds of thousands of tickets when the movie was released there. As Canada prepared to celebrate its Sesquicentennial in 2017, the film was identified as one of 150 essential works in Canadian cinema history.

The final movie Julien performed in, *Le Temps d'une Chasse*, is an exploration of the male psyche as surfaced in a weekend hunting trip. It was the first full-length feature film by Francis Mankiewicz who went on to produce several award-winning films. *Le Temps d'une Chasse* was presented at both the Venice Film Festival and the Cannes Film Festival in 1973. Though it won no awards, it has been recognized as a classic in Québec cinema.

Julien gets a high up perch in the tree so he'll have a superior view to stimulate his imagination. And now, please get back to your seats as we continue our journey. That speck in the distance is Knockaderry.

Nanny, 1969. Credit Marie Bruce Bengle.

Philipp II Ernst **La Fripouille Fétide de la Famille Lippé** (Stinking Rogue of the Lippé family).

Anton Wilhelm Strack, Portrait of Philipp II, Count of Schaumburg-Lippe (1720-1787). Public domain.

Marie Bruce Bengle holding author with Jan Bengle Ruidl in 1960. Credit: Bob Bengle.

Below, Archange "Célina" Lamoureux Bengle, the author's great-grandmother.

Donald "Butch" Bengle, casualty
of Divine Retribution, right,
(Credit: Alston Studios) and Bob
Bengle, unrepentant fruitcake thief
below.

Elzier "Elsie" Monat Bengle and
Esther O'Brien Bruce, September

17, 1949 before the wedding of
their children, Marie Bruce and
Robert Bengle.

"Pépé," Emile Bengle, in his younger years, left, and
in his later years, center.

Above right, Private Johnson's Royal
Regiment of New York 1776 by
Charles M. Lefferts. This is the
uniform worn by Adam and John
Bangle. Public domain.

Bob Bengle, groom, Marie Bruce
Bengle, bride, Marie's cousin Avis
Damon Lessard, matron of honor, and
Emile L. Bengle, Bob's brother, best
man.

Gill, Massachusetts Town Hall.
Credit: Carol Bengle Gilbert.

Wittikind, the ancestor with neither a first nor a last name, kneels before Charlemagne. Ary Scheffer: *Charlemagne reçoit la soumission de Widukind à Paderborn* (1840), Galerie des Batailles. Public domain.

Jacques Bengle (1924-2005), the author's third cousin and genealogy mentor. Credit: Fédération québécoise des généalogie.

Members of the Three Rivers Volunteer Fire Dept. The author's grandfather Emile Bengle is in the front row, third from right. Public domain.

Above left, Narcisse Bengle with Archange (Célina) Lamoureux Bengle. Public domain. Credit: T. C. Blasse. Right, Agnes Mainville Monat and Frank Monat, "refugees" from Three Rivers, MA. Below left, Springfield, MA Bookmobile makes a stop circa late 1950s. This Bookmobile was a vital resource for the author during childhood and was instrumental in inspiring her literary talents. Credit: Wood Museum of Springfield History. Below right, Marie Bruce Bengle in First Communion dress circa 1937.

The Banshee Appears, by R. Prowse. Nanny believed in the call of the Banshee warning that a family member was about to die. Public domain.

Bob Bengle and the author, 1958, above. Jeannette and Peter Alessi, the author's paternal aunt and uncle and godparents, 1940s, left.

Right, some of the decades' worth of correspondence used in creating a family tree. Credit: Carol Bengle Gilbert.

Postcard images of Main St., Three Rivers, MA, circa 1910. Courtesy of Palmer Historical Commission.

A tattered news clipping about Robert Monat's deportation case kept by his aunt, Elsie Monat Bengle and passed down to the author. Credit: Carol Bengle Gilbert.

Right, signatures of Lancaster settlers, including John Prescott and John Rugg. Left, map of the original settlers' lots. From *The Early Records of Lancaster, Massachusetts 1643-1725,* Henry S. Nourse, A.M. ed., 1884. Public domain.

Monument to people enslaved by members of the Waterman family—Flora, Prince, Parmalie, Cuff, Cholie, and others—placed by a descendent in 1895 and later removed. The Warwick Historical Cemetery #103 where the marker once stood is a burial ground specifically for enslaved people associated with the Waterman family, adjacent to the Waterman Cemetery. Credit: Rhode Island Historical Cemetery Commission.

Front side of the original deed signed by Miantonomi January 12, 1643 granting Shawomet to Richard Waterman, Samuel Gorton, and others. Public domain. Credit: Yale Indian Papers Project.

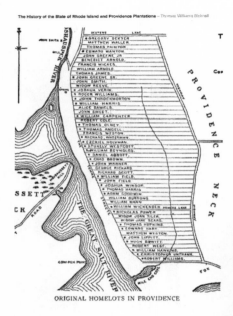

The History of the State of Rhode Island and Providence Plantations – Thomas Williams Bicknell

ORIGINAL HOMELOTS IN PROVIDENCE

Map depicts locations of property owned by Richard Waterman, Roger Williams, Benedict Arnold and Robert Cole in Providence. The men also owned property in Shawomet where the land dispute with the Gortonites occurred. Public domain.

Original grave Marker for Lancaster founder John Prescott, lying in front of a more recent commemorative headstone, above, Old Settler's Burying Ground, Lancaster, MA. The author's ninth great-grandfather.

Left, grave of Benjamin Tucker, Jr. with "Boston Tea Party Participant December 16, 1773" Commemorative Medal, Hope Cemetery, Worcester, MA, the author's fifth great-grandfather. Credit: Carol Bengle Gilbert.

Fear of vampires periodically led to corpse desecration in New England as noted by the *Boston Evening Transcript*, January 18, 1896. Public domain.

Chicopee Isolation Hospital, where Nanny's older brother John O'Brien spent his final days after contracting tuberculosis. Public domain. Credit: Russ H. Gilbert.

Below, Nanny's brother John Joseph O'Brien's obituary describes him as one of the most popular young men in the city.

Headstone of Ira Joyce and Nancy Waterman Joyce, the author's third great-grandparents, Pine Hill Cemetery, Sharon, VT. Credit: Carol Bengle Gilbert.

OBITUARY

John J. O'Brien

John J. O'Brien, one of the most popular young men in the city, died late Thursday evening at his home, 474 Maple street, after a short illness. He was born in Holyoke, and was a graduate of the Rosary high school in the class of 1910. He was a member of the alumni association of the school, Elder council, Knights of Columbus, and Court John Boyle O'Reilly, Foresters of America. He leaves, besides his father, one brother, Martin P., and four sisters, Mary, Lulu and Esther O'Brien and Mrs William Goss of Holyoke. The funeral will be held at the home of his father Monday morning, followed by requiem high mass in Holy Rosary church. The burial will be in St Jerome cemetery, the time to be announced.

The former Moore's Corner School in North Leverett, MA attended by Vivien Bruce. Outside, one of the student desks. Under the roof line, the writing reads "Empathy, Mutual Aid, Tolerant Skepticism Since At Least 1810." Credit: Carol Bengle Gilbert.

Vivien Bruce at the Moore's Corner Schoolhouse in Leverett, MA, second row, fourth from left. Courtesy of Leverett Historical Society. Above right, the old "two-holer" outhouse (boys' and girls' sides) at Moore's Corner School used by Vivien Bruce and her classmates in the late 1930s. Credit: Carol Bengle Gilbert,

FOUR GENERATIONS OF THE BRUCE FAMILY

Gravestone of Charles O. Bruce, Sr., (1869-1940) and Blanche Whiteman Bruce (1882-1927), North Gill Cemetery, Gill, MA, left, and Charles' father, Samuel Bascom Otis Bruce (1842-1918), Pine Hill Cemetery Sharon, VT, right. Credit: Carol Bengle Gilbert.

Lois Tucker Bruce (1815-1893), Otis Bruce (1799-1872), and Otis' parents Jonas Bruce (1753-1848) and Sarah R. Nott (1757-1849), Pine Hill Cemetery, Sharon, VT. Credit: Carol Bengle Gilbert.

WORKING IN THE MILLS DURING THE INDUSTRIAL REVOLUTION

Rag sorters at American Writing Paper Company, Holyoke, MA where Nanny's brother Marty O'Brien (1895-1980) worked before moving to Chicago. This image courtesy of the Wistariahurst Museum, Holyoke, Massachusetts.

A twister machine in the Merrick Thread Mill (American Thread Mill), Holyoke. Nanny's sisters Lizzie Mamie and Lulu worked in a Holyoke thread mill, initially as doffers and promoted to twisters. Courtesy of Holyoke Library.

Above, paper finishers at work in White and Wycoff paper mill in Holyoke in the 1920s. Nanny's brother Marty O'Brien worked as a finisher before deciding mill work wasn't for him. Courtesy of Holyoke Library.

A girl working in the inhospitable conditions of a paper mill. Courtesy of Holyoke Library.

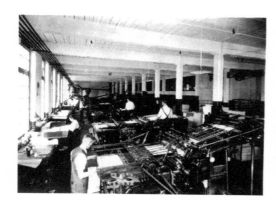

Cylinder presses used in papermaking. Courtesy of Holyoke Library.

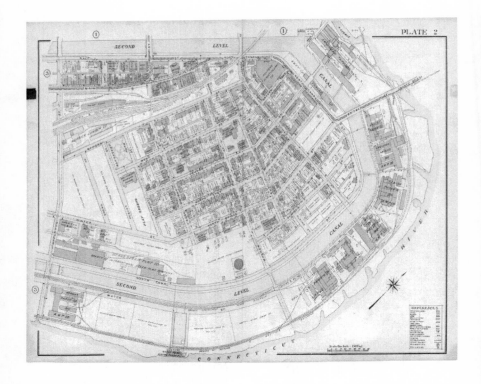

This 1911 map shows a section of Holyoke's tri-level canal system, constructed between 1847 and 1892, and the rings of mills it supported. According to the Society of Architectural Historians, the canals were designed so that the first tier of mills would use diverted river water flowing through a gatehouse into their waterwheels and turbines. These mills' wastewater would flow into the second tier canal for use by the second tier mills, which in turn would recycle their water to the third tier which would send their wastewater back to the Connecticut River. The locations of some of the O'Briens' addresses are also shown on this map— 52 West St., 58 West St., 98 Sargeant St., 35 East St., 36 East St., 17 Mosher St., and 13 Summer St.; the actual residences have been torn down. Many of the mills are shown, including American Writing Paper, bounded by Lyman, Summer and North Canal Sts., where Martin O'Brien, Jr. worked. His sisters likely worked in one of the nearby American Thread Company mills. Public domain. Credit: Harold H. Richards.

Sr. Julia Frances Killelea. Nanny spoke fondly of playing with her niece (then called Vivienne) during childhood and named her firstborn in honor of her. Sr. Julia Frances and her sister Roberta Gross Gasteyer were early contributors to the author's genealogical research into the Daleys and O'Briens. Credit: Sisters of St. Joseph, Springfield, MA.

Portrait of Charles O. Bruce, Sr. presented to the Town of Gill after his death, in commemoration of his 26 years service as Town Selectman. The portrait hangs in the museum of the Gill Historical Commission. Courtesy of the Gill Historical Commission.

An ad placed in the *Boston Gazette* August 13, 1733 by one of the author's least favorite forebears, who sold human beings along with rum and sugar. Public domain.

DALEY—Officer Timothy D. Daley, dearly beloved husband of Kate Daley (nee Casey), fond father of Daniel, Lillian, Patrick and Timothy Daley, brother of Officer Daniel D., Mrs. Eugene McKenna, Mrs. John Fitzgerald, Mrs. Edward Heaney; native of Knockaderry Farranfore, County Kerry, Ireland. Funeral Wednesday, Aug. 2, at 9:30 a. m., from late residence, 912 N. Springfield av. Autos to Mount Carmel. Member of Policemen's Benevolent association. For seats or limousines call Kedzie 2304.

"Native of Knockaderry Farranfore, County Kerry, Ireland." Critical evidence in the search for the Daly ancestral home. Public domain. Credit: Chicago Daily News.

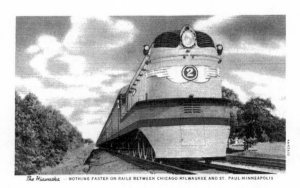

The Hiawatha, one of the finest locomotives operated by the Milwaukee Road, the railroad for which Daniel J. Daley drove freight trains. Public domain.

SS City of Richmond, the ship that brought Mary Daley O'Brien from Queenstown, Ireland to Castle Garden, NY in 1880. Public domain. Credit: Library of Congress, Prints and Photographs Division, Detroit Publishing Co. Collection.

INMAN LINE.

ROYAL MAIL STEAMERS.

Appointed to Sail as under, carrying on all occasions her Majesty's and the United States Mails.
These Steamers do not carry Horses, Cattle, or Live Stock of any description.

FROM LIVERPOOL VIA QUEENSTOWN TO NEW YORK.

	Captain	
CITY OF RICHMOND	..Leitch	......Thursday, May 6
CITY OF CHESTER	.....Brooks	.......Thursday, May 13
CITY OF BRUSSELS	.....Watkins	......Tuesday, May 18
CITY OF BERLIN	.......J. Kennedy	.Thursday, May 27
CITY OF MONTREAL	....Condron	......Tuesday, June 1
CITY OF RICHMOND	....Leitch	.......Thursday, June 10

FROM NEW YORK.

CITY OF BRUSSELS	.....Watkins	.....Thursday, April 29
CITY OF BERLIN	... .J. Kennedy	..Saturday, May 8

These well-known magnificent Steamers, built in water-tight compartments, are amongst the strongest, largest, and fastest on the Atlantic, reducing the passage to a minimum, and giving special comfort to passengers.
The Saloons, which are especially well lighted, ventilated, and luxuriously furnished, are amidships, occupying the whole width of the ship. The principal Staterooms are amidships forward of the engines, where least noise and motion is felt; and all are fitted with latest improvements, double baths, electric bells, &c. Ladies' and Gentlemen's sitting rooms, pianos, libraries, barbers' shops, bathrooms, &c. provided.
The Steerage accommodation cannot be excelled. Passengers of this class will find their comfort and privacy particularly studied, and the provisioning unsurpassed.
Experienced Surgeons and Stewardesses carried.
Saloon Passage 15, 18, and 21 guineas, according to accommodation.
Return Tickets at Reduced Rates.
Steerage Passage to New York, Boston, Philadelphia, or Baltimore, 6 guineas.
These steamers have through booking arrangements for Goods and Passengers with the Erie Railway Company, from New York to all points in the West, South, North-western States, and Dominion of Canada.
Passengers forwarded via SAN FRANCISCO, to AUSTRALIA, NEW ZEALAND, CHINA, and JAPAN, at lowest Through Rates.
Drafts issued free of charge from £1 upwards.
Letters by these steamers for Consignees and others must pass through the Postoffice. None will be received at the office of the Agents.
Parcels 5s. and upwards, according to size and value.
For Freight and Passage apply in New York to John G. Dale, 31 and 33, Broadway; in Manchester to A. W. Wilson, 33, Fountain-street; in Paris to A. R. Johnson, 9, Rue Scribe; in London to Rives and Allen, 29, Cannon-street; in Queenstown to C. and W. D. Seymour and Co.; and in Liverpool to WILLIAM INMAN,
61 and 63, Tower-buildings South, 21, Water-street.
Liverpool, May 1, 1880.

Saloon Passengers by the Royal Mail Steamer CITY OF RICHMOND will leave the Landing-stage, Prince's Pierhead, by the Company's Tender, punctually at Half-past Four o'clock afternoon To-morrow (Thursday), May 6. d

Advertisement for the Inman Line, owner of SS City of Richmond, listing the Captains and departure dates and boasting about steerage accommodations. Public domain. Credit: Liverpool Mercury, British Library Board.

Mary Daley O'Brien, (called "Maria Daly" in Ireland), and children John, Delia, Ella, and Daniel Francis O'Brien, St. Jerome's Cemetery, Holyoke, MA. Husband Martin is in a separate plot. Credit: Carol Bengle Gilbert.

Saloonkeeper Hussey spoke of the shooting as follows:

"Ald. Mulvihill and I were seated in my saloon playing cards when Fewer and a friend entered. The latter I know by sight and I have heard him called 'Steve.' They invited us to have a drink and we accepted. Neither Fewer nor 'Steve' appeared to be much under the influence of liquor. Suddenly the former drew his revolver and fired into the ceiling. 'Why, man,' said I, 'don't do that. There are people living up-stairs.' Fewer placed the revolver in his pocket again, and at the same time 'Steve,' as he started to walk out of the saloon, turned to Ald. Mulvihill and myself and said, 'You'd better take that away from him, for he's apt to shoot again.'

"The Alderman and I approached Fewer, when he fired another shot. His hand was in his overcoat pocket and it was this shot that struck Ald. Mulvihill. He fell to the floor as I sprang behind the bar to get my revolver from the cash drawer. I heard the Alderman groan and returned to him, for Fewer and 'Steve' had left the saloon. As I placed my hand under the wounded man's head I noticed blood on my wrist and then I realized what had happened. 'Are you hurt?' I asked. Ald. Mulvihill was still conscious and he replied, 'I don't know, but I think the shot struck me.' A moment later two officers entered the saloon and I told them who had done the shooting."

Margaret Daley Hussey's husband Ed's own words as he described the fatal shooting of Ald. Jeremiah N. Mulvhill in his Sangamon St. saloon. Snipped from "Ald. Mulvihill Shot," *The Chicago Tribune*, Jan. 26, 1894. Public domain.

Left, the Eastland on its side in the Chicago River, a disaster that killed 844 while Timothy D. Daley served in the Chicago Police Dept. Public domain. Credit: Chicago Tribune. Above, Chicago street scene from 1909 at Dearborn and Randolph Streets. Public domain. Credit: Chicago Historical Society.

Officer Patrick J. Daley is buried with his parents, Timothy D. Daley and Katherine Casey Daley and his sister Lillian Daley in Mt. Carmel Catholic Cemetery, Hillside, IL Credit: Kathy Dillon Kramer.

Statement of ███████████████, taken in the Captain's office of the 34th District Station 5327 Chicago Ave at 4.20 P.M. June 27th 1926.

Witness: Patrolman James Leonard Squad 22 A Detective Bureau.
         Michael Keane

Q. What is your name?

A. ████████████

Q. Where do you live?

A. ████████████

Q. What is your occupation?

A. Street Car Conductor.

Q. What do know concerning the shooting of Officer Patrick Daly?

A. While going West on a Chicago Ave Street Car at Springfield Ave I was looking North on Springfield Ave ,and █████ heard five (5) or Six (6) shots fired from an Automobile.

Q. What time did this shooting occur?

A. Between 2.05 AM and 2.10 AM 6/27/26

Q. After that what did you see?

A. Then I went up to my Motorman and asked him if he heard any shots.

Q. What did your Motorman say?

A. No. What is the Motorman's name. ████████████

Q. When did you hear of the Officers death?

A. About 3.20 AM I asked a Cadillac Squad at Cicero Ave And Chicago Ave and I asked them what happened at Spring field Ave and Chicago Ave. and one of them █████ laughed and said No. Then he asked me why I asked and I told him I heard the shooting ,and seen it also.

Q. At this particular time what were you doing at Springfield Ave and Chicago Ave.?

A. I was working on a run on a Chicago Ave street car at the time

Q. Did you see any men in the Automobile?

A. No.

Q. Could you identify anyone ?

A. No.

POLICEMAN KILLED.
Patrick Daley, who was slain by gunman near his home.
(Story on page 3.)

Left, a page from the murder investigation file of police officer Patrick J. Daley. Public domain.

Quiz Street Car Men in Death of Policeman

CHICAGO, June 28.—Six street car conductors were arrested Sunday night for questioning in connection with the slaying early Sunday of Patrick Daley, a policeman. One of the men had previously been arrested by Daley, and he carried warrants for the other five at the time his body was found in a yard near his home. The police believe the men shot Daley in an effort to destroy the warrants, but failed to obtain them in their hasty escape.

News clip and photo, public domain. Credit: *The Chicago Tribune.*

MISCHIEF AND HER ARCHITECTS AT PLAY
1978-1979

UGBC Tonight
FRIENDS Committee
invites you and your friends
to a PARTY

A FAREWELL PARTY for you and old
UGBC staffers; a day of
reminiscense and nostalgia to
share between UGBC and YOU
★ OPEN BAR ★
Free Beefsteak Dinner
ALUMNI HALL 7:00
Friday March 25

Christine Tetreault King, Carol Bengle Gilbert, Eileen Farrell Burk, Susan Liguori Davelman, and Stephanie Martin, rumored to be among Mischief's architects; frequently observed in communion with their favorite saints: St. Larry of Costello, St. Patrick di Carome, St. Mary "Guardian of Keeffedom," St. Paul "the Shepherd of McPartlands," McGrathius "Patron Saint of Boozehounds," the Most Pious Don Nathan, the Exalted John Fouhy, Our Blessed Muliebritas of Corso, His Holy Innocence Nathan Holt, St. James the Thespian, and the Immaculate Bob Holmes.

Am I available to card doors?
Well, I never! Really! You mean
you had to ask me? (How
could I resist such malicious
mischief.)

love and kisses,
me.

St. Patrick's Day at BC in 1979 started with some innocent fun— painting a regularly-graffitied walkway known as "the Dustbowl" green. Then Mischief showed up with politics on her mind. When economies of painting led her architects to drop the "Fr." in their painted comminiqué to the priest serving as University President, and the V.P. for Student Affairs sprung out of his car, startling them into flight prior to their finishing the job, the result was these unfortunate words on the sidewalk by the University President's office: "MONAN, YOU F". With the honorarium abandoned and "orgot your roots" in absentia, what chance did a handful of Mischief's architects have of convincing anyone the message was about scholarships for underprivileged Boston kids? Discredit: Carol Bengle Gilbert.

The author knew little but understood much about her ancestors' suffering in the Land War in Ireland when she helped organize a rent strike in 1979 in Cleveland, Ohio. Credit: Carol Bengle Gilbert.

Sketches about Moonlighters and the Land War

from *The Illustrated London News* near the time of the Castlefarm raid. The 11 images below are in the public domain.

Firies Parish- described as the center of the Moonlighters district.

Confronting Moonlighters in a cabin.

ARREST OF MOONLIGHTERS AT CASTLE ISLAND, KERRY.

Arresting Moonlighters, Castleisland.

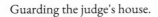

OUR SPECIAL ARTIST MISUNDERSTOOD BY THE CROWD

TRIAL OF MOONLIGHTERS AT CORK: GUARD OUTSIDE THE JUDGE'S HOUSE.

Guarding the judge's house.

Constables chasing an armed peasant.

Sounding the alarm at the approach of an eviction party, below.

Protecting Lord Kenmare's agents collecting the rents.

Scene at an eviction in County Kerry.

Carrying Moonlighters to Cork prison.

CONVEYING MOONLIGHTERS TO CORK PRISON.

Burning the house of evicted tenants at Glenbeigh.

Resistance to eviction in County Kerry.

Evictions of tenants were executed with extreme force in County Kerry, in this instance 79 military and 150 police, a combined force of 229, armed with rifles and batons, to evict two families! A crowd of local residents followed the police, with the girls and women "assailing police with their tongues" by hooting and making sacastic remarks to express their displeasure. When someone in the crowd threw stones, police charged and the crowd dispersed, re-gathering to follow the police to the second eviction site. Snipped from the full article in *The Irish Times*, January 8, 1886, page 5. Public domain.

CHAPTER 20

WELCOME TO AMERICA

The Dalys were Nanny's maternal family and the inspiration for my genealogical research. I knew bits and pieces of Mary Daley from stories Nanny told and inferred things about her from the way Nanny and Mom talked. No one else I knew used the word "eejit," so that peculiarly Irish word coming into our family lexicon must be Mary Daley's doing. Seeing as guests were a rarity in our house, Nanny's insistence that whenever we dropped a fork, a family member was coming to visit also must have been a hand-me-down from her credulous mother.

With actual facts in short supply, I linked anecdotes together in an effort to create a snapshot of my maternal great-grandmother's family. When I asked around, I got a dose of speculation with every fact delivered. The problem was, I couldn't distinguish the two. But eventually I came to find out I was looking for a family from County Kerry, or maybe County Cork, or possibly County Clare. Mary's mother was Elizabeth, or Eliza, surname Browne, maybe with an "e," maybe not. Her father was one of the 17,000 Irish answering to "Daly," and he didn't even have the wherewithal to adopt a unique nickname instead concealing himself among the droves of Daniel Dalys lumbering about western Ireland. And somehow this clod expected me to find him.

It's not like the occupying government in Ireland hadn't already set up sufficient roadblocks. From 1621 to 1829, Laws of Suppression of Popery ("the penal laws") inflicted by the British government with varying degrees of enforcement, banned Catholics from: the practice of their religion, while mandating their practice of Protestantism; education; land purchases and leases; residence in or within five miles of incorporated towns; voting; public office, trade, and professions; and even designation of a Catholic guardian for their minor children in the event of their deaths. Although "offenses" were not frequently charged, those committing them risked punishment by fine, whip, jail, or transportation (to colonial America or later to Australia.) During the time of the penal laws, a Catholic church register would have implicated practitioners in the crime of practicing their banned religion, so church registers were rarely kept, however exasperating for the progeny of those Irish folk whose steps on this Earth were obliterated.

Caving to Catholic Church demands for autonomy in record-keeping (because who would trust the Brits at that point?), the civil authorities excluded Catholics from the registration system set up in 1845 to track marriages. It took

19 more years, and the expansion of the recordkeeping requirement to births and deaths, before this mandate was extended to Catholics. The effects of the exclusion of Catholics from civil records unintentionally amplified centuries of policy aimed at wiping out Catholic identity.

American censuses were somewhat more promising, offering a glimpse of the life Mary Daley and her siblings made for themselves in America and the occupations they broke into after bypassing "No Irish Need Apply" signs. Working among strippers, teasers, heck makers, throstle doffers, and fire beaters, it's no wonder so many in the Daley family found their first work experience in their new country unpalatable. Keeping a keen eye out at all times for creelers, scutchers and slubbers in Holyoke's mills surely drained them.

The Dalys of Mary's generation were what Americans often call Black Irish, most or the lot of them fitting a singular description: medium-tall height, slight frame, black hair and blue eyes. Each of them was fluent in Irish and English. Where one went, they all went. Or almost all. The ones who immigrated ambled into Holyoke, Massachusetts each after the last, traveling in turn as the funds grew sufficient to purchase the next passage. First Mary, then, in uncertain order, Julia, Liz, Meg, John, and Dan. In all, six Daly children left the farm and made their way across the Atlantic. Mary must have been the brave one among the siblings, as she was first to make the trip. While she traveled alone, like almost all Irish immigrants of the era, she had kin at her destination, O'Sullivans related through her father's sister Catherine.

Though brave, Mary undoubtedly felt some trepidation as she followed the ship and mail news leading up to the embarkation. One such report received in Queenstown from the Cambria's captain, involved sighting a makeshift raft cobbled together from ship spars and ropes, with loose casks floating nearby. The steamer Helvetia, one of the largest steamships making the Queenstown to New York run, rescued a crew of a dismasted cargo ship that spent 10 days adrift on their way into Queenstown as Mary was heading out. Such were the risks of sailing in those times.

Mary booked on one of the last full-rigged hybrid sailing steamships before the newer double screw steamships without back-up sails usurped their place on the waters. Her ship was called the SS City of Richmond. Family and friends may have held an American Wake for her the night before she set out for Queenstown, as was customary among Roman Catholics of that era. The wakes marked the last occasion the emigrants would see Irish family and friends in their lifetimes. The ceremony involved plentiful food and drink, teary goodbyes, advice, presentation of good luck charms and gifts, and heavy reminders of the obligation to remember those back in the old country whose suffering was worsened for the loss of their companionship and labors.

On the day of her departure, goodbyes were said at home. Nellie Daly, whom you won't hear about again until you meet her in the Epilogue, related to me the story of a

Daly neighbor making the same trip as my ancestors and the parents standing waving at the edge of the farm until their children were out of sight, a practice considered typical. The distance to the train station was about a mile and a quarter. Traveling by train, Mary went first to Cork where she switched trains for Queenstown (lately called Cobh), timing her travels so as to punctiliously arrive the day before she was due to set sail. An overnight stay was mandated, to enable the shipping lines to check her papers and subject her to the customary showering and delousing required before boarding would be permitted.

Once on board ship, Mary crowded amongst 1324 other steerage passengers in an open bunked area where noise and stench and gloom were plentiful, privacy nonexistent. Had she sailed on a different day, she may have shared the space with fewer passengers, but then she'd have been cramped between bunks and cargo, for the ship owners avoided setting sail with any open space unfilled. The passengers carried their own bedding. The crew provided food, but unlike the more prosperous passengers in cabins above, the steerage dwellers were expected to cook it themselves in facilities that scarcely provided them the opportunity. Their access to the upper deck often restricted, Mary and her companions suffered stuffy air atop the other indignities for twelve days of forever until the ship finally docked at Castle Garden[35] at 6 p.m. Saturday, May 24, 1880. The passage included complimentary ground transport to Boston.

---

[35] Castle Garden was the predecessor immigration facilty to Ellis Island. The latter opened in 1892.

The Inman Line, owner of the RMS City of Richmond, put a favorable spin on the steerage experience. In its advertising it promised, "The steerage accommodation cannot be excelled. Passengers of this class will find their comfort and privacy particularly studied, and the provisioning unsurpassed."[36] It's tough to avoid having your privacy and comfort studied with 2648 eyeballs packed close, peering at you day and night. Steerage passage was six guineas, equivalent to about $950 today.

Mary may have chosen to leave Ireland to make marriage and parenthood an option as much as for income. In Ireland, marriage was still dependent upon dowries. Dowries brought in money for the parents of sons, but for a daughter to marry, her parents needed the means to pay a dowry to the groom's family. In families that weren't wealthy, the daughters' marriage options often depended entirely upon the dowries received by the family upon the marriage of sons, which could then be turned over to marry off the daughters, in turn, for as long as the funds held out. Records from the era show many adult children never marrying and living out their lives in their parents' households. While Mary was the eldest daughter and had brothers, western Ireland was in an economic slump worse than other parts of the country, and any dowry funds that might have come in may have been needed to keep the large Daly family afloat.

On arriving in Boston, Mary made her way to Holyoke, Massachusetts. Holyoke was a place unlike any

---

[36] Source 189.

Mary had ever known. From a small farm community where the same dozens of families and neighbors had mingled for generations, she was thrust into a bustling city of 22,000. In Knockaderry, Mary had walked everywhere of necessity, limiting her travels to a radius of about 12 miles. The only entertainment she had ever known was a monthly dance that drew up to 200 people from a cluster of neighboring townlands. The penal laws had denied her family education for generations; while Catholics were no longer forbidden schooling in Mary's childhood, the teaching was minimal and focused on the "three Rs," particularly learning to read.[37]

What Mary was well-versed in was religion, and it dominated her family's life. Her religion not only set her on the path to righteousness, it alerted her to the ways of the cunning Devil who would try to lure her into sinfulness with an endless variety of vile tricks, even assuming human form. Prayer and devotion were mainstays of her and her family's daily existence.

Shortly after her arrival in Holyoke, Mary one day endeavored to ride the streetcar, an entirely new experience.

---

[37] Before the law changed to allow Catholics to attend school in 1829, some were educated in secret "hedge schools." The schoolmasters risked fine or imprisonment for educating Catholics. A system of national schools was introduced in 1831, but attendance was far from universal; compulsory education laws weren't in effect until 1892. Thus, in 1871, for example, when Mary was still what would be considered school age today, nationwide voluntary attendance lagged at 37 percent.

Upon climbing aboard, the sight of one of her fellow riders startled her. This man, he had dark, almost black skin. With her provincial background and lack of education, Mary had no idea people with skintones so entirely unlike her own existed; she feared the man who looked so different from anyone she'd ever seen or heard of must be that devil in human form she'd been warned about. It was only when she later shared her streetcar experience with an acquaintance more cosmopolitan than her that she came to realize how much she had to learn about the world and its peoples.

Mary found work in one of the paper mills that gave the city its identity as the Paper City of the World. Three years later, the newly-immigrated Martin O'Brien came to work in that same paper mill. Martin worked as a paper maker, mixing chemicals, water, and pulp fibers to create paper, while Mary was a sorter, counting and inspecting the finished sheets.

They married in 1885. Within the year, the babies started coming, one after another: Lizzie, Ella, Mamie, John, Lulu, Martin, Delia, Daniel Francis, and at the tail end, as she always used to say, red-haired Esther (Nanny). Despite the family responsibilities, Mary continued working in the mills at least sporadically and through at least 1900, by which time she was mother to seven. The pay was low and the hours long, and it often required multiple family members working to keep a household afloat. A typical millworker in Holyoke heeded the loud whistle summoning employees to their workplace for a 5 a.m. start and went home at 9 p.m., with breaks totaling two-and-a-half hours, and worked six days per week. Inside the mills, they grappled with high humidity, airborne dust and lint, and exposure to carcinogenic chemicals. Mill work was notorious for causing:

dizziness,
fatigue,
fainting,
migraines,
respiratory problems including pneumonia and bronchitis,
byssinosis,
eye strain,
and deafness, the latter so pervasive that employees actually learned to lip read and employed makeshift sign language to communicate.

In the poorly ventilated cotton mills, women working with the spinning frames regularly fainted. Fainting was so common, the mill owners took pride in the ventilation systems they eventually installed, boasting of their effect in reducing the faint rate. Fires were also a serious risk with the close proximity of gas lanterns and rags.

The Holyoke paper mills were somewhat unusual in that they were owned and managed locally. To stave off unionization, the owners catered to certain employee needs including providing affordable housing and hiring relatives in search of work. They also instituted across-the-board hours cuts during slowdowns in lieu of layoffs.

Within a few years, Meg, Julia, John, Liz, and Dan in uncertain order had joined Mary in Holyoke, all working in mills of one sort or another. Disenchanted with the working conditions, the unmarried siblings moved on to Chicago in about 1888 after word of better paying railroad jobs caught John and Dan's attention, Sr. Julia Frances told me, and Liz and Meg joined them, certain anything they might find would be preferable to the filthy, clamorous mills.

The immigrant Daly girls remained close throughout their lives, with those living near each other sharing reminiscences of their childhoods back in Ireland whenever they gathered. One such memory the Chicago-based sisters, Elizabeth and Margaret, enjoyed recalling involved craftsmen such as quilters or thatchers staying with their family a few days, performing work in exchange for meals and a roof over their— Gasp! Is that Nellie Daly again?— apparently too eager to wait for the Epilogue to make her contribution, she's jumping into this chapter once more to describe for us how the Daly sisters spoke fondly of one man they called Paddy na Cuiltéir (Paddy the Quilter). Clothing was expensive and the people of Kerry poor so the men typically owned a single suit and the women a single coat. They wore the same suit or coat until it fell into such disrepair it could be worn no more. When a garment became old and faded but was still intact, Paddy na Cuiltéir would come to rip out the seams and turn the fabric, then sew it back together, giving the garment new life.

Although 900 miles separated Liz and Meg from Mary and Julia, they were there for each other when it mattered most. Mary's obituary indicated her Chicago sisters may have been in Massachusetts during her final illness. And, as you will see shortly, when one of Mary's children needed bed and board to start up life in Chicago five years later, Mary's sister Margaret welcomed him into her household.

As the O'Brien children grew, they followed their parents into mill work. By 1900, 14-year-old Lizzie worked as a cotton doffer in a thread mill that produced spools of thread, wool, and twine. Her work there may have started at an even younger age, since the mills were full of children working, many alongside their parents. Doffer was an entry level job and involved removing full bobbins, pins, or spindles from a spinning frame and replacing them with empty ones. When the 1910 Census was taken, Lizzie's little sisters Mamie, 20, and Lulu, 17, were working as doffers. By 1920, these younger O'Brien sisters had stepped up to the role of twisters, operating the machine that twisted threads and yarns together. This was a coveted sit-down job and paid considerably more than the doffer job.[38] Lizzie had left millwork behind by 1910 after marrying woolen mill worker William Killelea and giving birth to her first child (who would become "Fr. Bill" and work as an Army chaplain as an adult). Lizzie's husband died of tuberculosis later that year while Lizzie was pregnant, and Lizzie would return to millwork after her second baby Vivienne (later known as "Sr. Julia Frances") was born and both children entrusted to her aunt Julia Daley Fitzgerald. Julia and her husband John raised them for five years while Lizzie worked until Lizzie

---

[38] Cotton thread mill jobs paid from 75 cents to $1.60 per day.

remarried.[39] Lizzie's weaving in and out of the mill as necessity dictated, as her mother had also done, was typical of many married or widowed, female millhands.

Young Marty found work at the American Writing Paper Company, one of Holyoke's 28 paper mills which was singularly responsible for producing 75% of all fine papers in the United States. It was the umbrella company for Linden Paper, which came to employ his father before his father retired. Like his father, Marty was a papermaker. But Marty, like most of his mother's generation of Daleys, was deeply dissatisfied working in a mill. He decided to visit relatives in Chicago to explore job options. Nanny, at 16, and the other family members who made the trip with him, would choose to return to Holyoke, but Marty would remain in Chicago, living with his Aunt Meg-who-became-Maggie-on-moving-to-Chicago's family for the next decade until he married and started his own household. Marty secured employment as a drill press operator in a washing machine factory where he continued working until at least 1950 when he was 52 years old. That job involved heavy lifting, bending, and thunderous noise; still it was apparently a substantial improvement over the mills.

The O'Brien children may have become immune to noise by this time between working in mills and years of

---

[39] Lizzie remarried to William Gross, an aircraft toolmaker, in 1916. This would be another short-lived marriage as William died of blood poisoning in 1924 as a result of that fatal pencil prick that Nanny memorialized into persistent safety warnings. By this time, Lizzie was mother to five.

cohabitation with Mary and her old iron woodstove. Whenever Mary wanted the children's attention, she whacked that stove with the poker, unleashing a loud racket. The intensity of the poker strikes corresponded to the degree of Mary's annoyance. Mary's daughter Lulu picked up the torch after Mary's death but her preferred noise generator was the kitchen broom which made a mighty sound when its wooden handle contacted the plaster ceiling. In my toddler and preschool years, I lived in a duplex with my parents, sister, Nanny and me upstairs and great Aunt Lulu downstairs. When our noise disturbed Lulu, she'd hammer that broom handle on the ceiling in rapidfire staccato to demand quiet. But Lulu didn't limit her broom-banging to noisy children at a distance. When our family joined her downstairs to watch tv on Friday nights, Lulu made liberal use of that broom, in hopes she might be given an opportunity to hear the television. Jan and I laughed and laughed at her leveraging that broom handle against the ceiling with us right there in the room and made more noise just to see her do it.

For generations, a special sensitivity or prescience has often alerted the Dalys and their descendants to the Grim Reaper's impending visits before he sets off for his journey. I'm uncertain how many of the Dalys and Daly descendants share this quality but I know the group includes, at a minimum, me, one of my daughters, my sister, my mother, my grandmother, my great-grandmother Mary Daley O'Brien, my great aunt Lulu, Lulu's daughter Avis and Avis' daughter Mary. The latter was given the nickname "Scary Mary" at work after she alerted a coworker to her brother's imminent death based not on knowledge but this inscrutable sensitivity. During her final illness, on her last night on this Earthly plane, Mary Daley O'Brien announced she was taking to her bed to die, and she threatened to return from the dead and raise a ruckus, banging away on the stove with the poker if her children kicked up a crying fuss because she was gone. Shortly after she'd passed, her children, gathered around the stove, couldn't hold back their sobs at the mention of her. The sudden noise from the stove terrified them, and they vowed never to cry over Mary's death again. If the noise wasn't indigenous to the operation of that woodstove, it could have been the result of tinnitus brought on by the millwork and life with Mary, or perhaps it was Mary making good on her promise.

CHAPTER 21

A RAY OF HOPE

From what I'd heard about my ancestors' experience in the Holyoke mills, the very last thing I wanted to do at 17 was work in a factory. Like my mother, I loved learning. My mother had told me since I was four years old I would grow up and go to college, and that's what I planned to do. I'd spent the autumn and early winter months applying to colleges and seeking scholarships. Then the acceptances came, accompanied by meager financial aid offers. So the prospect of attending college faded away just as high school was ending. I'd reluctantly sent declines to the schools that offered me admission, including my first choice Boston College. BC cost $4500 per year, almost half of my father's annual income, I knew, since I did his taxes. That income barely kept food on the table and the lights on. Yet the College Board concluded that my parents, who also had no savings, could contribute thousands to my college tab.[40]

Work had been hard to come by and I'd worked only a few hours a week at a part-time job the spring of my senior year of high school. The economy had been in recession until recently and the slow comeback had yet to roll into our blue-collar community. I cringed at the thought of toiling away in a photo processing factory that first summer after high school, but they offered me a job when no one else did. What immediate options did I have?

Working conditions in a photo processing factory bore dispiriting similarities to the conditions my ancestors endured and I had planned to escape. The machines that printed the photos clank-clank-clanked all night long during my 5 p.m. to 1 a.m. shift. I often left work with a headache. The heavy rolls of photo paper would be ruined if exposed to light, so we had to learn to thread the machines in darkness while closed into a small space with an accordion-style vinyl door. We were cautioned that a dropped roll would crush a foot. Even when not sealed away in this dark closet, the lighting was intentionally dim, protecting the work at the expense of the worker. Our eyes were exposed to non-stop flashing from the machine making prints from negatives. As unpleasant as my job was, I was glad not to work with the carcinogenic chemicals some co-workers had to contend with. I hated those occasions when I had to walk past areas of

---

[40] The Springfield Teachers Club and the Jeffrey A. Parish Foundation had also awarded me modest scholarships but even with that assistance, I needed thousands more before I could enroll.

the plant where the toxic fumes resided.[41] I despaired of spending my life in the factory, this one or any other. But with my college plans so recently disintegrated, I'd yet to mastermind a Plan B.

One afternoon, I received an unexpected phone call. The preceding autumn, I'd written essays in hopes of being offered some scholarship help from the Pinkertons, where my father had recently started working. The man on the phone informed me I'd been selected as one of the recipients. He asked what college I was enrolling in. I explained to him that I'd had to turn down my acceptances.

"Where do you want to go?" he asked me.

"Boston College, but I already told them I couldn't come, and they gave my space to someone else."

He told me not to worry, the amount would depend on where I actually enrolled and hung up after promising to get back to me. I couldn't figure out what he meant. I wasn't sure he understood that colleges had already filled their classes for the fall and given away to others the little financial aid originally offered to me.

---

[41] It was illegal to assign women of child-bearing age to work with these chemicals and the company complied with the law, erecting barriers to entry by workers not employed in the chemical section. Nonetheless, I was filled with anxiety when in that general area of the plant.

The next call was from my father, his words a fast-flowing stream. This man from the scholarship committee was on the phone with his boss, and his boss had waved him into the room to surreptitiously listen in on a second phone. He got me on another line when he learned what they were talking about. He told me they were considering giving me five. Five hundred dollars was a lot of money and I'd be grateful for it, but with college costing nine times that amount yearly, it wasn't going to get me in the door. And there was the matter of the spaces having been filled. Still, I was counting in my head, trying to make that $500, with the $300 in scholarship money I already had, stretch.

"No, five thousand," he whisper-shouted.

And then the committee, in the room with the man talking to my father's boss, took a close look at the details and discovered a problem. They'd have to call back.

In their second call, the scholarship committee man explained the problem to my father's boss with my father eavesdropping once again and filling me in on the play-by-play. The scholarship application required a parent to have worked for the Pinkertons continuously for eight months. My father had been making his usual yearly job switches and had started with them less than eight months before I filed my application. My reactivated college hopes crumbled into sorry bits. I wasn't eligible for the Pinkertons' scholarship.

Now the scholarship committee had to figure out how to handle this awkward situation. As men of integrity, they wouldn't disappoint a young student by promising a scholarship and then withdrawing it, but since they hadn't offered any specific amount yet, they told my father's boss they thought it fair to give me a token award, maybe $100. Their written requirements didn't spell out how the eight month criterion worked after all, so they understood the innocence of what they correctly assumed to be my mistake in thinking the time ran from the award date, not the application date. The boss spoke highly of my father in case it might influence their decision. As they were about to settle on that token $100, one man on the committee proposed an alternative. He reminded the others I was their number one candidate in the region and the one applicant they'd been planning to give a full scholarship covering tuition, room, board, and expenses for four years. Since I was still the most qualified candidate and still needed the money to go to school, and the lack of clarity in their rules was no fault of mine, why didn't they go ahead with the offer they originally intended to make, he suggested.

Suddenly equipped with a full ride scholarship, yet having no college to go to and the application deadline long gone, I considered what to do next. I had limited experience and couldn't expect sound advice from parents who stumbled through life ducking to avoid decapitation by the perpetual crises falling from the sky and landing atop their unlucky persons. I settled on calling Boston College's admissions office as a first step on the off chance they had a space left. A tired-sounding admissions representative said they'd filled all of their seats two months previously. I persisted. I understand, I told her, but maybe if there's room in classes for one more, under these unusual circumstances, they could let me enroll even if I had to find a room off campus for a year? Even if I had to take all big lecture classes? She gave me no encouragement. Instead, with another sigh, she passed me off up the line to her supervisor, who turned out to be a Jesuit named Fr. Walsh. On hearing my story, he warmly welcomed me to Boston College, assuring me there'd be room for me in the dorms as well as in classes.

I finished that summer in the factory and returned during winter break and the following summer and next winter break. The conditions weren't any better, but I needed income and I reminded myself, it wouldn't be forever. I was making my way through college and toward a better life. And Shame had no say in the matter!

CHAPTER 22

MISCHIEF, IN *MY* TREE?

In 1979, two signs referencing penalties for "MALICIOUS MISCHIEF" disappeared from the Boston College mailroom. Mischief, by nature, is playful, so it's just as well those libelous admonitions vanished. You could say whoever removed those signs performed a public service. I daresay treks to the mailroom were more comfortable for all 8,800 BC undergrads once those derogatory signs no longer stared them down.

Certain students at BC had a particular penchant for Mischief. Mischief lured them from their dorms in the middle of the night to investigate obscure entrances to forbidden underground tunnels known to underlie the campus quad or to distribute flyers most sagaciously deposited in classrooms and beneath dorm room doors under the cover of darkness. Painting on a sidewalk a political message for the edification of the campus administration wouldn't emit the desired mystique if carried out in the noonday sun. Mischief acquired a vast collection of beer glasses in those years, though it was difficult to say who actually owned them. As one school year came to a close and students prepared to vacate the campus for the summer, it was hard not to scoff at the sight of the pathetic cardboard boxes placed in dorm hallways by the Dean of Students at the behest of pleading bar owners for no-questions-asked return of any of their barware that might have found its way in Mischief's collection. Once, when a corrupt student government hosted a self-congratulatory, formal dinner party for its officers, featuring steak and an open bar paid for with funds from the student treasury, Mischief invited the entire student body.

Mischief employs a camarilla of architects. While she safeguards their identity, some claim that wherever in Boston a spirited crowd balances atop tables on Thursdays at midnight singing chorus upon chorus of "When Irish Eyes Are Smiling," you can be certain some of Mischief's architects are present. My roommate Christine Tetreault was often rumored to be one of them. Christine was almost two inches shorter than me and wore shoes a half size larger. This didn't prevent us from sharing our wardrobes, treasured clogs and knee boots included. It wasn't unusual for one of us to awaken to a missing mascara wand or a favorite shirt absent from the closet, only to observe it on the other's person or in their possession later in the day. We often found ourselves in the same locales, whether that be the Heights student newspaper office or Molly's or Mary Ann's, the popular off-campus bars. We learned to shrug it off when friends chased one of us halfway across campus before realizing which one of us it was, and typically not the one they were looking for, or called us by each other's names. While there was an arguable resemblance, it was wholly superficial, the result no doubt of acquired familiarity, common interests, and prevailing styles, not to mention the borrowed clothing. Sometimes, that vague resemblance was useful to us. After one particular wintertime excursion which might have lent fuel to tittle-tattle about who was or wasn't in league with Mischief, I wore Christine's jacket for a week to avoid detection by someones who might have had an interest in my whereabouts. But our ability to stand in for one another had sinister potential and nearly led us to a dangerous precipice in our final college summer, with only our shrewd acumen to steer us elsewhere.[42]

Time and distance tamed— though it could never eradicate— our fascination with the elusive Mischief and the conflating of our public identities. Still, when 42 years had passed since our college graduation, I was taken aback to come upon a handful of Tétreaults weaving their way into *my* family tree. I surmised Mischief might be about. Like Christine, I have considerable French-Canadian heritage, but

---

[42] Sharing that tale does nothing to advance this narrative, but to satisfy your curiosity, I'll provide the "Cliffs Notes" version. We were hired by someone who was fascinated by both our fungibility and our association with Mischief, particularly our alleged role in acquiring and safeguarding her beer glass collection. This employer insisted we play a particular game in an environment fraught with manufactured tension and international intrigue all day instead of working. It took only two days for us to realize something was decidedly irregular, and we left that employment, never the wiser as to the true motives of our employer.

there were no Tétreaults sneaking about the canopy last time I was up there. What is this Anne Hélène Tétreault dit Ducharme doing in the midst of *my* relatives? Peering up further, I spotted another Tétreault name tag, this one belonging to Anne Hélène's father Gabriel who apparently lacks proficiency at spelling as his surname is missing its "l-t." And his father's there too, some guy named Joseph-Marie, combining the most vexatious of the deficiencies in the French-Canadian naming scheme. But it's Louis Tétreau who really grabbed my attention. Joseph-Marie's father, Louis was the original Tétreau to abandon old France for New France in 1658 or thereabouts. It was said of him,

> "The arrival of Louis Tétreau to Trois-Rivières did not go unnoticed, as he had red hair and his tongue hung out."[43]

If this man can't keep his tongue inside his mouth, he's going to have to find himself another tree to sit in, and as soon as I climb up a few hundred more feet, I plan to tell him that myself.

With four generations of Tétreaults taking refuge in my tree, my instinct was to contact Christine to find out if her tree had suffered some sort of calamity. She could report nothing of the kind and was as flabbergasted as I was to find her ancestors loose in my tree. If these Tétreault invaders weren't arboreally-confused, we soon realized we might each have our own set of Tétreault ancestors. *Or...* preposterous!

---

[43] Source 216.

That's the stuff of fantastical musings and sloppy fact-mining.

"Mischief?"

"Mischief!"

I rooted out a book titled *The story of Louis Tétreau (1635-1699): the ancestor of all Tétreau in North America.* All? Did this literally mean all, and if so, was that conclusion the product of sound research? The only way to find out if Christine and I had common ancestors intermingling up there I reckoned was to comb through the records of entirely too many of my/her/our presumptive arrière-arrière-arrière-arrière-arrière-arrière-arrière-arrière grand père Louis' 75,000 North American descendants in search of a common link.

A few years back, I installed a penny floor in my laundry room. It took me four months to obtain, clean, glue down, and cover with polyurethane the 50,000-plus pennies necessary to complete the job. I swore off big numbers afterwards, promising myself that if any project involving tens of thousands of anything at all presented itself to me, I'd run like a wolf was breathing down my neck. But despite the looming Tétreaults numbering 75,000, well it was just a quick peek, after all. Or maybe a couple.

The red-haired specimen with the lolling tongue was a child of Mathurin Tétreau and Marie Bernard from the Poitou region of Brittany. No one has established with any certainty the reasons he emigrated but the grounds for guessing are said to be as fertile as the farmland this overtaxed tenant farmer vacated when he set sail for the New World. My guess is that if growing up in a country ruled by a four-year-old King whose pursuits included climbing the Hôtel de Villeroy railings, dipping his Royal feet in the murky water of the Seine, and developing phobias didn't prod Tétreau to plot his escape, perhaps Louis XIV's notorious stench and accompanying halitosis did the trick.

New France may have been under the same rule as old France, but at least there was an ocean between Louis and the tax-happy mother country with its by-then adolescent king after he signed on as a domestic servant for the Jesuits and sallied forth. Those Jesuits sued Louis when he reneged on their 36 month agreement by abandoning the job early, one of a string of lawsuits that earned him a reputation for litigiousness. Or, as one descendant chose to characterize Louis' litigation litany, it showed him to be a clever businessman— such as when his own pigs trampled his crops and he professed himself unable to honor the obligation to pay the property owner the required measure of produce for the right to use the land.

My putative Tétreault trail stretches back from my paternal grandmother Elsie Monat Bengle, of fruitcake-baking renown, who was the daughter of Frank Monat, the same Frank Monat, who with wife and family was forced to abandon Three Rivers in favor of Detroit. Frank's mother was Philomène Dubour Monat. Philomène's father was said to be Louis Dubour whose father was François

Dubourg, whose mother, in turn, was the first Tétreault discovered to have surreptitiously slipped into my heritage, Anne Hélène Ducharme Tétreault. If I could find the proof to support Philomène's parentage, then I was a Tétreault descendant without a doubt. Or maybe with some doubt. I still needed to keep watch for signs of Mischief, whom I suspected might be responsible for hoisting those Tétreaults into the upper branches of my tree and creating the illusion they belonged there.

Thanks to Tétreau being a well-documented lineage, proving Philomène's relation to Louis Dubour was painless. The examination of this putative line of descent revealed none of Mischief's signature tricks. Now the roommates who shared shoes and mascara in college were sharing a common surname in their ancestry and might be sharing family. My remaining task was determining whether somewhere in our respective lineages, we had a common Tétreault ancestor.

Christine's genealogy on her paternal side consists of Tétreaults of various spellings— and there are 67 known variants amongst all of the North American Tétreau descendants— with Ducharme appendages popping in and out from generation to generation. Ducharme is a "dit" name, a well-intentioned but poorly-conceived naming tradition allowing a person to adopt an additional name, usually drawn from a place, a personal characteristic, or other descriptor, that distinguishes him from others with the same name. Joseph-Marie Tétreault dit Ducharme's compound surname, for example, means "Tétreau, called Ducharme," with the Ducharme depicting association with a hornbeam tree. Sympathies to those living next to the town dump who might find themselves answering to "Tétreault dit Garbage Heap." Once adopted, a "dit" name can be used with or instead of the actual name, and the actual name alone can still be used. There was apparently no Melvil Dewey or Edwin Seibels[44] in the years leading up to the 17th century to alert dit-name-devisers to the pitfalls this practice would foist upon their genealogically-inclined descendants.

Anne Hélène is not among Christine's ancestors. Nor did Anne Hélène's father Gabriel find his way into Christine's Tetreault King's line. My college roommate descended from Tétreaults I'd not yet encountered, with names like Nazaire Seraphin— Seraphin, oh what irony that my cherished roommate boasts angelic roots, albeit ones with devilish associations! And Hyacinthe, that name choice founded either in laziness, copping from the city Saint-Hyacinthe that many Canadian Tétreaus called home, or lunacy, if the parents of said Hyacinthe knowingly chose a legacy of beheading[45] in naming their precious offspring.

Angelic, Christine? Laughter spills forth like a waterfall.

---

[44] Edwin G. Seibels invented the vertical filing system in 1898.

[45] During the reign of Emperor Valerian (257-269), Hyancith, along with his brother Proteus, was arrested for practicing Christianity and beheaded. A century and a half earlier Hyacinth of Caesarea was likewise arrested for practicing Christianity and deliberately starved to death by his captors who served him only foods forbidden by his religion. Both men came to be known after death as St. Hyancinth. In later years, there would be other men accorded this title. I refer here to the first of these, of course.

But look! Christine's seventh great-grandfather was named Joseph-Marie, that same silly name one of my ancestors has. Like my own Joseph-Marie, Christine's was born in Trois-Rivières in 1678 and died in Verchères in 1762. And his wife was Anne Jarret dit Beauregard, just like my Joseph-Marie's wife. With this shared ancestor, my BC roommate and I learned— 42 years after graduating— that we're cousins. Eighth cousins, but cousins nonetheless. This discovery fully exonerated Mischief of any role in the tree-mingling. Maybe all of those friends who said we looked alike back in our college days were onto something.

CHAPTER 23

BLACK SHEEP RECONSIDERED

In a herd seemingly burdened with a genetic predisposition toward "black sheep," Charlie wore the deepest pitch of them all. It's hard to pinpoint any particular reason for this reputation, but the impression was pervasive. When I think back on it, my grandmother said very little against him, other than fretting about his drinking, and, of course, his abandoning their marriage. My mother said nothing against him until their falling out, when he declined to come to Springfield to see Bobby at death's door in the hospital.

"He's your son!" my mother prodded his conscience, aghast. But Charlie wouldn't budge. Nanny sobbed. Mom, overcome with disbelief and dismay, swore she'd never talk to that disloyal father of hers again after she hung up the phone. To the best of my knowledge, she didn't, not even to inform him years later when Nanny died and the year following when word came that Bobby had been found dead in a fleabag hotel downtown. I don't think Mom herself visited her brother in the hospital but that apparently was different. Many moons later, Dad told me he suspected Charlie didn't have the bus fare to come to Springfield and was too proud to admit it.

Having never known Charlie or Vivien,[46] or anyone else in Charlie's family, I was vulnerable to Suspicion, which snickered at the mention of Charlie's name, cashing in on my lack of familiarity with the subject. If Charlie is so bad, imagine what the rest of his family must be like, Suspicion chortled. I shuddered and turned away. Even when I grew up and began researching my genealogy in earnest, I struggled to push away the distaste that had come to envelop all things Charlie. It wasn't until I turned up records demonstrating his father Charles O. Bruce Sr.'s social contributions that I began to strongly reconsider Charlie's family's reputation and Charlie's own. What did I really know about them? Almost nothing.

Charles O. Bruce Sr. was the son of Sam Bascom O. Bruce, who survived Andersonville, and Belle Joyce. Born in 1869, he grew up on a farm in Hartford, Vermont with three brothers and sisters, two of whom died in early childhood. Though I'd been led to believe, and had believed for decades, I was the first in my line to go to college, I wasn't. Charlie's father was. He attended the Graduate School of Theology at Oberlin for a year or more, preparing for the ministry, in an

---

[46] They met me once when I was an infant but I, of course, have no recollection of the encounter.

environment that required students to be in their rooms by 10 p.m., strictly forbade card playing, and mandated attendance at not one but two church services on Sundays.[47] He abandoned his studies when his eyesight proved inadequate to the task. Then he returned to Mt. Hermon School, where he and his brother Herbert had attended high school, took up a paint brush and bucket and headed up the paint department for the next 41 years.

It confounds me that my mother never told me about Charles, Sr. going to college. She must have known. It's the sort of thing that would have interested the mom who made honor roll in school, the mom who told her daughters since before they started school that they'd grow up and go to college one day. And yet: Not. A. Mention. Not even when her "~~first~~ second in the family to go to college" daughter secured her spot in the BC class of '79 and set off.

Mom claimed never to have met Charles Sr. and that may well be true. She was 11 when he died, and I don't have any knowledge of them being in the same place ever. But Charlie must have told her about his father. What kid doesn't ask?

Mom had a broad, rational streak I always assumed she inherited from Charlie, since it sure didn't come from Nanny. And she was open-minded about religion and race, something I attributed to her having lived in that crucible of ethnic, racial, religious, and social diversity, New York City. Though a devoted Catholic, she didn't have any airs about

---

[47] These rules were eliminated in 1898.

her religion trumping anyone else's, including her father's vague Protestantism. She accepted my having Jewish friends and a black friend at a time when it wasn't uncommon for parents to balk at such mixing. Yet with all of her open-mindedness, there was one religious type Mom tolerated, but didn't care for, and that was proselytizers. I wonder if she knew of her paternal grandfather's fellowship with the evangelist D.L. Moody, and what she thought of it if she did? It's almost inconceivable she didn't know. Nanny, Charlie, Mom and Bobby moved into a house on Charles Sr.'s property shortly after his death, where they stayed for about three years, living alongside Charlie's sister Frances and her eldest two children, Libby and Charles "Edward" Wiberg. That house is located on Main Road in Gill on the Mt. Hermon School property.[48]

D.L. Moody was a prominent and charismatic evangelist with expansive goals that crossed continental boundaries. He was founder of the Moody Bible Institute, but more importantly for this story, founder of the Mount Hermon School and the Northfield Seminary, boys and girls boarding schools in neighboring Gill and Northfield, Massachusetts, schools which, in those early years, aimed to educate the masses to become Christian evangelists. By the 1890s, Mount Hermon had already adopted defining traditions that continue to this day, such as the Rope Pull, featuring the junior and senior classes lined up on opposite shores of Shadow Lake where the junior members inevitably find themselves splashing about; and the spontaneous Mountain Day when teachers announce an unexpected

---

[48] It was while they were living there that Vivien moved in with them.

reprieve from the classroom to go hiking amid the New England fall foliage. The founder's respect for the value of manual labor meant every student performed janitorial, laundry, kitchen or farm work, another tradition that endures. The school reached out to prospective students without privilege, enrolling many Native American, black, and foreign students as well as orphans and students from impoverished families. As a student at Mt. Hermon from 1892-1897, Charles not only came under Moody's religious and social influence, he became the man's friend. Charles' adoption of his friend's life philosophy is apparent from his choices. He didn't look down at the job he took supervising painters at the Mt. Hermon School when his hopes of ministry fell apart; he enjoyed it and found fulfillment in it. And, like Moody, he kept his sights on the larger social good.

Charles was elected Selectman for the first time in 1913 and continued to be elected every two years until he declined to toss his name in the hat again after 13 consecutive terms. Even then, he was talked into running for Town Assessor, an election he won, and serving as a member of the Gill Finance Committee.

Charles' duties as Town Selectman were as varied as the interests of the town. In 1925, he and his fellow Selectmen were charged with obtaining bids for the paving of a town road. As Board Chair in 1929, Charles worked with the electric company and his Gill neighbors to negotiate reasonable terms for bringing electricity to the town's 74 houses. By 1932, he sat on the dais with various dignitaries when the French King Bridge, a three level, cantilever arch spanning the Connecticut River between Gill and Ervin at the Mohawk Trail cut-off, was dedicated. It was the only bridge of its type in the state and, so far as anyone present knew, in the country. The towns had worked this project together and savvily obtained full funding from the state so the towns benefitted from the new bridge without having to foot the bill. Sixty-thousand people came to the ceremony, kicked off with a howitzer salute. Then came the inevitable speeches and a parade featuring some 60 floats designed to highlight the history of transportation, followed by outboard motor boat and canoe races on the river.

In May 1937, a less glamorous task fell to Selectman Bruce, erecting a sign at the the Gill Community Club dances reminding the dancers to keep the noise down when they ventured outside. Charles was a charter member of the Club, which attended to the town's social interests, sponsoring flower shows and fairs, dance lessons, picnics, and charitable drives including creating quilts for donation to families that lost their homes to fire. The 1929 club's run spanned 61 years.

By 1938, the Selectmen had to weigh the value of a new, consolidated school with the added tax burden to the larger property owners. Charles came down on the side of the property owners, suggesting that the timing wasn't right for committing to such a large-scale plan.

A Republican, Charles served as a delegate to the state convention for many years and claimed a spot on the town Republican Committee. He was a correspondent to the

Landmark, a Vermont newspaper, which you will remember was the source of some good-natured teasing about elections, pitting his Republican loyalties against the Democratic allegiance of his maternal grandfather, Ira Joyce. His correspondent role involved sharing the social news of the town with the editor, something he was quite familiar with given his many friends and political interests.

What better tribute could anyone hope to receive than the one paid to Charles O. Bruce on his retirement as a town Selectman? The remaining Selectmen voted unanimously on a resolution praising him for his service that was recorded for posterity in the town records. It reads in part:

"...And, whereas, during Mr. Bruce's entire term of office, he has stood forth as a man of honorable character and high purpose, whose counsel and judgment have always been sought by the citizens of Gill, who have come to respect him for his sterling worth, honor him for his splendid qualities, and love him for his sympathetic understanding, Be it resolved, that the citizens of the Town of Gill, In annual town meeting assembled, express to Mr. Bruce their continued affection, their keen appreciation of, and their deep gratitude for all that he has done for the town, and their earnest hope that he may spared for many more years for counsel and advice, and their firm belief that his years of faithfulness will serve not only as an inspiration for his successors but as an example for other town officials throughout the commonwealth of Massachusetts..."[49]

---

[49] Source 233.

With Charles, Sr.'s suspected "black sheep" status debunked, did Charlie also deserve an upgrade? If it's hard to place yourself in an ancestor's head, it's an equally daunting task to place yourself in their time. The analysis of Charlie's proper ovine hue takes shape as a series of points and counterpoints in my head:

Point: Charlie left Nanny and the kids.
Counterpoints: Nanny and Charlie's relationship was corroded by rancor. At least he agreed not to seek a divorce so as not to disgrace Nanny. And he gave her his interest in their house.

Point: Nanny had no income and had never worked. Charlie knew his leaving would force Mom to drop out of school to go to work.
Counterpoint: It was the 1940s. Women's education wasn't taken seriously by society.

Point: He drank too much. Even he conceded there was a period when he drank heavily.
Counterpoint: Despite his drinking, he managed to go to work regularly and support the family. And eventually he came to see his drinking too much as a problem and toned it down.

Point: Their life was unstable because Charlie kept uprooting them.
Counterpoint: Charlie was a hard worker and took jobs where he could find them. Counterman, sadwater, rayon

mill worker, dishwasher, janitor, he did what he needed to do to earn a living through the Great Depression, moving where the jobs were.

Point: Charlie didn't insist on keeping Vivien.

Counterpoint: If Nanny ultimately refused to care for the baby, what could he do? Did he know his father couldn't keep her when he brought her there? What advice did his father give him? Did he ask other relatives to take in Vivien? How much did things I know not about this situation influence the outcome? In the end, when Vivien returned to the family, Charlie stood by her for the rest of her life. That has to count for something, right?

CHAPTER 24

MUDDLED

Muddled. That's the ideal adjective to describe my family tree. Mary Daley O'Brien's sister Liz Daly married "Edmund" Hussey who apparently was born, worked, died, and answered censuses as "Edward." Edmund v. Edward might be a "so what?" if Liz' Edmund/Edward didn't happen to have a brother named Edward,[50] and if that Edward didn't happen to be married to Liz's sister Maggie. But the Edward-Edmund muddlement keeps good company. There was a story told to me about Dan, Liz and Maggie's brother, which turned out to be not the story of Dan but the story of Patrick. Not Liz and Maggie's mystery brother Patrick who showed up in our history without even a "how do you do?" but Patrick the son of another brother, Timothy, who himself

---

[50] While naming multiple children the same name was common in Irish families, the second and any subsequent child given the assigned name was typically born after the death of the first child given the name.

appeared like a lighting bolt in a sunny sky.[51] Keeping these muddled busybodies out of each other's tree branches is a nightmare.

I spent decades trying to track down the story about Dan Daly, the one which turned out to be not about Dan, but about Patrick, but not *that* Patrick. It was the story of a cop turned detective, out to serve a warrant in 1930 and returning home from the unproductive effort late at night, only to be shot dead on his own doorstep by the very man for whom he'd spent the day searching.

Dan was one of the Dalys who moved to Chicago from Holyoke in the late 1880s, abandoning despised millwork with hopes of signing on with the railroad. He

---

[51] Two mystery brothers would have been an adequate number, but before long I came upon a third, Jeremiah. Jeremiah evaded detection by clinging to his homeland's soil when the pull of emigration gripped his siblings. Those siblings apparently forgot to mention him enough for awareness of his existence to have filtered down to all of the American Daly descendants.

ended up becoming a cop, likely because his older brother Timothy secured a job on the police force. Not a shred of corroboration supported the story of his death. For the longest time, all concrete evidence of his life, as well as his tragic death, eluded me. The Chicago Police Department was a dead end with no record of a murdered cop named Dan Daly. No 1930 obituary. No published account of a detective named Daniel Daly getting shot in 1930 in Chicago, which surely would have made the news. I tried searching with and without his name, with reference to his being a police officer and without. I expanded the timeframe. Nothing brought results until finally I searched "Daly shot," with no first name, no occupational reference, a broad time frame, and the state. The search uncovered a story so remarkably similar to the one I'd been told about Dan, I knew I was finally hot on the trail. But the story subject's name was Patrick Daley. I checked Dan's middle initial in the hopes it was "P." It was not.

Officer Pat Daley pulled the patrol box at Chicago and Kedzie Avenues at 2 a.m. June 27, 1926, signaling the end of his shift, then climbed back into an automobile driven by his partner that day, Patrolman Arthur Neville. Neville, who had to pick up his wife before going home, dropped Pat at an intersection a block and a half from the house at 910 North Springfield Avenue where Pat lived with his mother and their cousin, police officer Dennis Lyons. When he exited the car, Pat carried with him a square, one-pound box of Cupid Fruit and Nuts in white wrapping. His partner later recounted his purchasing the candy as a gift for his mother for $1.25 at a cigar store on Division Street earlier in the day.

In the two years Pat Daley had been on the police force, he'd progressed from patrol officer to plainclothes detective, achieving a reputation as "an exemplary officer." Wearing police star 1178, he was a familiar sight in his neighborhood, recognized by most everyone. Those who knew him described "a clean, good-natured young man," one they emphasized didn't touch liquor and had no apparent enemies. But it didn't take known enemies to cut his life short. In those wee hours, Pat commanded an unknown person to "Halt!" while pulling out his service revolver. No witnesses could fill in the details of what happened next, or why; they could say only that five, six, seven, or eight shots rang out in the night. By the time anyone looked out, there was nothing to see. One of the neighbors, Dennis Sherlock, set out to investigate the source of the shots and discovered a man with a gun face down on the grass on the northeast corner of N. Springfield Avenue and Iowa Street. He didn't recognize this gunshot victim as his neighbor Officer Pat Daley until the police arrived and turned him face up.

A lead bullet pierced Pat's right arm two inches below the shoulder from the back, traveling in a downward direction, ripping through his right lung, passing beneath his liver and kidneys and coming to rest below his lowermost left rib. The first responding officer observed that Pat, though not moving, was still alive and urged Sherlock to hurry and fetch the doctor living nearby. By the time the doctor pulled on his trousers and scurried over to the crime scene, Pat was no longer breathing. He was brought to St. Anne's Hospital in the squad's Cadillac T-63, accompanied by his cousin, Police

Sergeant Dennis Lyons, who had arrived on the scene shortly after the shooting. It was too late.

Italian-wedding crashers, a drunk man with a bloody hand, a handful of pugilistic streetcar drivers, and a possibly-cuckolded husband of a woman who may have been more than a friend to Pat competed for top billing on the suspect list. Yet, with all these prospective candidates, the Chicago Police had trouble choosing even one perpetrator. The decision was so perplexing, they still haven't settled on their guy ninety-seven years later.

The "clews" led the police exactly nowhere. The murder could have been perpetrated by a random stick-up guy only if his stick-up skills were so subpar he took none of Pat's money and walked away from both Pat's First National Bank of Chicago passbook and that delicious Cupid candy, tantalizingly wrapped and begging for consumption. And this hypothetical deficient stick-up artist would have needed an equally incompetent accomplice, for the shot that killed Daley came from behind, possibly from an automobile, while he pursued someone on foot in front of him.

The number of drunken Chicagoans wandering about Pat's neighborhood at that late hour in a time when Prohibition was in full force is mind boggling, but none of the stories laid out by these inebriated souls drew sufficient police skepticism to provoke continued digging. When the scheme to crash the Italian wedding in hopes of scoring free beer was concocted, for example, one of the participants claimed to have gone home and grabbed his Sunday pants, running them over to a tailor for pressing, before dressing the part of an invited guest. Such effort and the payment of a tailor's fee to boot for one purloined beer? And almost to a man, the wedding crashers, drunk on their single beers, reported turning their noses up at the one glass of wine that each was provided with the beer once an insider snuck them into the basement of the wedding house. A brother of the bride denied the wedding crashers succeeded in gaining admittance at all, describing an encounter with them on a porch and a successful repellence. The legitimate wedding guests, unlike the chameleonic crashers who were at once there and not there, simultaneously drunk and sober, were paragons of sobriety, one and all.

A drunken man wandering about with a bloody hand looked promising. But he readily admitted punching in an acquaintance's garage window out of spite, and the window testified to the truthfulness of his account.

The police treaded lightly with the potential paramour lest Patrick's pristine reputation be sullied. Mrs. Putative Paramour attested that Patrick supplied her silk stockings and candy while she gifted him silk shirts. The Cupid Fruit and Nuts cried out for acknowledgement at this juncture, but the officer questioning Mrs. Paramour never second-guessed the identity of their intended recipient. Not-a-Couple preferred riding around in her husband's Overland sedan in lieu of going to the movies, dinner, or the ice cream parlor, weather permitting, though she denied any professions of love exchanged between them or any unseemly contact during these excursions. Pat called her on her home telephone, yet her husband remained ignorant of the eighteen month dalliance, she was certain. The investigators took her at her word, never questioning the husband whose wife vouched he was in their bed with her by 12:30 a.m. and didn't leave the house before daybreak the night the man, who to all appearances cuckolded him, was shot dead.

Ah, let us not forget the streetcar operators! As Pat chased the unknown suspect in the night, he proved his relationship to me by tripping over a pipe railing and going "splat!" on the ground, sustaining facial and leg lacerations. It's believed that this is how his pockets disgorged their contents, including two warrants, two "bad character" cards, and a letter of investigation, in addition to the aforementioned bank passbook. The warrants were members of a larger set, one of which Daley had already served, arresting streetcar operator Joseph Kowald. There were six in total, all naming streetcar operators and all sworn out by ice cream parlor owner Clarence Hand who reported being attacked by these men weeks earlier, allegedly in retaliation for a brass knuckles beating inflicted on the brother of one of them two years before. Daley had stopped these men on an unrelated suspicion just after the beating and, upon questioning, told them to get on home. Only after Hand later swore out warrants did the men face consequences.

Kowald denied seeking revenge on Daley for arresting him on the warrant.

Q: After you were released at the North Ave. station, didn't you state that you would get him (meaning Daley) if it would be the last act of your life.

A: No sir I did not.[52]

Kowald was riding the rails just before Daley was shot, boarding the eastbound North Avenue streetcar with run number 76 about 1 a.m, getting off at California Avenue and then transferring to a Western Avenue car southbound to Augusta Street, where he arrived home about 2 a.m. His route placed him close in time and location to the shooting of Pat Daley, but his mother, up late sewing, was his witness to being home by 2 a.m. and promptly going to bed. The other streetcar operators likewise offered alibis. Thus ended the theory that Daley's killing was an act of revenge by the streetcar operators named in warrants and subject to arrest for beating Mr. Hand, a crime several of them readily admitted committing.

The theory that the men shooed away from the Italian wedding went home for a gun with the intention of returning to break up the celebration at which they weren't welcome, but were instead interrupted by Daley, collapsed for a lack of evidence.

The Police Department Annual Report for 1926 describes the circumstances of Pat's murder as unknown due to the absence of witnesses. The report didn't say so, but Pat's was obviously a cold case almost immediately after his death.

[52] Source 246.

Even his inquest record is a bare bones recitation of his being found dead of a gunshot with no witnesses. I knew this was "the" story. Now I needed to decode the trickery that transformed Dan into Pat. Remember Mary Daley's brother Dan, the guy we were trying to track down when Pat jumped in and usurped his life story?

By 1926, Dan should have been in his sixties. Pat was 32. My experience in the Land of Muddlement wouldn't let me exclude Dan calling himself Patrick, despite having an older brother with that name, but hiding the 30-year age difference? Not so simple. As I mapped my next move, it hit me. Brother Timothy was a police officer. Who's more likely to have a police officer for a son than a police officer? Some birth certificate research established that Timothy had a son Patrick.[53] Bingo! Tracking this Patrick proved him to be the true subject of events previously known as "the Dan story."

With young Patrick installed in Dan's former life, I was stumped; what was I supposed to do with Dan? Timothy's obituary mentioned brother Daniel D. as a fellow police officer. So he did become a cop. Why was he otherwise incognito? I had one more bit of information to work with, knowledge that he was alive and working in Chicago as of the date of Timothy's death. Eventually, with an unexplained time gap, I found him a nice wife and six lovely children.[54]

---

[53] Dan was a cop, too, supposedly, but I'd had enough of Dan's evasiveness. And at the time, I was still on the hunt for him and had no information about his offspring.

[54] Two of these children, Daniel J. and Timothy, died of heart ailments in their teen years. A third, Thomas, died at age 21 during WWII.

One of his sons was named- ahem!- Daniel. Let me mention here that my great-grandmother, Timothy and Dan's sister Mary, also named one of her sons Daniel. As did Liz. And Jeremiah. And Timothy.[55]

If you spot an unclaimed Dan Daly sprinting through the streets of Chicago, give me a shout; one of ours is probably on the loose.

---

[55] While the number of relatives with the same names can be confusing, it's a result of the Irish naming customs, not strictly followed, which call for the first son's name to honor the paternal grandfather, the second the maternal grandfather, the third the father, and the fourth the father's eldest brother, while the first daughter's name honors the maternal grandmother, the second the paternal grandmother, the third the mother, and the fourth the mother's eldest sister.

Chapter 25

The Milwaukee Road

Dan Daley achieved his dream of running a locomotive, but in muddled Daly fashion, it wasn't the immigrant Dan who went to Chicago looking for railroad work with his brother John. Instead, one of the numerous nephews sharing the name, a son of Timothy Daley, took up the mantle and became an engineer on the storied Chicago, Milwaukee, St. Paul and Pacific Railroad. Inasmuch as our stories are the product of our times and cumulation of our works, this younger Dan's experience can be viewed through the railroad prism.

The Chicago railroads' clout was undeniable. They employed nine percent of the city's workforce in the decade before my forebears arrived. From 1870 to 1900, the number of railroad employees more than quintupled and continued to grow through the 1920s. In those early decades of the Twentieth Century, the railroads were in their heyday. The

Chicago, Milwaukee, St. Paul and Pacific Railroad operated 11,000 miles of track in 12 states by the time it reached its 90th birthday in the 1930s. Newspaper archives reveal the role the "Milwaukee Road" played in the lives of Chicagoans. The train brought disabled children to a summer camp in Wisconsin. It carried mourners to the gravesite after the funeral of a woman named Mary Kennealy, as it did for many other families. And when the plane derby pit flyers against each other in daring races in 1930, it was the reliable Milwaukee Road that brought the crowds.

The cast of characters arriving in the Windy City by train included both the predictable and the surprising. Governor Franklin D. Roosevelt rode the rails to Chicago in 1932 when campaigning for the presidency. Alaska Bishop Joseph R. Crimont rode in on the all steel luxury train Olympian in the early stages of his journey to Vatican City to meet with Pope Pius XI. The colorful orange and maroon Olympian cars carried broadcast radio receivers, still somewhat a novelty at the time, and were equipped with roller bearings for passenger comfort. The Bishop traveled in August so undoubtedly he arrived in one of the cars featuring an open gondola, operated only in the summer months. The electrified Olympian generated so much enthusiasm that Lionel Trains featured one of its engineers in its 1931 holiday ads, selling its models as the authentic trains "real railroad men buy for their boys."[56]

In between the Governor campaigning for the presidency and the Bishop en route to visit the Pope, a person

---

[56] Source 269.

of notoriety made use of the Chicago, Milwaukee, St. Paul and Pacific Railroad. The *Tribune* detailed "Madcap Congressman" Marion Zioncheck's escape from a mental hospital in Maryland and subsequent six hour "whirlwind of excitement that rivaled his antics of the last six months in the national capital"[57] as he passed through Chicago en route to his home Seattle, flanked by detectives. Those Washington antics included dancing in fountains and driving on the White House lawn. After what the Tribune characterized as his "dizzying evening" in Chicago, Zioncheck was kicked off his plane at the airport and hopped aboard the Milwaukee Road for the final leg of his trip.

Dan Daley drove trains when the acclaimed Olympian Hiawatha made its debut, cutting the travel time to Minneapolis to seven hours. On its 20-mile test run, the Hiawatha maintained consistent speeds of 106 to 108 miles per hour. The regular high-speed trains in 1935, whose fleetness was touted just months before the Hiawatha entered into service, moved a mile a minute. Mile a minute speed is something Nanny marveled at often, though her references may have been mostly hyperbole applied to her grandchildren's bursts of unrestrained motion. As one of those grandchildren, I failed to appreciate the wonder of moving from the horse and wagon era to the age of motorized travel. I dismissed a mile a minute then as no big deal. With the perspective of age and having experienced my own generation's technological leaps, I belatedly understand how impressive these speeds were to those encountering them for the first time.

---

[57] Source 270.

Competition among the rail lines for business encouraged the owners to go to great lengths to establish their dominance. The post office trains competed to quickly deliver mail and newspapers along their routes. Always up for a challenge, and ever supportive of its railroad family and customers, the Milwaukee Road management responded with enthusiasm to an appeal by Riley D. Cronk. Cronk used the train to deliver newspapers at a mark-up and found himself undercut by the appearance of a competitor using a shorter route on the Northwestern line in 1895. This was before Dan's days as an engineer but captures the spirit of railroading which continued into his tenure. Rumors spread of a locomotive race, soon confirmed. The Milwaukee Road undertook to beat the Northwestern Elroy Flyer, outfitting its competing train with its top engineers and best equipment. The race pit a Milwaukee Road train from Chicago's Union Station to Janesville, Wisconsin against the Northwestern Elroy Flyer whose route was a full 21 miles shorter. Milwaukee Road's Vice President Edward Ripley told his men to beat the Elroy train to Janesville "at all hazard."[58]

The Flyer started late, 20 minutes off schedule, but a gung-ho engineer, warned of the Milwaukee Road's competing run, determined to make up for lost time and reached Harvard, Illinois five minutes ahead of schedule. The papers for the small towns were thrown on the fly so as not to slow down the train. Despite extraordinary efforts, the Milwaukee Road train arrived 14 minutes behind its

---

[58] Source 274.

competitor. Not prone to failure, the railroad executives resolved to race again the following Sunday.

The majesty of train travel didn't come without a price tag in lives lost. One in 357 railroad workers died on the job in 1889 and the risk of death for employees remained high through about 1910. The engineer job, while highly skilled, was dangerous, with crashes and deadly boiler explosions among the risks. The engineer needed to keep a complex boiler system running. With the trains weighing thousands of tons, it was critical the engineer regulate the train speed. The railroads assigned engineers to individual segments of track where, for safety's sake, they needed to know the location of every signal and the locations of the curves, and every subtle change in grade.

Some of the headlines of the day include these:

November 1928: Milk Truck Hit By Fast Train, 1 Killed, 1 Hurt
January 1930: Body Found on Tracks
June 1932: Engineer Killed, 15 Injured When Train Is Ditched

Dan Daley was the engineer on freight trains involved in gruesome crashes in which deaths occurred, an experience no doubt devastating. When William Miller, an employee of the Carnegie Illinois Steel Corp., tried to beat the train by driving against flashing warning signals in Summit, Illinois in 1936, it was Dan Daley who disembarked his freight train and pulled the body from the wreckage. Again, in 1940, when Dan was driving a 64-car freight run, an auto driver came onto the tracks too suddenly for him to timely stop the train. This time, an executive of the Joseph B. Klicka Company, Joseph B. Hanzel, failed to heed the warnings of crossing watchman Edward Geary and crashed into the train's tender. Hanzel later died at the hospital.

Pedestrian encounters at grade crossings were all too frequent. News reports contain the sad stories of all manner of people inattentive to passing trains, from schoolchildren, to young men carrying lunches to workers, to elderly women trying to cross the street, mowed down when engineers were unable to stop on a dime.

By 1932, freight loadings for the Milwaukee Road line reached about 40,000 bi-weekly. While stolen rides by "bums" or "tramps" as well as adventurers atop and between freight cars has been romanticized in movies, the danger was proven by the death tolls, and trying to prevent such unauthorized riders was one more burden of the engineer. Alfred Alioto lost his life when he and friends rode atop the Milwaukee Road for a fun outing at the Washington Dells. Two companions jumping before him shouted to alert him to the oncoming passenger train, but he couldn't hear them above the locomotive roar and jumped to his death. Thirteen year old Raymond Kleba slipped under the train wheels and was crushed after hitching a ride to his father's workplace, intending to bring him his lunch. Thomas Doyle was a transient who is believed to have jumped from the Milwaukee Road freight train in Buffalo in 1937. While he avoided being run over by the train, the jump caused skull and leg fractures, killing him. Fourteen-year-olds Joseph Palmer and Jack Wassery and their dog companion named Bum were among the lucky ones, caught by railroad detectives in Minnesota as they prepared to re-board the freight train for the second leg of a multi-day adventure. They were deprived of the ride and lived to tell their story.

The camaraderie of Railroad engineers and crews was legendary. The company had its own *Milwaukee Road Magazine* to promote good relations. Soda Ash Johnny, whose real name was John Michael Horan, was one of the most famous railmen of the time. Nicknamed Soda Ash for a boiler cleaning process he'd devised using that substance, he spent 83 years with Milwaukee Road and his lifetime contribution was celebrated by the company management as his 100th birthday approached. When he died, the railroad sent a delegation of 200 railroaders on a special train, from the president and other top executives to workers in the railroad shops, to honor his memory and mourn his death. In his lifetime, Horan, who started out piling wood for the trains, had the opportunity to shake hands with every company president overseeing his 83-year work history.

But it didn't require a life's work to gain company appreciation. When a heat wave felled Cook County residents in droves in June 1931, killing 16 by June 28, Milwaukee Road management took extraordinary measures to try to save one of their own. Fifty-year-old Frank Malek worked as a car inspector in the Galewood railyard. After he collapsed in the 100 degree temperatures, managers ordered the tracks cleared and provided a special train to race him to a waiting ambulance at Union Station. Despite the heroic efforts, Malek passed away. The exceptional effort to save him was consistent with long-term practice. In 1902, when two freight trains collided in Iowa, with both engineers killed and 30 workers injured, the company likewise had arranged special trains to get its workers to the hospital.

Unfortunately, Dan's home life lacked the luster of his railroading experience. He developed a reputation for womanizing and gambling. One story handed down among family concerns his second daughter, Caroline, nicknamed Carrie. Carrie was born in 1913. Unlike the one sibling before her and two after, whose births were timely registered, she didn't show up in official records until she sent word of her own birth to the State of Illinois in 1973 when she was 60 years old. This delayed registration lends possible credence to the old family account of Carrie's origins. Kinfolk described Dan returning from work one day with a baby girl in his arms and handing her to his wife, Elizabeth. No one in the family besides Dan, with the presumed exception of Elizabeth, knew where he'd gotten that baby. And Dan and Elizabeth never revealed the secret of Caroline's parentage. But from the day she arrived in the Daley house, she was held out as their daughter.

Dan's wife did not seem especially fond of Dan. She stuck a gigantic knife in the pantry where it remained for decades; that knife, it was said, was intended for use on Dan, should circumstances requiring its employment arise. On his deathbed, Dan called out not for the woman with whom he'd shared pallet and pantry for thirty years but for some stranger by the name of Clementine.

Railroader Dan Daley and his wife Elizabeth Jacobs Daley raised four daughters. They had 16 grandchildren, 51 great-grandchildren, and 11 great-great grandchildren by the time Elizabeth died in 1981. Dan was long gone by then, having died in 1942 at age 52.

CHAPTER 26

THE LODESTAR

The headlines, *Napoleon Monat Must Die* and *Monat Goes to the Electric Chair* with accompanying articles referencing Sing Sing, co-conspirators, and an insanity defense, threatened to uproot my family tree. Napoleon Monat is one of my great-great-grandfathers' names. This monster couldn't be one of us! I can't have such detritus defiling the tree I so carefully nurtured. Where are the pruning shears?

Further reading placed this Monat's roots in Holyoke. Uh-oh. That's under our canopy. The danger was imminent. A mad scramble for birth certificates and an in-depth plunge into old news reports with a microscopic scanning for dates freed our tree from this impending scourge. This man was too young to be my Napoleon. And to be sure he wasn't any other kind of close relative, I sealed his fate with an examination of his birth certificate. Napoleon-Monat-the-murderer wasn't one of ours!

While the worst of the lot, Napoleon isn't my tree's only brush with unjustified infamy. Information often surfaces in awkward order. A quaint story, an address, a crime, a relationship— these scraps of someone's life, or maybe different someones' lives— cluster together in a messy pile, awaiting the corroboration that will assign them their proper owner. Like our Napoleon Monat, Mary Daley O'Brien's brother, Chicago police officer Timothy D. Daley suffered a near miss, only in his case, he might have experienced some teasing in real time.

The *Chicago Tribune* reported on August 28, 1889 under the header *Gleanings in Local Fields* that police officer Timothy Daley "unearthed a great conspiracy in his own mind yesterday morning."[59] And all his cop friends were laughing at him. The *Inter Ocean* carried the same story under the headline *A Policeman's Imagination*, describing Officer Timothy Daley as "a victim of a too vivid dream."[60] Believing he'd heard his landlady and a boarder named Dean discussing murdering a baby and himself as he was drifting off to sleep, he later called in five fellow officers to arrest the plotters.

He insisted to the judge the next morning that he heard the landlady say, "I solemnly swear that the child shall

---

[59] Source 297.
[60] Source 298.

die and I will keep the murder secret, so help me God."[61] Witnesses alibied Dean's absence from the house during the hour in which this proclamation supposedly spilled from his mouth. The arresting officers testified to finding both the landlady and Dean asleep in their respective rooms, out of earshot of Officer Daley's room, by the time they arrived. Said the *Tribune,* Daley "stuck to his extraordinary story on cross-examination by the judge, who gave it as his opinion that the officer was demented."

Demented might find a limb on my family tree, but Timothy's notch is not on that limb. The story was about a different police officer from an adjacent police district. Working under the Chicago Police Department's motto "At danger's call, we'll promptly fly; and bravely do or bravely die," Timothy D. Daley served through the era starting just after the Haymarket Riot, through the 1903 Iroquois Theater fire and continuing right up past the Eastland Disaster of 1915 when a steamboat overturned in the Chicago River, killing more than died in the sinking of the RMS Titanic three years earlier.

As a young child, I learned about the tragedy of the RMS Titanic from Nanny who recalled it in the 1960s as if it were yesterday. She was seven years old when that ocean liner went down, taking some 1,160 souls to the ocean floor and killing 340 more whose remains were recovered. Of the 110 Irish Titanic steerage passengers boarding in Queenstown, the port where Nanny's mother, father, aunts and uncles, started their American journeys, 67% percent were lost, with

---

[61] Ibid.

children and men hit hardest. Five of the six Irish children traveling in steerage and 46 of the 51 men didn't make it out alive. The Irish women fared better with 30 of 53 rescued. When Nanny told the story of the Titanic sinking, the message about the owner class hubris came through loud and clear. Cautiousness was in my nature, so it hardly took a ship crashing into an iceberg to convince me to hold back in face of the unfamiliar. It struck me that this ship sinking carried a tragic air more personal than run of the mill bad news but I passed it off as part of Nanny's fixation on all things Irish. Looking back now, my breath catches as I notice how close in time it was to her own parents' overseas journeys, how there-but-for-the-grace-of-God-go-I imprinted itself in a most personal way on Nanny and her Daley and O'Brien kin. Timothy in particular must have been confronted with Titanic emotions on seeing close-up the subsequent sinking of the Eastland.

Police duties in the City of Chicago in that era included taking abandoned children to the foundlings home and "wayward" girls to Home of the Good Shepherd, fielding complaints about unlit street lamps and defective fire hydrants. Police issued notices to property owners to repair their sidewalks. They took possession of stray horse teams and chased down runaway horses. In August 1910, detectives from Timothy's precinct arrested twenty Greeks, Turks, and men of other "foreign" nationalities for the crime of insulting (in our era, we might say hitting on) women pedestrians at a street crossing.

Initially working at pay of about $1,000 per year, Timothy Daley put in extraordinary hours. Like all patrolmen, he was expected to patrol approximately 63 hours weekly, while remaining on reserve for 49 more. In the Chicago Police Department Annual Report for 1903, the police chief noted that his officers had had scant opportunity for days off in the previous two years due in part to a massive railway strike and other labor disputes. Timothy was injured on the job that winter but was back in service no later than mid-summer when he arrested one James Fitzsimmons for larceny.

Timothy saw horse-drawn police wagons begin to retire as the first police cars came into use. The year prior to his death, the Department still spent $22,000 on horseshoes and $42,000 on feed. And he witnessed the introduction of women police officers, though their roles were limited. He died on what was so far the hottest day of the year in July 1916,[62] with 28 years in service.

When Sister Julia Frances scratched her memory for wisps of information about forebears long passed, the name Timothy did not find its way to the surface. But once my research uncovered him, he became the lodestar guiding me to County Kerry. It was one of his death notices that not only linked his name to those of known Daley siblings but tied the

---

[62] The next day proved hotter with the high temperature 102 degrees and the low 84 degrees. This was and still is the hottest day ever recorded in Chicago history based on the average daily temperatures at the official recording station at the University of Chicago. Hotter unofficial temperatures were actually recorded at Midway Airport in 1934.

family to a particular locality in Ireland with these magical words: "native of Knockaderry-Farranfore, County Kerry, Ireland."[63]

---

[63] Source 300.

CHAPTER 27

HOW *EN ROUTE TO KNOCKADERRY*

WAS BORN

We both knew the answer would be "Ireland," when, for Christmas 2019, my son Andy surprised me with a trip to "wherever [I] want to go." Tickets bought and the trip calendared for three weeks beginning in June 2020, I pulled out my genealogy files and scrambled to fill gaps, to know as much as I could before my arrival. This book resulted in part from my preparation for this dream trip.

2020 had its own surprises in store, of course; with Covid-19 getting its miserable grip on the world and refusing to let go, we had to postpone our British Isles caper twice. But the postponements weren't all bad. In their own way, 2020 and 2021 became an adventure, not so much for their novelty to our generation, with mask-wearing, social distancing, and

Zoom meetings, but for the astounding new details of my family history I would unearth when I decided to continue researching and compile my genealogy into a book rather than brood for the indeterminate time that eventually extended beyond two years.

The book I planned to write was for my three children. It was to be a compendium of my research, organized by ancestor, a reference book of sorts, with stories supplemented with vital documents, maps, wills, and property records— a book, it didn't take long to realize, that they would never read. Shortly after starting that tedious project, while I was taking a walk one day, the inspiration hit me to change gears and instead tell the story of my experience discovering those ancestors.

After writing furiously and completing several chapters, I encountered a problem. I had a mental block when it came to making the story about me and my journey. Without me as the fulcrum, *En Route to Knockaderry* would become a manuscript in search of a plot. I instinctively knew I had to prop up these ancestors, but I struggled to write about myself. My daughter Cindy, who holds an Occupational Associates degree in Acting, suggested wearing a mask like she did in acting classes, figuratively or even literally. Thanks to Covid, I was wearing a mask, though not the type she meant.

"You don't have a story, without you," she reminded me.

Cindy had not seen the book-manuscript-in-progress or heard its specific contents described when she suggested I start with Nanny at the dinner table as we ate a typical meal with her telling stories.

"Get out of my head," I told her. "You're scaring me."

Chapter One then was already structured as Chapter One now, featuring Nanny telling stories at dinner and teatime. We talked about screenplays because this book, like most of my writing, is heavy with imagery.

"How could you best write a screenplay linking all these different stories?" I asked.

"You're the common link," she said, again. Not because I didn't hear it the first time, not because I didn't get it, not even because I hadn't figured it out on my own. The message needed repeating because I was fighting it, hesitant to reveal too much of myself.[64]

Determined to shelf my self-consciousness and craft the story that needed to be told, I analyzed each chapter in my nascent manuscript. Why did I choose this person? What made this person's story need to be told as part of my exploration of my ancestry? How were their traits or experiences relevant to me? And most importantly, how did this person's story contribute to my own transformation

---

[64] Were I to write that screenplay today, I'd center it on Chapter 28 and use the Sullivans' eviction as the backstory.

from that little girl hiding in the shadows for fear of her differences being discovered to the woman who kicked Shame out of the equation and now celebrates her ancestry without regard to either who her forebears were or who they were not?

Ecstatic to find I could trace my Dalys back to the very street where Daniel and Elizabeth, parents of Nanny's mother, raised their family, I was not so lucky with Nanny's father's family. I looked for a genealogy group that might be able to help, and finding mention of Irish Genealogy on Facebook, I posted to it about my inability to find Jeremiah and Annie O'Brien, hoping someone would have tips. To my amazement, Mary O'Keeffe, a friend from Boston College, responded. Not only was she a member of that group, she had developed considerable expertise in genealogy tracking her own family history. Within a short time, Mary produced a document clarifying that my great-grandfather Martin O'Brien was from County Clare, cutting my work in half. Previously, I had inconsistent claims of Clare and Cork provenance. But even with that massive workload reduction, I have not been able to find records of a Jeremiah and Annie O'Brien who had children named Martin and Bridget in the correct time frame. They may be people who grew up in an area where Roman Catholics weren't documented, or it may be their parish's documentation has yet to go online. My deepest fear is that they may be among those people identified only by initials in the workhouse records. Martin's death certificate indicates his father's name was John, conflicting with the marriage records for him and his sister, but a search for John and Annie was similarly disappointing. Since every other source from family lore to marriage records pegged him as a Jeremiah, I suspect his name might be John Jeremiah and he was known by his middle name due to sharing the same name with others in his family.

Members of other online genealogy groups proved immensely helpful in locating ancestral records as well. But some problems have proved intractable to date. I plan to keep searching for those missing links, despite the seeming impossibility. With my research, so many other "impossible" barriers have been broken to bits, just like few church pews you will learn about shortly.

There are more exciting discoveries, so keep on reading. And there's also some necessary housecleaning to be done; don't bother yourself trying to set right any irregularities you may have noticed, as they'll be cleared up soon enough.

CHAPTER 28

MOONLIGHT RAIDS AND LITURGICAL

REBELLIONS

When the Bishop of Kerry made the extraordinary decision to cancel Mass in Firies parish for 18 days leading up to Ash Wednesday in 1886, neither an epidemic nor a natural disaster forced his hand. There was an atypical burst of heavy snow that spring, but it didn't arrive until April, well into the Lenten season. The Most Reverend Doctor Andrew Higgins was instead confronting an interpersonal calamity of the most unusual nature.

Dan Daly was at that time "indisposed," so there's no blaming him for the goings-on. Remember Dan Daly? No, not *that* Dan Daly, and not *that* one, either. I refer to the particular Dan Daly who was said to have harbored railroad dreams but who experienced cop realities instead, the Dan Daly who laid low while I chased him all over Chicago. Long before Dan landed in the Windy City, he had made his home in Knockaderry, in the civil parish of Molahiffe, and the Roman Catholic parish Firies.[65] Dan may have joined an organization whose members dressed in white and made moonlight raids— or maybe he didn't, it's hard to say— but either way, you understand he was not a member of the Ku Klux Klan; that organization had entirely different goals and operated solely in America, a country in which Dan had yet to step foot. So, despite the same-colored clothing and nocturnal preferences, the KKK had no hand in the events that led Kerry's Bishop to close up the church and tell the parishioners to stay home. Nor did Dan Daly, at least not directly.

When Dan requested his little sister Elizabeth wash his trousers November 12, 1885, two-and-half months before the church closure, she complied without noticing whether

---

[65] From 1695 through 1829, the British banned the Irish Roman Catholics from practicing their religion. Under Cromwell, the Brits burned Catholic churches to the ground, including the Molahiffe Church. Those who practiced Catholicism did so secretly, using Mass rocks in the woods whenever a traveling priest came through town. Those priests were risking death for saying the Catholic Mass. When the laws were relaxed, a church was constructed of wattle and straw in about 1832; however that church caught fire and burned to the ground. Luckily, parish birth and marriage registers were rescued and did not suffer significant damage. After the fire, the parishoners walked eight miles each way to attend church in Ballyhar on Sundays. A new church was constructed with funding from the community during Mary Daley's childhood. It's that new church, St. Gertrude's, where the events described in this chapter took place.

the pants had pockets in them or not. She set the trousers in a pot to steep that Thursday, and they remained in the pot until Saturday at which time she observed while scrubbing them that the pockets were missing but neglected to inquire as to the pockets' whereabouts. As one of ten children, and a girl who was expected to clean her brother's trousers in lieu of throwing the wash pot at him for presuming her provision of such service, it's easily understood why Elizabeth was content to let Dan figure out for himself where his pockets had gotten off to. And so when the trial came around, that is— er, more or less (with a smidgeon of creative enhancement)— what she told the judge and jury.

Dan is singularly responsible for upending the family immigration narrative which I myself believed right up through Chapter 27. There were events happening in Ireland that prompted my ancestors to emigrate alright, but the Great Hunger two decades gone was not chief among them. It was the time of the Land War, when high rents imposed by the few, and often absentee, landlords twisted every last cent out of a population increasingly pressed to pay it, especially in the west where local agrarian conditions exacerbated the general economic depression felt throughout the country. The activists called for rent strikes and used tactics from intimidation to boycott to pressure those choosing to pay rent to reverse course and to keep new renters from taking up properties recently subject to evictions. The boycotts kept farmers who declined to oblige from obtaining help with farm work and other necessities and were prohibited by law.

My mother vehemently denied our Irishness when I asked about our heritage, insisting we were American and nothing more. She may have had more Irish in her than she cared to acknowledge. Once when the subject of buying foreclosed properties arose, she reacted with intense emotion, insisting that it wasn't right to profit off someone else's troubles. Of course, we lived with foreclosure bearing down on us. In those days when the mortgage collector came door to door to pry cash out of those who missed payments, hand-wringing and muttered worries were followed by rushed curtain and door closing and disappearing from view whenever the mortgage man was spotted walking down the street. He could knock or ring the doorbell as long as he cared to; no one was going to open up. It may have been only fear of losing the home that represented security that was responsible for my mother's impassioned reaction to mere talk of foreclosure sales, but I believe it went deeper. She grew up listening to Nanny, after all.

When the Royal Constabulary grabbed up Dan Daly, the official charge against him was na Buachaillí Bána, or Whiteboyism. When the court finished with him, he was sentenced to 14 years penal servitude. The judge suggested he should be grateful for that sentence, , , intimating he'd squeaked by on a Whiteboyism charge in lieu of answering a murder charge with his life only thanks to moderation by the prosecutors, and he expressed doubt in the sufficiency of the 14 year sentence he himself imposed.

Never accuse the Dalys of being overly fashionable; the crime with which our boy Dan managed to get charged, Whiteboyism,[66] had been out of vogue for more than a century. There were other names for what the tenant rights activists were doing— contemporary journalists preferred the term Moonlighting— but with the Whiteboy Acts still on the books, Whiteboyism proved a convenient label to slap on poor Dan. And a Hail Mary for the prosecutor who otherwise had no case against Dan he could put forward.

The Moonlighters of Dan Daly's era descended from secret societies created more than a hundred years earlier, groups aimed at protesting excessive rents, forced tithes to the Church of England, and evictions. Determined to crush this political activism, the British ruling class enacted harsh "Whiteboy" laws, punishing participation with death. The death penalty initially applied not only to cases in which a murder occurred but even in the more typical cases of gun theft or distributing threatening handbills. The laws let up somewhat by the time of Dan's arrest, but formal charges continued to be proffered and convictions had on insufficient evidence, and the penalties remained disproportionately harsh compared to those imposed for like crimes not prosecuted under the Whiteboyism taint.

Contrary to the impression of the Moonlighters as depraved, violent, antisocial criminals deliberately laid by British law enforcement personnel, the Moonlighters purposefully sought to right the wrongs of an oppressive

---

[66] The name is derived from white smocks worn by those original night raiders.

system imposed by a hostile foreign government occupying their land. With most of the native Irish population relegated to tenant farming the lands of absentee British landlords who charged rents usurping most of their farm income, the tenants were being evicted at alarming rates and with brutal force. Between October 1880 and January 1886, some 86 residents of the small local area where the Dalys lived were cast into homelessness, as a result of 13 evictions. To evict just two families from Kenmare Estate in January 1886, the British sent a contingent 229 strong, comprised of military and police armed with rifles and bludgeons. These removals presaged an "extremely large number"[67] of evictions scheduled to take place there before month's end, enough to empty an entire townland.

When these swarms of military and regular police arrived to displace tenants, they often burned down the tenant houses to ensure the tenants couldn't return to them once they left the area. Poor laws allowed vagrants to be arrested and forced into the fearsome workhouses with their alarming death and long-term inmate residency rates and despised mandatory family separation policies. The cruelty of these practices and the repressive nature of the government left the local Irish people few options for protecting themselves and their communities.

The Moonlighters engaged in acts of charity and support for displaced tenants, including building new houses in a single day for some of those cast out. They collectively sought out rent reductions for those desperate not to follow.

---

[67] Source 342.

They organized rent strikes when landlords refused reasonable accommodations. When necessary to persuade their own neighbors, fearful of opposing the occupying government, they resorted to force. Yet even as Moonlighters raided homes for guns and money to support their mission, they as often met with camaraderie as with resistance. They habitually collected resigned "donations" from the householders they raided. Violent encounters happened, but so did a drink or meal with a homeowner; in one reported case, Moonlighters joined a wedding celebration that was underway when they arrived. The purpose of including this information is not to dismiss or validate the violence sometimes associated with Moonlighter raids but to add perspective so as to provide a more accurate picture of the Moonlighters and their motivations.

Our Dan may have been guilty of a crime. I take no firm position on this but feel some skepticism, for his criminality would require labeling his seemingly honorable father, brother, and sister perjurers. Yet if your country were invaded by a hostile power seeking to slowly inflict genocide on your people, and your son or brother stood up for those in his community using the few tools available, would you not tell a lie in the invading power's courtroom to save your beloved from the retribution the invader would pass off as justice? It's hard to know one way or the other what happened, but as you will soon see, a testifying police officer acknowledged Dan's good reputation and the judge likewise commended his father's integrity.

Poor John O'Connell Curtin did lose his life in a murderous act. But acknowledging that someone murdered Mr. Curtin is in no way the same as establishing that Dan was in the group that did it, and the prosecutor barely tried. He didn't need to try. With a jury terrified of Moonlighting and a judge almost uniformly disparaging of the nation's youth, the Whiteboyism charge ensured a conviction and hefty sentence without evidence of any substance.

John O'Connell Curtin was a gentleman farmer, controlling one of the largest tenant farms in the area. He was also a member of the National League, an organization devoted to abolishing landlordism in favor of tenant land ownership. He was sympathetic to some of the aims though not the means of the Moonlighters, having himself unsuccessfully joined forces with the local priest Rev. Patrick O'Connor to seek reductions in Kenmare[68] tenant rents in the year prior to his murder. However, when the denial of reductions led to a general rent strike against Lord Kenmare, Curtin broke ranks and paid his rent. Despite his strike-breaker status, Curtin's murder was believed by police to have been solely the result of a gun raid gone awry and not revenge.

The travesty masquerading as a trial began with the seating of a man hard of hearing on the jury— a jury which, consistent with practice of the time, was limited in membership to male landowners and long-term leaseholders, predominantly Protestants of relative wealth. In Dan's case

---

[68] Lord Kenmare was one of the principal owners/lessors of property in the area of County Kerry where the Dalys lived.

the jury consisted of 12 "gentlemen," distinguished in news reports from the "farming class." Prosecutors enjoyed the right to strike any potential juror they suspected of sympathy with the defense, a right they were known to employ liberally with any Roman Catholics who slipped onto the jury lists. In Dan's case, they struck 11 potential jurors. The prosecutor's chief witness in Dan's case, George Curtin, son of the deceased, stated on the night of the attack that the Moonlighters wore masks fashioned out of pockets, and he couldn't identify them because he didn't see their faces (but for the co-defendant identified as Thady Casey who became unmasked but whom he did not know by sight.) Six days later, he couldn't pick Dan out of a line-up as the one man he'd told police had a familiar physique; yet at trial he testified that he recognized Dan as one of the raiders by his physique because he'd seen him in passing at church over the years. So sure he was of this identification, he declined to swear to its accuracy:

Q: Will you swear it was Daly who was there that night?
A: I will not...[69]

No other witness put Dan at the crime scene. The prosecutor himself told the jury that the case against Dan was weaker than the case against Casey and hinged upon Daniel Curtin placing him at the crime scene.

Like so many young men imprisoned for Whiteboyism, Dan had no criminal history. While men

---

[69] Source 311.

known to have participated in the raid went into hiding immediately thereafter, Dan was in his father's yard working up until his arrest. His father Daniel, his brother Jeremiah, and his sister Elizabeth all testified he was at home on the night the Moonlighters went into Mr. Curtin's house to steal guns and unintentionally killed him in a shootout that erupted after his children resisted their demands, and Mr. Curtin fired two shots, one straight into the face of the young Moonlighter Thady Sullivan.[70]

The senior Daniel Daly testified that shortly before 7 p.m., Dan's brother Jeremiah had come in to fetch Dan to help him point spars for thatching in the barn, and Jeremiah confirmed this. The Dalys lived almost two miles as the crow flies from Castlefarm. Putting aside Jeremiah's testimony about pointing spars together, if Dan spoke with his father on their farm just before seven, there was scant time for him to get to the Curtin residence in time to participate in the raid which was said to have occurred between 7 and 8 p.m., likely starting about 7:15 and continuing for 10 to 20 minutes. Dan came in to his supper between 8 and 9 p.m., his father said, while Dan's sister Elizabeth remembered calling Dan into the house for supper shortly after hearing the Tralee train pass on that fatal night. She told the court that he remained inside, going to bed an hour later.

A police officer testifying for the Crown said he'd known Dan for years and never knew anything against him.

---

[70] There were multiple Thady Sullivans present at the Curtin home that evening, including, at a minimum, two servants and the Moonlighter who was shot.

The judge himself, while bashing young people testifying on both sides of the case with generalized complaints about the youth of the day, spoke highly of Dan's father's testimony, saying he appeared to be under the influence of morality and good conduct. This would suggest to most people that his alibi testimony was credible. The smoking gun wasn't a gun at all but a pocket, and we all know a pocket can't smoke without soon disintegrating. In the days after the raid, police found several fallen pockets snipped from clothing, with eye holes cut out and a strap attached, on and near the Curtin property. A police officer said he was able to sew one of these perfectly into Dan's trousers. Yes, that says "sew," as in contaminating the evidence. Remember the trousers with the missing pockets? Frustrated police who suspected Dan had been present at Castlefarm but couldn't pressure a soul in County Kerry to implicate him, took him into custody in that failed effort to get George Curtin to identify him by his physique. While on the premises arresting him, the constables snatched Dan's pants off the clothesline where they were drying.[71] Dan was 5 foot 9 and 170 pounds. His pants size was probably similar to half the young men in County Kerry, and any one of them might have been convicted on this untethered pocket match.

George Fitzmaurice's play *The Moonlighter* is a work of fiction yet captures the tenor of the Whiteboyism prosecutions:

---

[71] Some reports indicated Dan was wearing the pants and they were confiscated at the police station, but that seems less likely given Elizabeth's testimony about scrubbing the pants that very day.

A man is as safe in the moonlighters as out of them. And if the choice fell on a man to do a bad deed itself, 'tisn't him might be hung at all but some one as free of the crime as Jesus Christ himself, if he hadn't his alibi correct or was about the vicinity. The peelers don't care a devil but to make a case; the judge don't give a whack but to choke you for an example, and a jury of Cork Scotchmen would swing the nation on circumstantial evidence.[72]

Four days before Christmas, and three days before Dan's twenty-second birthday, the Court of Assizes, after an extended jury deliberation lasting a full 15 minutes, convicted Dan. The youth-disparaging judge, Justice William O'Brien, sentenced him to the aforementioned 14 years. He was instantly remanded to gaol in Tralee, to be transferred in the following weeks to the Mountjoy prison in Dublin, colloquially known as "the Joy."

Breaking the code of silence by ratting someone out to the constables or testifying against them in a felony case were cardinal sins in rural County Kerry, far more grievous than any Dan's brother Jeremiah or his cousin Catherine "Kitty Teadgh Tom"[73] Brosnan were about to commit, inspired by none other than Mischief herself. It was Jeremiah

---

[72] Source 328.

[73] With so many people sharing the same names, nicknames were essential but ultimately insufficient. The Irish began using nicknames that incorporated the lineage of a particular person such that Catherine Brosnan was called "Kitty," her nickname, with "Teadgh," her father's name and "Tom," her grandfather's name appended to distinguish her from other Brosnan women called Kitty.

and Kitty's beloved brother and cousin who had been wronged by these particular transgressions, and they determined to teach the slow-to-learn Curtins, whom they never did like, a lesson. When the Curtins set out for church one Sunday morning in January, they were confronted by a massive crowd of neighbors recruited by Jeremiah and Kitty Teadgh Tom who left them no room to doubt that they were unwelcome at Mass. That first time, the Curtins turned back toward home. The following Sunday, the Curtins made it into St. Gertrude's vestibule without incident, only to be greeted by widespread jeering as they made their way up the aisle to their pew and again when Mass was over. So it should have come as no surprise to anyone when the next Sunday proved eventful.

Four weeks post-trial, the preponderance of the parish continued to seethe over what they perceived as an unjust conviction of Dan and a heinous crime against the popular young Thady Sullivan, shot dead by Mr. Curtin. Remember, this was a tiny collection of townlands populated by family and neighbors who'd lived side-by-side for generations. While it may not suit modern perceptions, to those people in that time it was obvious the local band of Moonlighters had no intention to hurt anyone, and none of them would have shot Curtin had he not fired his gun. Too, it was understood that when the Moonlighters came for your weapons, you gave them up in support of the cause, however reluctantly. These factors were compelling in any assessment of fault for the raid gone wrong.

As the Curtins made their third excursion to church since the death of their patriarch, they had to walk the one mile distance as their horse needed shoeing, and boycotters deterred the farrier from approaching the Curtin barn. Wealthier than most of the local farmers, the Curtins owned Castlefarm near the ruins of the old Molahiffe Castle. Some sixty years before John O'Connell Curtin was murdered at Castlefarm, his father-in-law, Maurice De Courcy, Esq., the home's prior owner, had faced a Whiteboys raid there. John himself had experienced a Moonlighter raid four years before the one in which he was murdered. So it wasn't surprising that on this Sunday excursion to church and back, in light of the tensions of the past weeks,[74] the well-heeled Curtin family brought a hefty contingent of police to guard them.

Rev. O'Connor said the Mass without incident and retired to the sacristy. As the congregation dispersed, one small knot of girls gathered inside the churchyard gate talking, while another formed just outside the gate. When the Curtins exited the church and proceeded in their direction, both groups of girls hooted. The 25 police employed to protect the Curtins decided to ward off any trouble from the throng of churchgoers milling about by preemptively beating them with bludgeons and stabbing them with swords. A dozen parishioners received severe slash wounds, including to the face and scalp. One man was so badly cut, he had to be

---

[74] Another source of tension was the relative attendance at the funerals of the two men killed in the raid. The common farmer's son Timothy "Thady" Sullivan drew the largest crowd ever amassed for a County Kerry funeral whereas Mr. Curtin's was poorly attended, particularly for a man of his stature, respected in life.

carried off. The enraged crowd pelted the police with stones. After the Curtins were ushered away from the melee, some of the devout church ladies, chafing at the the Curtins' audacity in showing up for Mass with a veritable army on the offensive, returned to the sanctuary, wrestled the Curtin pew out of the building and smashed it to smithereens. Then, they returned inside, seized the pew usually occupied by the constabulary and carried that out, shattering it for good measure.

In the following weeks, hostilities continued. Rev. O'Connor, who had been reduced to tears when he learned of the brutality outside the church, pleaded with his parishioners to refrain from violence. In an interview later included in the Special Commission on Parnellism[75] and Crime report addressing Moonlighting violence, the Reverend Father offered insight into the parishioners' newly developed antipathy for the Curtin family. There had been numerous evictions of farmer tenants and the Moonlighters sought to forestall future evictions by ensuring no one would thereafter rent the land. Many people faulted the Curtins, who were fully cognizant of these goals, he said, for not peacefully relinquishing their guns when the raiders appeared.[76]

---

[75] Parnellism, named after Charles Stewart Parnell, Irish Nationalist leader and member of the House of Commons, was the advocacy of Home Rule in Ireland, then under British domination, and the methods of agitation used in that aim.

[76] John O'Connell Curtin had relinquished guns in a previous Moonlighter raid in 1881 and was said to be determined to hang onto new guns he had purchased, which purchase in Cork, a few days before the fatal raid, reached Moonlighter ears.

With the church ultimately unable to persuade the warring parties to come in peace, the Bishop kicked the entire parish to the curb. But fierce Irish loyalties did not abate with this brief Mass hiatus. The Curtins continued to face boycotts, and the boycotters were called to account in court. Six weeks passed before the Bishop deemed it safe to reopen the church after his original announcement of an eighteen-day closure. A short time later, in late March, the deceased Moonlighter Thady Sullivan's friends and family waylaid a new pew being delivered to the church for the Curtins. Afterwards, that pew, like its predecessor, lay in the church yard broken into splinters.

Jeremiah Daly, his sister Elizabeth Daly, and Kitty Teadgh Tom Brosnan were among a large group arrested following the Curtins' church troubles, but in an amazing stroke of luck for Kitty, the authorities in Tralee were compelled to release her due to a law preventing detention of a woman with more than two children. Kitty had sixteen! (She would go on to have five more in the years following.) Elizabeth's and Jeremiah's charging sheets accuse them of the laughable crime of "abusing" members of the Royal Constabulary "by hooting and booing at them" and otherwise obstructing them in the discharge of their duty as such peace officers whilst protecting Daniel Curtin, George Curtin, Norah Curtin, and Elizabeth Curtin. Those arrested were ordered to post bail and released on the expectation that they would remain out of the law's sights for six months. Mischief evaded arrest altogether and may have been glimpsed escaping into the faerie mound at Boolacoullane.

By January 1887, with no let-up to their troubles in sight, the Curtins deemed it advisable to put their house on the market and move to Limerick where they owned another property. The widow Agnes O'Connell Curtin requested leniency for the men charged for boycotting her, telling the court all was well between them since the boycotters showed up at the sale of her Castlefarm household goods and bought from her at fair prices. When their cases were heard, crowds cheered the defendants.

One more relative makes an appearance— or rather a disappearance— in this tale. While three Thady Sullivans would seem to be a sufficient number to populate any place or story, there was in fact a fourth Thady Sullivan present in the vicinity of Knockaderry who was neither a servant to the Curtins nor a dead Moonlighter. Thady Sullivan #4 was a Daly cousin. When this Thady's cousin and close companion Dan Daly was arrested and hauled off to Cork Gaol, Thady feared their association might find him accused next and his freedom curtailed. In desperation, he sought out Mischief and associates who swiftly arranged for him to be smuggled out of Ireland in a barrel. That barrel was loaded onto a ship at Kenmare port, and before long Thady Sullivan #4 found himself in America.

The Castlefarm raid quickly assumed folkloric dimensions and was memorialized in a ballad whose meaning is subject to variant interpretations. A listener might wonder was this ballad was composed as a secret communication intended to pass a message? Or perhaps it was intended to influence public opinion or the course of the investigation?

The ballad lionizes the Moonlighters responsible, particularly the deceased Thady Sullivan. It suggests that Curtin's shooter escaped and emigrated, with the line "God prosper him over the water." This might be a reference to Thady Sullivan #4, yet it would be simplistic to assume he was the triggerman, if he were there at all. Wouldn't he, being out of the reach of the law, be one to blame if one goal of this ditty were to throw police off? The ballad expresses sympathy for the men in jail deemed innocent[77] by the balladeer. Yet, the lines about Mr. Curtin's grandfather bringing croppies to the gallows are said to be false, whether grounded in malfeasance or misinformation. This leaves us to wonder whether the balladeer had inside information about the Moonlighter raid on Castlefarm, some of it contradicting the official account, or whether this ballad was an exercise in misdirection. Either is possible. The ballad[78] goes like this:

> Now listen awhile the truth I will state,
> How those moonlighting heroes of late made a raid,
> Down in Castlefarm in John Curtin's place,

---

[77] With respect to Daniel's co-defendant Thady Casey's involvement, Curtin children testified that when his mask came off, they asked him his name and he gave it. Servants who knew Casey, who did not see the unmasked man but heard his voice, insisted that the voice they heard was not Casey's. The judge disparaged those servant witnesses at trial, chastising them before the jury for not putting their lives in jeopardy to try to aid their respectable employer, strongly implying their lives were expendable. The servants testified inconsistently but ultimately said the man was not Casey. One of the servants, Bryan Sullivan, was so traumatized by the trial, he attempted suicide inside the courthouse hallway.
[78] Source 334.

They entered the kitchen with masks on their face,
Demanding firearms, they followed his son
Right into the parlour in search for a gun,
From the top of the stair two bullets did come,
Which murdered the poor widow's darling....

A young lad in the ranks, a dashing
young blade,
With a darling young heart that was never
dismayed,
He leveled his rifle that ne're him betrayed,
And left the old blood-hound there squealing.
They fought and they rallied through parlour
and hall,
Outside in the kitchen old Curtin did fall,
But for damp ammunition we would settle
them all,
Which is but the fate of informers.

His grandfather, too, I'm informed of
late,
He brought to the gallows in the year '98
Four dozen croppies, the truth we must state,
For which he was highly rewarded;
But the blood of those martyrs for vengeance
does call,
It was heaven decreed it that Curtin should
fall.
Success to the right boy that gave him the ball,
God prosper him over the water.

Nora and Lizzie with Agnes the three
Came tumbling downstairs in the midst of the
spree,
With Doran that evening they drank in full
glee,
But little expected the slaughter.
It's a pity the lapdog of Kenmare Estate
Was not caught in the den, we would give him
a taste
Of some powder and ball that would send him
in haste
Far away from tormenting poor sinners.

So now to conclude and to finish my song,
May those boys that's in jail be at home before long,
Those two innocent men that are in the wrong,
That the Lord he may keep them from harm.
Not forgetting Thady Sullivan shot through the
head,
May the powers above for his soul find a bed,
And his loving mother is now nearly dead,
Lamenting the loss of her darling.

Dan left Mountjoy in May 1895, at age 31. By then,
most of his siblings had emigrated to America and within a
short time, he joined them. He went straight to Chicago
where family waited.

CHAPTER 29

PUZZLE-ING PIECES

How could Dan Daly have been up in the Joy in Ireland when his siblings relocated to Chicago if he were one of the brothers who hankered to move there after life in Holyoke's mills proved miserable? No matter how muddled the Daly story is and how self-promoting family tales, the man could not have been in two places at once.

The conviction timing, December 1885, corresponds with Dan's immigration to the United States, that is, his immigration date as reported by him on the 1910 and 1920 Censuses.[79] That immigration date is a cautionary tale about cross-referencing data when doing genealogical research. This

---

[79] In 1930, he reported his immigration date as 1900. This date is also incorrect. His marriage in Chicago took place in 1889. His most likely immigration date is 1898 based on ship passenger manifests and known locations on specific dates.

man had a reason for choosing a fictional 1885 immigration date; if he were here, he couldn't have been there. There, where some convict named Dan Daly had done hard time. And who would doubt his recounting of his travel date as 1885 even if they heard of a Dan Daly in gaol when he came from an area where the name Daly was top two in popularity and arrived in a locale where you couldn't pass along the sidewalk without bumping into one or a dozen of the same? The record of Dan's stay in the Cork Gaol firmly establishes that he was transferred to Mountjoy Prison in Dublin on January 19, 1886. And he remained there nine years and four months.

And what about John? Why do we never hear of him again once he moved to Chicago? Did John die young after he got there? One thing I can assure you, he would not have broken with the family. This clan was tight. When Nanny's brother Marty moved to Chicago, and she returned to Holyoke, they exchanged weekly letters for decades to come. Another relative in Eastern Massachusetts upon becoming widowed hustled right off to Chicago to move in with extended family living there. So John, wherever he may have ended up, wouldn't have strayed far from his kin.

In piecing together the puzzle, remember that we have Timothy to account for, Timothy who was omitted from the telling of the Holyoke-to-Chicago migration. I'm confident Sr. Julia Frances' account was as truthful and accurate as she knew. But I was asking her to recall details about relatives she'd probably never met, whom she presumably hadn't thought about in years, they having died when she was young after them never having been an active part of her life. She joined the Sisters of St. Joseph and moved into the convent when she was but 19 and spent the next decades traveling to parishes across Massachusetts in need of her teaching services.[80] By the time I had occasion to ask her about our shared ancestors, she was retired and well into her 80s. Just as she recounted the detective Patrick story with sufficient accuracy that I could immediately recognize it when I found news accounts about it, despite the mistaken attribution to his uncle Dan, Sr. Julia Frances seems to have gotten the essentials straight about Timothy while getting tripped up on his name, instead pulling a name from the next generation. It makes sense for those railroad dreams driving a man westward to have belonged to Timothy, whose son Dan followed through and made them a reality. Timothy, Elizabeth and Margaret were indisputably already in Chicago—Timothy a patrolman in the Chicago Police Department, Elizabeth selling milk from a pushcart, and Maggie keeping house— by the time Dan was released from Mountjoy and booked passage to America.

Sorting out this confusion required revisiting potential immigration records and whittling them away one by one until the immigration pattern emerged. Timothy and

---

[80] Sister Julia Frances taught elementary school at Our Lady of Hope in Springfield from 1933-1939 and from 1959-1967, at St. Mary's in Milford from 1939-1942, at St. Louis School in Webster from 1942-1949, at St. Michael's in Northampton from 1967-1969, at St. Peter's in Worcester from 1969-1971, at Sacred Heart in Pittsfield from 1971-1979, and at St. Mary's in Westfield from 1979-1980. She held a B.A.from Our Lady of the College of the Elms, another relative holding a college degree unbeknownst to me as I was growing up.

his sister Margaret emigrated together on the SS Wyoming in 1881. Their journey started out pleasantly from Queenstown on Sunday morning the 17th of April, with sunshine above a calm sea and fair winds. Three days in, their fortune plummeted. The head winds set in, and the ship began to pitch and roll, nauseating many of the passengers. These conditions persisted from Wednesday until Saturday, when their luck changed again. The sea became calm, and smooth sailing followed until they reached the Castle Garden dock at 4 p.m. on April 26. Upon arriving in Holyoke, they took up residence in the same boarding house on Lyman street. Timothy secured a position at D. Mackintosh & Sons textile mill and Margaret at Winona Paper Co. where they worked until those railroad dreams seduced Timothy, and the pair moved on to Chicago. Elizabeth, the youngest child in the family, emigrated to Chicago after the Holyoke exodus. Daniel, still indisposed in Dublin, arrived last, joining the siblings in Chicago. The timing of Julia's arrival is uncertain but Census entries indicate a 1883 or 1885 arrival, and she married in Holyoke in 1891 and remained in Holyoke for the rest of her life.

My Daley line stems from Daniel Daly and Elizabeth "Bessie" or "Betty" Browne who married and settled in the civil parish of Molahiffe and the Roman Catholic parish Firies in Knockaderry, County Kerry in about 1852. Knockaderry, or Cnoc a'Doire in Irish, is a tiny townland .59 square miles in size, a wee bit north of the crossroads in Farranfore Village along the N22, a stone's throw from the

Kerry Airport.[81] The Firies parish records detail the baptisms of eight children born to Daniel and Elizabeth, starting with Jeremiah in 1853 and continuing through Elizabeth in 1868. No records of them baptizing a son named John Daly exist. An extensive records search as well as discussions with other descendents indicate there never was a John Daly in the generation that emigrated. Daniel and Elizabeth did, however, baptize children named Timothy, Patrick, and Jeremiah, whose existence seems to have either been forgotten or muddled in the American telling of the Daly story. Irish census documents reveal a ninth child, Norah, whose story likewise seems to have been omitted by the American Daleys.

Jeremiah and Norah are easy enough to explain as they stayed behind in Ireland. When the Daly migration started, the eldest Daly brother Jeremiah was already settled in Knockaderry with a wife and children. He was never part of the American story. Norah, too, chose to stay in Ireland. She stayed on the farm with her parents and was their caretaker in the years prior to their deaths in 1907. Daniel and Elizabeth died within a week of each other in March of that year, and not from a communicable disease. As Nanny would say, Elizabeth died of a broken heart after losing Daniel. As their death records do say, they both died of senile decay (a catchall term used to refer to death from unspecified causes associated with the declines of age), which they'd suffered

---

[81] Genealogy's propensity for tossing surprises at people surfaces once again with the exploration of records from this tiny townland. Home to 21 census tracts in 1901, Knockaderry was one-third populated by a combination of Dalys and my BC and genealogist friend Mary O'Keeffe's Sullivan forebears.

together for two years. Norah was beside each of them at their deaths. Elizabeth was 80 and Daniel 79 at their passing. They outlived their golden wedding anniversary by five years.

Tracing the Daly and Browne stories back prior to Daniel and Elizabeth has proved extraordinarily difficult due to the dearth of Irish records. With large families and every cousin among them naming kids after grandpas, dad, brothers, grandmas, mom, and sisters, finding the precise Whatever-his-name-is-Daly or What's-her-name-Browne and being sure it's the correct one is a colossal undertaking. What's worse, you can't even rely on the naming pattern due to superstition that forced deviations whenever using the prescribed name would result in "three in a yard" or three living generations of persons on the same farm with that name. If that were to happen, it was said, one of them would die, and so an alternate name was chosen.

Nanny was but two years old and living an ocean away when her maternal grandparents died, so she never had the opportunity to know Daniel and Elizabeth or to hear about their lives as they lived them. By this time, three of her own siblings were deceased and the remaining siblings were significantly older than baby Esther, ranging from the eldest Lizzie at 21, who would be married in a few months' time, to the closest in age to Nanny, Marty who was already 12. And just after Nanny turned 11 years old, her mother Mary Daley O'Brien died. With Mary gone and all but one of Mary's American immigrant siblings in Chicago, Nanny lost much of her connection to the ancestral Dalys. She may have heard stories from her siblings, earlier passed down by Mary, but they were likely infrequent and less detailed than the stories she heard about those still living or those who had been members of her immediate family. In any case, despite the regularity of Nanny's dinner and teatime stories, and the talk about Ireland itself, I don't remember hearing about the relatives back in Ireland other than her grandfather's name. My impression was that everyone who didn't emigrate had died beforehand, and maybe that's what she believed.

CHAPTER 30

WRONG, WRONG, AND WRONG AGAIN

Norah Daly was as carefree as Timothy and Patrick when it came to introductions. Until she slipped into a Census return, I was unaware she existed. But there she was on the 1901 Irish Census form at the home of Daniel and Elizabeth, listed as their daughter.

Like so many others in my family tree, Norah stashed secrets in the family vault. The first hint that all was not as it seemed with Norah was her absence from parish baptismal records. All of the Daly children were born in Knockaderry in Fries parish. Norah's presumed birthdate estimated from Irish Census records fell smack in the middle of the bunch. The children before her and those after were duly recorded in the parish records but Norah was AWOL. Norah's approximate birth year calculated from the Census records would place her birth in the same year as Daniel's, giving her the status of actual twin to Daniel, or, since he was born in

December, possibly an Irish twin born at the start of the year. It troubled me that there was no mention of her, and I searched for evidence of her baptism by my Daly great-grandparents in the entire range of Elizabeth's childbearing years and turned up nothing. In 1800s County Kerry, first-time mothers often returned to their childhood homes to give birth. If Norah were actually the oldest sibling, this might explain her absence from the Firies baptismal register. But I found no other church register in the area with an Elizabeth Browne and Daniel Daly christening a daughter who might be our Norah. I looked for potential cataclysms bedeviling western Ireland that might have kept her religious parents from the baptismal font. Nothing. So maybe she was inadvertently omitted from the record. As is typical for Roman Catholics of the era of her birth, Norah found no mention in civil birth records. This left me to wonder, who was Norah, really, and where did she come from?

I tried to put the Norah question aside, but it kept niggling at me. I consulted with other genealogy buffs. Was the problem simply that Norah's baptism wasn't recorded? Was the name Norah a pet name, standing for something other than the traditional Hanorah or Honor? But if it was, why didn't I find a record of a child with another name? Perhaps Norah was Daniel's illegitimate daughter, someone suggested, while another posited that she may have been household help mistaken for a daughter by the Census taker.

If Norah were a niece whose parents died, responsibility for raising her may have fallen to Daniel and Elizabeth. This explanation would be more likely if I could find a Norah born in the correct timeframe and location with either Daniel, Elizabeth, or both as godparents. I found such a Norah, born five years earlier than my Norah should have been based on the Census record. The five year age difference is inconsequential. In that era in Ireland, many neither knew nor cared about their actual age, and the ages given in Census records are often incorrect, sometimes wildly so. Daniel was this Norah's godfather.

I thought I was on to something. But this Norah's parents were very much alive when the 1901 Census came around. ...Very much alive and living right next door to Daniel and Elizabeth. Daniel's brother Timothy (another one!) and his wife Julia filed a 1901 Census return that included a married daughter and her large family. But their return did not include their unmarried daughter Norah, who typically would have lived with them in those times. So it appeared that Norah was Daniel and Elizabeth's niece. This conclusion tied the evidence together nicely. For a period of months, I believed I'd learned the truth about Norah. Except once again looks are deceiving. Timothy's daughter Norah, I would come to learn, was omitted from his Census form not because she was next door caring for relatives but because she died at the age of four. Who then was the Norah living with Daniel and Elizabeth?

While I never did find Norah's baptismal record, I found a better source, a Daly descendant familiar with Norah's story. She was Daniel and Elizabeth's daughter after all. Her absence from the parish birth record was apparently random error. Born in 1860, Norah grew up to become a nun. She did not live on the family farm with her parents during most of her adulthood but this devoted daughter did return home to care for them in their twilight years. Her presence at their deaths was recorded in official records without describing her relationship to them. Upon her death, Norah was buried alongside her parents in the old Molahiffe cemetery.

CHAPTER 31

BARGAIN WITH THE WEE FOLK

With the Timothy-Dan mix-up sorted, Norah's mysterious appearance resolved, and John moved down to the generation where he belongs in the family tree, there's still one member of the Daly family out in limbo. The elder Patrick Daly's a slippery character with seemingly little interest in his tree perch, but as Knockaderry came into reach, with my determination to find him in overdrive, I put together clues to nail him onto his branch. First, I spotted in the newspapers a Constable named Patrick Daley who became a Chicago police officer, distinct from the Patrick who became a detective and was murdered. With Patrick-the-Missing's brothers and nephew on the police force, it seemed reasonable these stories might be about the very Patrick I was seeking. As we can deduce from the excess number of Timothy Daleys on the Chicago Police force, though, the mere existence of a Patrick Daley in their midst is alone insufficient to prove a relationship. On close inspection, Patrick the Constable-turned-cop failed the test, having run for Constable when our Patrick would have been but 18 years old, more than a decade before any of our Daly clan was known to have emigrated to America.

While I long suspected Patrick might be walking in the mythical John's shoes or at least alongside Timothy who himself might have borrowed the generationally-confuddled John's footwear, I had no actual evidence Patrick was in Chicago, or even that he was alive when Timothy and Margaret moved from Holyoke to that city or when Elizabeth and Dan subsequently joined them. Like Timothy, he was omitted from the account of the Holyoke exodus, thus once I discovered his existence in Firies birth records, I had no idea on which side of the ocean I might find him.

The next clue made me laugh out loud. It happens that those mix-and-match Hussey boys, married to Daly sisters Maggie and Liz, had a sister of their own. Her name was Hannah Hussey and who do you suppose she married? It couldn't be a coincidence that her husband's name just happened to be Patrick Daley, now, could it? Well, yes, actually it could. And is. According to his obituary, that Patrick Daley had a brother Charles in Boston, something our Daly clan lacked, and no local sisters or brothers to mourn his death, something our Daly clan had aplenty.

Those "Hussey boys," it seems, were not brothers after all but likely cousins. The one whose name appears to have been recorded in his parish birth registry as

"Edmondum," ironically, was not the one mistakenly called Edmund on the transcription of his marriage record, Liz's husband, but the other one, Maggie's husband. From collateral evidence including the birth year and Margaret and Edward's two children having the same names as Edmund-factus-Edward's parents, it appears Edmund-from-Ireland transformed into Edward upon emigrating. Edwards, Edmunds, no matter, both men attracted disaster. Liz's Edward was a firefighter credited with saving lives but experiencing serious burns when he neglected to wear a coat under his rubber suit. Margaret's Edward, who died only seven years after emigrating and four years into their marriage at age 30, kept a saloon[82] of not entirely stellar reputation. An Alderman was murdered there, and Ed himself was shot by a cop there, both shootings the product of inebriation. News reports described both men's faces in the latter shooting as "frightfully battered up."[83] Regardless of whatever relationship these "Hussey boys" may have had, what an unfortunate coincidence for the genealogist that sisters from a family already flush with duplicate names would marry men with the same name and one of their sisters would marry a man with a name identical to that of her brother's brother-in-law.

---

[82] Saloons played an important role in the social life of Chicagoans as did the saloonkeepers. As described in *The Saloon in Chicago,* "The saloonkeeper, usually a man their [the customers'] superior in intelligence, often directs their thought. He has in his possession the latest political and sporting news. Here in argument each has fair play. He who can win and tell the best story is, not by election, but by virtue of fitness, the leader. The saloon is, in short, the clearing-house for the common intelligence—the social and intellectual center of the neighborhood."

[83] Source 362.

Back to the starting line, I wasn't letting Patrick get away that easily. My next insight sprang from the discovery of the theretofore unknown brother, Jeremiah. Two years Patrick's elder, and a master of disguise, Jeremiah never left much of a trail for those intent on posthumous classification from afar. On rooting him out, I remembered one of my potential Chicago Patricks having a daughter whose name was recorded "Iermie," an obvious mistake. What if Iermie were Jeremie, the female companion name to Jeremiah? The Dalys did have a fancy for repeating names from generation to generation. On review and comparison to later documents, Iermie turned out to be mistranscribed as I suspected, but the correct name was Jennie. And thorough investigation of Jennie and her parents left me no closer to trapping Patrick. He's a wily one. Patrick's wiliness, however, is no match for my determination.

The Daly death records for those who remained in Ireland were easy to trace as they clustered in the Knockaderry area. If Patrick stayed true to this pattern, he did not die in Ireland unless he died before age nine, when the civil registration system was expanded to include deaths and births, including those of Catholics. Nor could I find any record of a marriage in Ireland.

American obituaries provided another pattern of interest. Julia Daley Fitzpatrick's mid-1933 obituary, which I obtained late in my research, mentions one surviving brother in Chicago (Dan) and one in Ireland (Jeremiah), indicating Patrick's death likely preceded hers. When Chicago Dalys

died, their obituaries mentioned the other local siblings as
mourning their loss and sometimes their Massachusetts
relatives but not the relatives left behind in Ireland. None of
their obituaries mentioned Patrick. He could have been the
first to die in America, or maybe he was never here. Not here,
of course, would mean a whole world to search to find him. I
had the daunting task of proving which one it was. I still had
one prime suspect in Chicago when a search entry stopped
me cold: a Patrick J. Daley born in our Patrick's birth year
(1855) in Knockadarough, County Kerry, and residing in
Washington, D.C. There is no Knockadarough in County
Kerry. Was it Knockaderry?

Patrick setting up house in the nation's capital, far
from any American siblings, seemed doubtful, except for one
fact, the ready availability of secure government jobs. So, the
Patrick married to Julia Long in Washington, D.C. became a
top contender for my family tree. I hoped this would not turn
out to be our Patrick. The poor couple had two sons named
after their father who died in infancy before a third survived,
and their daughter Mary Patricia died in young adulthood. A
very sad Patrick, this one. It took awhile to trace him, but
once again I'd stumbled upon a red herring.

Although I never knew him, I was ready at this point
to bet anything that our Patrick Daly had been one annoying
man, in life as in death! Having ruled out most of the Patrick
Dalys in the target territories of Ireland, western
Massachusetts, and Chicago, and lacking source material to
fully evaluate the stragglers, I was losing confidence in my
ability to turn up the evidence that would identify his proper

place. But despite the challenges, I've finally come to understand the truth about Pat. Had I bet Patrick was one annoying *man*, I'd have lost my bet. The reason I've been unable to pin down our Pat? That scoundrel schemed with the Wee Folk to transform him into a racehorse. At nearly the same time Timothy and Margaret were boarding the train to Chicago to start their new lives, the equine Pat Daly showed up in the paddock at Chicago's Washington Park Race Track. Happenstance? He attracted as steady a following in the newspapers as he did on the track where he performed admirably, winning races and being given low odds on account of his capable gallops. Steady, competent, hardworking, all Daly qualities. If you need further proof, just ask yourself, when was the last time you heard of a racehorse with a first and a last name?

So we finally have the story down. Jeremiah remained in Knockaderry, farming like his father. Norah likewise stayed close to home, joining a convent, then returning to care for her aged parents. Their siblings emigrated. Mary and Julia built lives in Holyoke. Timothy left Holyoke for Chicago with locomotive whistles awakening him from his dreams each night. Margaret tagged along, and Elizabeth soon joined them in Chicago where both Elizabeth and Margaret opened their hearts to men named Ed Hussey who came from townlands in Ireland nearby their own. Dan— well, our little troublemaker Dan has one more wrench to toss into our story. His success at remaining invisible for so much of my search stems from that surfeit of Daniels in our family, which led to his being called by his middle name "David" to avoid confusion. "David" joined the Chicago crowd later, upon his release from Mountjoy, identifying himself as Daniel D. and David in different situations just to confuse us. Patrick mysteriously appeared in Washington Park one day, and no one but the Wee Folk can say how it happened.

CHAPTER 32

THEY CAME FROM COUNTY KERRY

Secrets were among my worst enemies and Shame's best friends. Secrets sprouted everywhere, too close to avoid, yet skittering out of my grasp. They were bosom companions of not only Shame but the men looking in the windows and all of the outsiders who would do us harm.

The Secrets did not start with Mom. They traveled from Ireland to America in the steerage compartment of the SS City of Richmond in 1880, sticking as close to Mary Daley as if she'd packed them in her trunk. I suspect their tenure in County Kerry had been a long one, for back then it was essential to thwart anyone who might be listening for survival's sake. The best way to keep "them," whoever they might be, from hearing was to avoid speaking of sensitive subjects outside of the four walls of the home. What happened in the family stayed in the family. While such caution apparently met knowing acceptance among my ancestors in Knockaderry, who'd been marked for extinction for two centuries by the time Mary Daley was born in the mid-1800s, the Secrets found themselves in a less hospitable environment in 1960s America. It didn't stop them from wreaking havoc.

Henry Lessard was one casualty of the Secrets. Henry was a welder, acclaimed for his extraordinary expertise. He was also a devoted family man. But neither occupational excellence nor familial steadfastness brought him within the Secrets' embrace. He would sit in his car in our driveway for hours on end. If it happened once, it'd be an anomaly. But poor Henry did not sit in the car in our drive, from well before twilight past the time the evening sky darkened and stars appeared, one time only. It was his estate, and Henry made the best of it, rolling down the windows and listening to ball games on the radio. He'd been married to his wife Avis, Nanny's niece, for some thirty years by this time. Yet when Avis had "family business" to discuss with my mother and Nanny, Henry would dutifully drive her to our house and remain in the car for the duration, as instructed. He was not among the few souls permitted to be in the know.

Henry was in good company, though he may not have been aware of it at the time. Children of both families, my sister Jan and me, and our cousin Mary,[84] were likewise shooed away when the Secrets were on display. We might catch a word or two, if we were quiet enough on the stairs, but our stealth was never sufficient to outwit the Secrets, and

---

[84] Mary had three siblings but they were older and not around at this time.

our presence was inevitably detected too soon for any real understanding to develop. The Secrets had over three hundred years' experience in deflecting outsiders, after all. And outsiders we were, even as we were indoctrinated into the family responsibility of protecting those Secrets at all peril. Dad might quit a job precipitously leaving us no assurance we'd have groceries at week's end, but that was no one else's business now, was it? We might see Uncle Bobby stumble up the front walk but sure he wasn't there if a neighbor were to mention it. If it happened in the house, it stayed in the house. If the outside world saw, why then it never happened at all and how dare anyone say otherwise!

When it came to extended family or ancestors, there were none but saints among them. If oddly unsaintlike behavior came to light, or if overzealous prodding threatened to expose one of the Secrets associated with our saints, a vigilant Daly descendant summoned others in the know and together they constructed a wall so hastily, there wasn't time to watch it going up. Their expertise at wall-building ensured no one would trespass, try as they might. I was born in 1957, one of the youngest members of the extended family in my generation. By the time I was old enough to ask questions, there were so many walls, most of my clan was out of sight and out of reach. I learned innocuous details about them through Nanny's stories. Most of the rest of my impressions were formed from a jumbled clutter of whispers patched with assumptions borne of Suspicion.

The Secrets fed on lies. Not the kind of lies you might expect. Not "I wasn't there; I didn't do it." No, these lies were of a different nature. These lies altered the core of our existence, distorted our understanding of our place in the universe. If you will trust official birth records, then there's no disputing that Avis was born to Lulu and her first husband Ralph Damon in 1921. My mother came along in 1928, joining the shared household established by Nanny and Lulu and their husbands after a brief time in Lizzie's house (Ralph had died and Lulu was remarried to Fred Schmidt by this time). With minimal competency in mathematics, you can compute their age difference, seven years. Once the Secrets went to work, that age difference became 12 years. The Secrets ensured the 12-year span was hammered into our memories with regular mentions. Why, we will never know, but it was Gospel throughout the extended family that Avis was 12 years older than Marie, and nobody broke ranks to say otherwise, even those who'd witnessed their growth firsthand. The Secrets added two years to the age difference between my mother and her older sister Vivien, while removing two years from the four-year gap between Mom and her younger brother Bobby. And that's how the Secrets made reality sway so that neither we nor anyone else would ever pin down the pivotal facts defining our family.

My father came from a boisterous family, each sibling more opinionated than the last. They talked over one another, eager to claim the spotlight and profess their know-how. They corrected each other's assertions without hesitation, never mind whether any correction was warranted. Not so with my mother's family. The Secrets demanded adherence to a loyalty code barring authenticity testing. The truth could dance on the table in front of them and they'd deny it to support one of their own. You could consider this evasion a self-delusion to avoid discomfort, but that wouldn't fully capture its essence. Everyone sticking together and taking each other at their word served a more salient purpose: warding off any fuss that might inadvertently expose the Secrets. The results could be preposterous, as you will witness for yourself in the upcoming chapter when Nanny thumbs her nose at the same Catholic Church she'd venerated her entire life.

There came a time in my young adulthood when I had occasion to talk with my mother about the unfortunate "fact" of her birth occurring in the weeks after Black Tuesday, the Stock Market crash of 1929 that spiraled into the Great Depression. I imagined her coming into the world at that time made her family's circumstances challenging and said so. Nanny and Mamie had been dead for more than a decade by the time of this conversation, Lulu even longer and Lizzie the longest of all, so perhaps Mom felt unconstrained enough to expose one mouthful of Secret fodder to me.

"I was born in 1928," she said.

"You always told us you were born in 1929!" I protested.

"I was born in 1928."

And that was that. There was no denial or admission of the longstanding lie and no explanation. Reality changed, and a lifetime of understanding was shuffled off to the shredder.

If you're an astute reader, you might have picked up my hesitation some chapters back to accept my mother's word that she never knew her paternal grandfather. I tried to pin her down on that before she died. I had given birth to the first of my children, and I told her I wanted information about our family for him, so he'd know his roots. I asked who Charlie's parents were and where they had lived. Sadly, her loyalty to the Secrets outweighed any obligation she might have felt to share the family history for the benefit of future generations. She admitted the safe truth that Charlie's mother had died before she was born. From there, she adapted the background of her mother-in-law Elsie, a woman she admired, and presented it as her own, falsely telling me that her father's family, like Elsie's parents, had lived far away in Michigan. Nanny's family? She barely knew any of them. Well, except Lulu, she acknowledged when I pointed out the obvious, and maybe Mamie, but she swore she never heard a thing about the relatives in Mary Daley's generation or life back in Ireland. Did I know she was lying? Yes, instinctively I detected more of her lies than I believed. But there was nothing to be done about it I knew from a lifetime of running head on into Secrets and limping away bruised.

As my work on this book was coming to a close, I began hearing eerily similar stories from across the world of Secrets shutting out post-immigration generations of Daly descendants, skewing their perceptions, obscuring their heritage, and isolating them from their kin. It seems the Secrets were sufficient in force that they were able to maintain a second-line presence in Chicago with Timothy, Margaret,

Elizabeth and Daniel David, and even with a branch of the family that emigrated to New Zealand. But, generations removed and long distances strayed from their origins, the Secrets had become rancid.

CHAPTER 23

NANNY HOLDS THE KEY

My genealogical journey began with Nanny, so I should have anticipated the inevitability of it leading back to Nanny in the end. The Nanny I knew was not the Nanny my mother knew, her siblings and parents knew, Charlie knew, or even my own sister knew. My Nanny used an old fashioned curling rod with turquoise wood handles, heated on the stove, to curl her gray hair upon awakening in the morning. She liked to remind me, or maybe it was herself she was reminding, that in her younger years her hair had been auburn red. Nanny didn't mind too much her hair turning gray with age, but she hoped it would never turn white like her sisters' had as, to her, that represented everything fearsome about growing old. Nanny sang. *Mocking Bird Hill, When I Was a Chicken, Too Ra Loo Ra Loo Ra, How Much Is That Doggy in the Window?* and *Easter Parade* were among her favorites. But *Carolina Moon, Deep in the Heart of Texas, Oh Dear, What Can the Matter Be?* (the *Seven Old Ladies Got Stuck in a Lavatory* version), *Who Threw the Overalls in*

Mrs. Murphy's Chowder?, *McNamara's Band*, *76 Trombones*, and *Playmate* were also heard often on Agnes Street.

Nanny was a chain smoker, a late sleeper, and a worrier. "Oh dear!" was a frequent utterance. No one exited the house without her warning, "Look out for traffic!" So ingrained was this caution, she once directed it at my sister as she was leaving the living room in her pajamas to head upstairs to bed. As much as Nanny worried, she never blamed. If a reckless driver zipped by at breakneck speed, she'd exclaim, "Oh, dear, he better slow down or he's going to get hurt," with no assumptions, no judgments. Nanny never extended a compliment without tacking on a blessing for her Irish mother had instilled in her that to do so would be to endanger the person she meant to admire.

Nanny was the clock that kept the household running. She got up each day as the sun crept close to the meridian and went to bed after the 11 o'clock news. It was she who invariably said it's time to put the kettle on for tea or to start the potatoes for supper. Dad found it grating that Nanny always insisted on being last to bed. She would go downstairs and run the water in the kitchen sink, seemingly forever, to get a cold glass before going to sleep. Checking that the stove burners and the lights were turned off completed the routine. The repetitiveness, the inflexibility, the insistence that she be the one to perform these tasks, it drove my father crazy. While that's relatable, Nanny's clockwork repertoire lent the household a rhythm that rescued it from chaos.

In the same way Nanny marked out our daily rhythm, she kept us abreast of the changing seasons. We got spring coats and straw hats for Easter each year, and winter coats and boots when the leaves began to turn. Nanny brought home festive pins for our lapels from the Five and Dime, marking the passage of Halloween, Thanksgiving, Christmas, St. Valentine's Day, St. Patrick's Day, and Easter.

I was a little jealous of Jan for her time with Nanny in her youngest grandmothering years. Jan got to ride the bus downtown with Nanny to the shops or the movies. Jan and Nanny shared a common interest in movie magazines, and they both knew all the latest gossip about this movie star and that. When it came to celebrities, I was more like my mother, suspicious and even a bit disdainful of the activities of those who displayed their business on marquees for all to notice. While Nanny never took me downtown or to the movies and I barely listened to chatter about the latest scandal emanating from Hollywood, Nanny would sometimes play with me when I was lonely. We played pick up sticks or jacks, games she'd played in her youth. She gave me a dime for candy almost every day after school, or a nickel if it was nearing month's end. Nanny no doubt sparked my love of Broadway musicals, chirping out their lyrics and those of moving picture show tunes and pop tunes from the radio, morning, noon, and night.

In her later years, Nanny always asked me to read her the banner headline when the evening news was delivered. When she had to read something, she'd supplement her eyeglasses with her Kresge's magnifying glass. During the years Bobby was in Vietnam, before she needed that magnifying glass, Nanny scowered the news pages herself for any hint of trouble from wherever he'd reported his unit was stationed in his most recent letter. When the World Trade Center construction began, she followed the reports with awe, comparing the immediate mirabilia to her wonder at the erection of the Empire State building back when she was young. The Troubles plagued Ireland during my growing up years, and Nanny kept up with the tit-for-tat, the car bombings, no-gos, peace walls, prisoners, and protests. She knew the who's who and the what's what because this news was about Ireland, after all.

Nanny's favorite news day was Wednesday. That's when Forbes & Wallace and Steiger's, our local department stores, published their weekly sales ads in time for "shopping day," otherwise known as Thursday. Nanny would examine those ads with a critical eye, expressing delight or amazement at the stylish outfits, though her shopping days were mostly past. When the spring fashion pages came, Nanny would marvel at the latest designs from Paris or sometimes shake her head in consternation, wondering aloud who would wear such a get-up.

When Mamie appeared on our doorstep, suitcase in hand, that summer day long ago, Nanny implored my mother to let her move into Nanny's bedroom. Taking care of one old lady was enough, my mother screamed, and she wasn't taking in another. I cringed in the middle of them, torn between my loyalty to Nanny and my lack of enthusiasm for this prospective new housemate. It made me angry to hear my mother attack Nanny like that. Nanny was our family. She loved us, and we loved her. Besides, she wasn't some beggar we took in; she contributed to household expenses from her Social Security check every month[85] and she cooked and cleaned, and took care of us kids, too. I appreciated Nanny's devotion to her sister and her desire to do the right thing. Yet the thought of living with Mamie, who stood before us with white mane wild and uncombed, her cotton dress wet from incontinence, mumbling words I couldn't quite follow, intimidated me, and though I was ashamed of my feelings, I selfishly hoped Mom held her ground. Amidst the fury flung at Nanny by Mom and the desperate pleas Nanny pitched back, no one paid me any notice, and my concerns went unspoken.

There were ways in which my mother was the adult taking care of Nanny, most notably the time when Nanny started bleeding and chose to ignore it rather than face what it might mean, but in a day-to-day sense, it was Nanny who assumed Mom's responsibilities, filled in when Mom sat vacant and stiff atop her bedding in her darkened room while the sun moved lower in the sky and the kids clamored for attention or sustenance.

"Bob'll be home in a half hour, shall I put the spuds on?" Nanny would call upstairs.

---

[85] Before she started receiving Social Security, back in Feeding Hills, Nanny had hustled over to Dairy Barn and gotten herself a job when Mom and Dad explained the necessity of her earning her own spending money. She also babysat for the children of my eldest cousin on my father's side of the family.

Sometimes my mother would stir, but most often Nanny would get the nod to peel the potatoes and set them on the stove to boil.

Going to Church on Sunday didn't fulfill Nanny's prayer quota, so she prayed at home, too, often in front of Mary Holding the Sacred Heart of Jesus on the Half-Shell atop her dresser. Nanny prayed so often and so fervently, I lost track of most of the things she prayed about. Her prayer requests could be weighty, like when she begged Jesus to spare her son Bobby's life as he lay hospitalized with pneumonia, or frivolous like her frequent pleas to St. Anthony for intercession to help her find her watch or her glasses when she misplaced them after taking them off to wash the dishes or rest her eyes. When Nanny and Jesus or Nanny and her Saints got to bargaining, Nanny was sure to keep up her end. She suffered terrible indigestion. Once when it kept her awake in agony, as the hours ticked by, she promised St. Jude she'd never again eat her favorite strawberry preserves that she blamed for that bout of indigestion if he'd intercede with God to make the pain go away. From the following day forward, due to some hours of untortured sleep, Nanny buttered her toast. I slept through that bargaining session, but Nanny made sure I knew St. Jude had come through for her and she owed him.

As important as Church was to Nanny, her loyalty to family and steadfast unwillingness to challenge the word of relatives trumped it. When for no discernible reason Mom came to believe she'd been excommunicated from the

Catholic Church (she wasn't), Nanny didn't question the absurd claim. Instead, Nanny took Mom's side in the fictional battle and declared if the Church wouldn't let Mom in the door, they wouldn't see her gracing their pews either. And that was that for going to Church.

When I was 20-something, I was visiting my Auntie Marie, my father's sister whom you would have been well-advised to avoid when she had an iron in hand. She mentioned how shy my grandmother had been. Nanny, shy? She greeted strangers in the street, she sang in public, she let her opinions be known and didn't much care if her audience agreed with her. But then Auntie Marie showed me an old photo of her dating to my parents' marriage, standing next to other relatives, with her posture slightly hunched and her head down. I had to admit she looked less social than the Nanny I remembered, so maybe my Nanny wasn't the same Nanny the world saw.

So it was with Nanny's temper. Her fiery temper came with the red hair, she told us. She'd suddenly get "madder than a wet hen" over some trivial frustration and just as quickly get over it. Once when tween Jan mocked something she said, she threw the pot of hot soup she'd made us for lunch at the kitchen wall. Vegetable beef, if that sort of detail interests you. With the soup dripping down the wall, she wailed, "Now, look what you made me do," as she reached for a dish towel to clean up the mess. Nanny's eruptions didn't scare me like my mother's anger did. When Nanny's temper boiled over, it was never personal. Nanny just got flustered and overwhelmed, and I knew no matter how agitated she got, she wouldn't harm a fly.

That was *my* Nanny. The O'Brien family's Nanny was a welcome and probable surprise baby born when her mother Mary was 47, not long after the deaths of two siblings immediately before her in the birth order. She was protected and cared for by her much older siblings as well as her parents. Their Nanny had grown from a coddled infant everyone doted on to a wild and wilful pre-teen whose activities bore a hint of peril by the time of her twelfth year, when Mary Daley O'Brien's heart gave out. Nanny was so headstrong and hard to handle at age eleven— she described herself as having been somewhat of a hellion, bent on doing things her way and unwilling to yield to anyone else's— that an entire household of adults had difficulty containing her. I don't know the details, but her 21-year-old brother Marty, the next youngest in age to her, became her legal guardian even though her father and two much older sisters still lived at home. Something must have prompted this guardianship, but it's a secret still stuck in the bottom of the vault, the vault for which no living person holds a key. It wasn't Nanny who told me that Marty was her guardian but my cousin[86] Mary. I found verification in Marty's World War I draft registration where he is listed as guardian and sole support for his by then twelve-year-old sister.[87]

---

[86] She's technically my second cousin, as our lines meet at great-grandparent.

[87] Although Nanny was Marty's ward, they apparently lived together with the rest of the family. His draft registration dated June 1917 gives his address as 98 Sargeant St. and that is the same address the family lived at during the 1920 Census.

Charlie's wife was another Nanny I don't recognize. That reverently Catholic and devoutly Irish Nanny would marry a Protestant, and a Brit, no less, is fathomable mainly by considering her facility in rebranding him a full-blooded Irishman and not looking back.[88] He didn't become a Catholic of his own accord, or even in her imagination, but he agreed to her raising their kids in her religion, so good enough. Since the priest wouldn't marry them, they headed over to Springfield City Hall and were pronounced husband and wife by Wayland V. James, Justice of the Peace, in August 1924. They'd filed their notice of intention just four days earlier, with Nanny skimming two years off her two decades in the official records. They registered using the same Liberty Street address in Springfield's Hungry Hill neighborhood for both, an address blocks up from her sister Lizzie. Ironically, the marriage that began in Hungry Hill moved through a variety of intermediary locations to reach its functional end in Feeding Hills in nearby Agawam. What a metaphor!

More than a decade after Nanny and Charlie separated, when I was a baby and before my mother's permanent estrangement from Vivien, and her subsequent estrangement from Charlie, my mother and father paid a visit to Charlie and Vivien in upstate New York. While they were there, they encouraged Charlie to come spend some time with them and Nanny. They persuaded him Nanny had changed, and there might be a reconciliation. As the day of Charlie's arrival approached, they coached Nanny. Let

---

[88] Charlie's ancestry is substantially British, with some Irish, German, and Abenaki.

bygones be bygones, they told her. Go easy. But Nanny's anxiety— she did want to reconcile— must have gotten the best of her. Charlie had nerves of his own to contend with and took a single drink to calm them. As my Dad told the story, Charlie arrived and immediately upon his entering the apartment, Nanny barked at him, "Have you been drinking again?" and he turned and walked back out the door.

Nanny's much older sisters— Lulu, the closest in age, was eleven years older than Nanny— held the sway of high priests. While unfalteringly warm and loving toward most family, they eventually found their goodwill dwindling when it came to Brucie, as they called Charlie. During the later years Nanny and Charlie were together, their suspicions about him, communicated during tête-à-têtes over tea and sweets in Lulu's or Lizzie's kitchens[89] became facts before Nanny made it home. Charlie was scorned for his drinking, which though heavy in those years didn't cause him to miss work, and especially for his contribution to Vivien's predicament. The bad guy motif that disrupted Nanny's marriage started up again some time after Nanny moved in with us, this time culminating in Nanny accusing my father of cheating on my mother. He blew his top that evening, ordering her to leave the house. Nanny sobbed all the way to the rectory where she told the priest her sorry tale.

"What am I going to do?" she no doubt asked him, because Nanny was not a problem solver. She placed her troubles in others' inboxes and awaited their resolutions.

---

[89] Mamie lived with Lizzie back then.

On this night, the priest accompanied her back home, intent on negotiating a truce. The priest proposed that Bob accept that his home was also Esther's home and not throw her out again if Esther would respect the privacy of Bob and Marie's marriage and not interject herself into their business. A deal brokered by a priest was as hallowed as a bargain with the Heavenly Father in all his glory with all of the angels about him, so when a by-then-cooled-down Bob assented and Nanny gave her word, the issue was settled in perpetuity.

For most of my first seventeen years of life, Nanny and I shared a household. We saw each other every day. Yet I never got to experience the Nanny who cheered on the suffragettes, the Nanny who thrilled to the introduction of "talkies," who enjoyed listening to the War of the Worlds broadcast with her children on the radio back in October '38 (and who despite her belief in Leprechauns and the Banshees did not succumb to the fear of Martians invading the Earth). Nor did I get to spend time with the Nanny who primped before the mirror and pranced outside in the bargain variety of the latest styles, living in New York City and following the happenings on Broadway as closely as she followed the tidbits in her church bulletins. Even the Nanny who was mother to Mom and Bobby and strove to ensure they stayed heads above the riff-raff around them was a mystery to me. The Nanny who cast aside Vivien, leaving her to live with strangers in the country, is a Nanny alien to me in every way. I heard stories about Nanny marveling at the sights of Chicago when she went there with her brother Marty in 1920 and managing her ration coupons during World War II. But by the time I knew her, the Nanny who did all those things had become a Nanny who took the bus downtown once a week to visit her older sister Mamie and who often sat in the chair in her room rocking when she wasn't cleaning house or watching evening television.

If the Nanny I knew so well had lives I knew so little about, how could I take direction from a flighty bunch of ancestors who'd not once crossed my doorstep? Did I want Richard Waterman sticking a poker in my ribs, prodding me to speak up and defend the downtrodden? Or Old Benny taking offense at some random imposition and tossing my tea packets out on the lawn? I might enjoy a chat with the Monats, but if they got me banished to Detroit or kicked out of the country altogether, they might feel a chill in no way related to the polar vortex. And while Ira might whisper some quiet words of encouragement, what if it turned out like the time Jan promised to tell me a secret only to let her get close enough to spit right inside my ear? I won't tell you how old she was so you can keep imagining her seventy-year-old self sneaking up on people this way.

Here I was, in the midst of all these newfound ancestors whom I'd hoped would boost my stature, only to find that their achievements came hand in hand with their miscues, their genius with their nescience, their integrity with their shortcomings, their idiosyncrasies overrunning their conventions. They were neither better nor worse than me, even as they were both better and worse than me. I was no different with them than I'd been without them for they'd inconspicuously slipped their best and their worst into the metaphysical pool from which I would be created long before I had any say in the matter.

Here I was, in the midst of all these newfound ancestors whom I'd hoped would boost my stature, only to find that they needed me more than I needed them. Whatever scraps of their lives could be recaptured so long after their time on Earth, no one would ever see unless I pitched in and wrote their stories. Our stories, for their incremental experiences in moving the generations forward, contributed to my becoming who I am as surely as if those ancestors were sitting at that kitchen table with Nanny and me so many years ago.

* * *

There are people in this world who pass on the Epilogue after devouring a book such as this one. Such folks are destined to forever yearn for the richness of a complete story.

EPILOGUE

On an October day yet undecided on the question "Sunshine or rain?" the GPS instructed us to turn up what appeared to be a dirt and gravel road, passing between tall hedges. Soon after we obeyed, that same GPS announced we'd reached our destination. Knockaderry. In front of the car stood a livestock gate, and we realized we'd driven up a private driveway. So where was Knockaderry? There were no other roads save the main road in sight. No welcome sign. The distance from the crossroads suggested we should be in our ancestral townland. I looked left in hopes of spotting a dwelling old enough to have once housed my great-grandmother. That's where I thought it ought to be (if it still existed) based on my interpretation of the 1852 Griffith's Valuation, a property compilation designed to determine who was liable to pay the poor rate. (If you've never tried to decipher it, consider yourself lucky.) There, where I turned my gaze, and all around us, I saw only rolling farmland and a couple of modern houses. Determined to explore, I set in motion the first of two serendipitous events that changed the course of our visit. I stepped out of the car and headed down the drive, peering between the hedges as I meandered from side to side, looking for something I couldn't quite identify. Something that would tell me this was home.

A vehicle approached the gate from the other side, and I saw a man get out and open it and speak briefly with my son Andy, then return to the driver's seat. That man was influenced by the other serendipitous force guiding our destiny that afternoon. He approached me with his window open, and asked what I was looking for.

"Knockaderry," I told him.

"This is Knockaderry," he replied.

Out of my mouth tumbled a garbled narrative of great-great-grandparents living in Knockaderry more than a century ago, of my great-grandmother emigrating, of trying to find where they'd lived, or something about them, anything.

"Their name?" he asked, seemingly unperturbed by my disjointed presentation.

"Daly."

"I'm Daly," he said. After a moment, he added, "Batt Daly."

Batt Daly's presence in the same place as I found myself resulted from the second bovine-inspired watershed in my family history. You'll recall the first involved a wandering cow, an angry colonist, and a slap. That slap sent Samuel Gorton first to court and then to Warwick where his ideas so intrigued my ancestor Richard Waterman that they both got dragged to jail in Massachusetts, forced to defend their beliefs, and ultimately re-banned from the colony on pain of death. The current bovine influence is a bit less dramatic though arguably more important. Batt happens to be a cattle farmer, as were my Daly ancestors and virtually everyone else living in Knockaderry. Had his cattle not been stomping around demanding his attention at the very moment we parked in that neighboring drive, he wouldn't have been out tending to them over that hill, as he had other plans, and would not have spotted our rental car stopped at the gate. And what follows wouldn't have followed, and our story would be forever incomplete.

I told Batt my great-great-grandparents were Daniel Daly and Elizabeth Browne. He recognized those names. The same Daniel and Elizabeth were his great-grandparents. He recited tidbit upon tidbit that floored me once and again, starting with us sharing some relative named Timothy O'Sullivan who had lived within the range of an imprecise gesture. Timothy O'Sullivan's name indicated he was a son of Sullivan. All I knew about Timothy Sullivan with no "O" was that he had lived in Knockaderry a hundred-plus years ago and was second great-grandfather to my friend Mary O'Keeffe. I'd promised to keep an eye out for any word of his doings during my travels. As Batt's information spilled out, this unbidden and surprising O'Sullivan connection with my college friend Mary got left behind, our exact relationship yet undiscovered.

I identified my great-grandmother as Daniel and Elizabeth's daughter Mary.

"Mary..." He pondered a moment. "She married an O'Brien."

She did! He knew of her eldest daughter, Lizzie, but not the eight children who came after, including Nanny whom you will remember arrived at the tail end of near-twenty years of childbearing. He'd been to Chicago. American Daly descendants had visited Knockaderry. He knew two of Mary's brothers became cops, that a cop relative had been killed in the line of duty, and that two of Mary's sister Elizabeth's grandchildren with the surname Grace were priests. These two priests, long ago mentioned to me by Sr. Julia Frances, are still alive, Batt told me. Some of his grandfather Jeremiah's children created a second wave of Daly immigration to Holyoke, one of whom, Julia Daly, married Martin Dunn of Galway and was grandmother to former Holyoke mayor and one-term state senator Marty Dunn. It saddened me to learn that of all of Daniel and Elizabeth's children who emigrated, only the youngest, Elizabeth, once made it home for a visit. The others revered their parents and their homeland but were left with only fond stories of childhood to carry with them once they left Ireland.

When Mary Daley was growing up in Knockaderry, newness abounded. The Farranfore train station was but a few years old. The Church of St. Gertrude was erected with funding contributed by local families during Mary's childhood. Built to last hundreds of years, these structures stand today looking much like they did when she padded through Knockaderry fields and trod the horse-path roads. The church pews, unanchored now as they were then— you'd think three pew attacks in quick succession might have caused the parish to rethink that leniency— have no names inscribed on them; yet it's easy to imagine the fashionable Curtin family striding purposefully up the aisle to the front row, the teens perhaps glancing side-to-side, noting which members of the opposite sex turned eyes their way. The gray and white marble baptismal font with a polished wood cover is almost certainly the same one to which many of my Daly forebears gingerly stepped up, white-gowned newborn in hand, for the ritual of baptism which would not only welcome their latest family member into the communion of the church but also spare the baby's soul an eternity in Purgatory were the Grim Reaper to visit in the night.

At our second get-together with Batt, we were joined by his wife Nellie who prepared a delicious spread of tea and scones and who is finally getting an introduction. We exchanged stories of ancestors we each knew about, and they shared the few existing photos they had of the members of prior generations of our family. Batt took us down the road and up a drive to the house hidden among the hills where our ancestors Daniel Daly and Elizabeth Browne set up housekeeping upon their marriage in 1852, the home where my great-grandmother Mary and her brother Jeremiah, Batt's grandfather, were born and raised, along with their seven siblings. And where Batt himself grew up. The thatch roof was replaced with tin back in the 30's, and the current landowner has allowed the house to begin to fall to ruin. Yet many things remain unchanged from the days of Mary and Jeremiah's childhood, including the furniture and the wall decor which includes religious pictures and a Sacred Heart lamp. Even the old chamber pots and ice boxes remain.

Our next stop was the Molahiffe Cemetery where we visited the graves of our Daly and Browne ancestors. There was a surplusage of Dalys buried in that cemetery and without Batt's guidance I'd have been hard pressed to figure which were my forebears and would have erred in laying claim to all of them. But Batt, a Daly on both maternal and paternal sides, knows his Dalys and readily distinguished those in my line from those unrelated.

I am sorry to be the one to inform you of something you are destined to experience as a great tragedy. Patrick Daly's bargain with the Wee Folk was badly misinterpreted by me in that he never asked to be transformed into a racehorse at all. Alas, we are down one racehorse in the Daly family, which was our only racehorse it seems, so the position is open should you know of a suitable applicant with the particular connections required to make it happen! Although my interpretation of events seemed reasonable enough at the time, Batt has provided irrefutable proof that Patrick did not run the track at Washington Park and indeed never stepped foot in Chicago in his lifetime. Whatever the constituents of

Patrick's secret transaction with the Wee Folk, it resulted in Daniel and Elizabeth's second son popping up not in Washington Park but in Wellington, New Zealand. Research subsequent to the trip established that he went into business as a carter, married Margaret Green, and with her had three children.[90] He secured municipal contracts, including at least one for the not-so-glamorous work of carting away "night soil," a euphemism for human waste, discreetly removed in the dark so as not to offend anyone's sensibilities. Patrick's earnings enabled him to secure his place among the half of the Wellington men able to buy their families a modest house, but that house was situated in a most unenviable location, alongside a massive manure dump.

Although Patrick achieved some success in his work, he unfortunately developed a fondness for whisky. In this, he shared common ground with many of the flock of immigrants struggling to survive the long depression that gripped the capital city from the late 1870's until well into the 1890s. The scarce jobs to be found typically required grueling physical labor. There was no public poor relief for those who couldn't make the cut. With men turning to alcohol in alarming numbers, a temperance movement sprung up, though it never gained sufficient support to shutter the pubs. Patrick's affinity for the spiritus frumenti earned him more than 99 convictions and occasional sojourns in the clink. In the courtroom, his lawyer disputed that his

---

[90] He did not emigrate alone. He traveled with a member of the extended Daly family named Eneas Daly who went into business with him. Another relative, John Daly, was already in New Zealand; he would later stand up for Patrick at his wedding.

language during drunken dust-ups was obscene, insisting it was merely indecent. Patrick seemed especially smitten with prefixing objectionable adjectives to the epithet "scab." But he must have been gifted with an outsize portion of Irish charm, for hoteliers in whose establishments he over-imbibed and even his brawl victims came to his defense when the law came after him. It was a few words resulting in a "little rough and tumble,"[91] one old man testified in court after Patrick knocked him down and brutally beat him. For his part, Patrick blamed "a drop of drink."[92]

Some of Patrick's more colorful violations involved driving his cart furiously, weaving from side to side, belligerently refusing to pay tram fare, and unleashing such cascades of profanities toward police that he drew a crowd to gawk. When Patrick wasn't causing mayhem in the roads himself, his animals took up the baton, rambling through the streets unrestrained. Called into court for the common offense of letting his horses run loose on Adelaide Road and again, on Riddiford Street and then on Normanby Street, and Donald McClean Street, Patrick apparently reformed and kept the horses at home; he was subsequently charged with permitting his cattle to wander. On one occasion, a horse in Patrick's employ somehow tumbled from a wharf and drowned; Patrick then attempted to recoup the expense from public coffers, arguing the horse was engaged in Council work when it took the plunge. Maybe, just maybe, Patrick would have been better off as a racehorse.

---

[91] Source 386.
[92] Ibid.

Knockaderry introduced me to the identity of my great-great-grandfather Daniel Daly's parents. Can you guess? Another Daniel, this one married to Nora Clifford. They married in about 1810; their offspring included, in addition to Daniel and his brother Timothy whom I'd once mistaken as Norah's father: Patrick who married Juliana Daly and Jeremiah who married Johanna Allen, Mary Daly Sullivan, Nora Daly Brosnan, Julia Daly Glissane, Margaret Daly O'Leary, Elizabeth Daly Donovan, and Catherine Daly Sullivan.

Mary Daly Sullivan and her husband Peter Sullivan, aunt and uncle to my great-grandmother and her siblings, embody the suffering inflicted on the Irish people by inhumane British policies. The Sullivans were among the many souls evicted from their homes in County Kerry during the Great Hunger, known in Ireland as An Gorta Mór, leaving them and their seven children without a roof over their heads. Despite their despairing condition and responsibility for a brood of seven, somehow they managed to scrape up the passage for all nine of them on the sailing ship Ashburton in September 1852.

Although An Gorta Mór had persisted for seven years by then and was nearing its end, coffin ships[93] were still running at full tilt, the captains treating passengers like cargo,

---

[93] "Coffin ships" referred originally to ships designed for transporting lumber from Canada to the British Isles on which Irish emigrants were transported as "paying ballast' on the return trips. In time, the term seems to have been expanded to encompass other ships of dubious seaworthiness hastily put into service to transport emigrants or ships setting sail with those emigrants in unsafe conditions.

showing little regard for the high death rates— up to twenty percent. Whereas previously the month-long transatlantic journeys were limited to spring and summer, dangerous autumn and winter sailings were instituted during An Gorta Mór, subjecting even the passengers on the seaworthy sailing ships to the dangers associated with rough seas, storms, and ice. In the mid-1840's, the British Parliament had enacted new taxes on landowners in an effort to fund relief for those destitute and at risk of starvation in Ireland. The landlords' fear of these taxes becoming a permanent burden led many to pay passage to Canada or the United States for their non-paying tenants on those ships of dubious seaworthiness, pejoratively called coffin ships. Other evictees pulled together whatever resources they could to pay their own fares. The passengers who survived the journeys were sometimes barely alive on arrival and most were without any means of subsistence. The United States tried to deter this immigration with fare increases but ships carrying the desperate immigrants continued to sail into American ports.

Ship's fever, a euphemism for typhus, was common on the coffin ships and due to the overcrowding spread among the passengers unchecked. There was no bathroom in steerage, only buckets, which overflowed when the ships rocked. Ellen-Marie Pederson described the squalor confronting the passengers in *Star of the Sea: A Postcolonial, Postmodern Voyage into the Irish Famine*[94]:

---

[94] Source 393.

Hundreds of men, women and children huddled together in the dark on bare wooden floors with no ventilation, breathing a stench of vomit.

By the time An Gorta Mór let up, up to a million Irish had died at home and another one to two million emigrated, about three-eighths of the Irish population. For County Kerry, the statistics were bleaker: a third of Kerrymen emigrated or died during the peak years alone. This was not for want of food in the country. As was noted by a contemporaneous letter writer to the *Irish Felon* in 1848:[95]

> ...the corn crops [in 1846] were sufficient to feed the island. But the landlords *would* have their rents, in spite of famine and defiance of fever. They took the whole harvest, and left hunger to those who raised it. Had the people of Ireland been the landlords of Ireland, not a human creature would have died of hunger, nor the failure of the potato been considered a matter of any consequence.

The Sullivans survived their journey on the Ashburton intact and took up farming in Macomb, Illinois upon their arrival in the United States. But their eviction-fueled emigration experience was not theirs alone; the entire Daly clan bore its effects. The harshness of the British landlord system and the pain of eviction were thus desperately real to my Irish family and still stinging-fresh and personal in the 1860's as Mary Daley O'Brien and her siblings were growing up. When, in their early adulthood, the Land

---

[95] Source 402.

War brought a new round of evictions, their determination to conquer the forces holding them back no doubt sprang in significant part from their family's past collective injury. One of my own inheritances from Nanny was the seeds of indignation and injustice Mary Daley O'Brien passed down to her, coupled with vigorous, reflexive Pride in our shared Irish heritage.

The Sullivans have a second role to play in this story: Peter Sullivan is an ancestor of my BC friend Mary O'Keeffe, relating us by marriage. But that isn't Mary's and my only familial connection. Mary Daly Sullivan's sister Elizabeth married John "Jack" Donovan from the nearby Skahies townland, a son of Mary O'Keeffe's second great-grandfather.

My great-great-grandmother Elizabeth Browne's birth family, I learned, came from Limerick to Ballybane, another townland near Knockaderry. Her father and mother, John Browne and Mary Cotter, were parents of eight, including John, Nicholas, Patrick, Thomas, Margaret and two others whose names have yet to be uncovered, in addition to Elizabeth herself.

Now what of that other subject, you must wonder. Surely, she would have asked. It isn't most graceful to blurt out that kind of business with people you've only just met, you know. Such a delicate topic, I hesitated to introduce it too abruptly, but as our tour of Knockaderry was nearing its end, I asked. And this was the answer:

"Yah, Timothy and Dan were Moonlighters."

Views of the exterior and interior of the Daly ancestral home, now falling to ruin. Knockaderry, County Kerry, Ireland. Credit: Carol Bengle Gilbert, except as noted.

Original photo above courtesy of Batt Daly; image re-photographed by Carol Bengle Gilbert. This photo depicts the home exterior as it looked in the past.

This home was one of the properties associated with the Browne family who were the Viscounts Kenmare; it is one of the Browne estates forfeited during the Penal Laws and recovered in about 1720 by the Third Viscount Valentine Browne. During their exile, some of the Brownes are believed to have lived in Castlefarm, the home in which John O'Connell Curtin later lived.

The second Viscount Nicholas Browne and third Viscounts Nicholas Browne (c. 1670-1720) and Valentine Browne (1695-1736) were patrons of the Gaelic poet Aodhagán ó Rathaille. In ó Rathaille's poem *Epitilamium do Thighearna Mara*, one of two poems written in commemoration of Viscount Valentine Browne's marriage to Honora Butler, he refers to the Viscount as "the prince of Killarney." He also wrote songs for their children. At some point, there was a disagreement, and he penned angry verses about his former patron. Due to a break in records, it cannot be determined whether Elizabeth Browne's family has any relationship to the Viscounts Browne; however her brother Nicholas Browne indisputably lived at Boucheens.

The Browne family monument in the Old Molahiffe Cemetery. Nicholas, Thomas, and Patrick Browne, brothers of Elizabeth Browne Daly, are buried here. Credit: Carol Bengle Gilbert.

Memorial to four generations of the Daly family, Old Molahiffe Cemetery. The dates given for the couple Daniel and Elizabeth's deaths on the gravestone do not match the dates given in death records. The Index of Names at the end of this book contains dates from the official records. Credit: Carol Bengle Gilbert

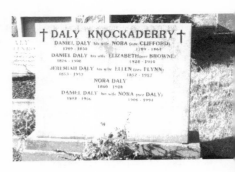

View of cemetery entrance. Credit: Carol Bengle Gilbert.

Above, the Farranfore train station where Mary Daley and her siblings began their immigration journeys. Sign in Irish and English identifying the station, below right. Credit: Andrew Bengle Gilbert. Below, left, the view looking out from Cobh (then Queenstown) Harbor as Mary Daly and her siblings would have seen it as they set out for America. Credit: Carol Bengle Gilbert

The Church of St. Gertrude in
Killahane, site of multiple pew
attacks in the 1880s. Credit:
Carol Bengle Gilbert.

Daniel D. Daly whose missing pockets landed him in "the Joy." He subsequently emigrated and became a police officer with the Chicago Police Dept. The Chicago Police Dept. at that time was known for providing institutional assistance to Moonlighters fleeing County Kerry and to set them up with jobs on their arrival in America. However, not all Kerrymen in the Chicago Police Dept. were ex-Moonlighters and not all Moonlighters fleeing Kerry for Chicago became police officers. In Daniel's case, his brother Timothy was already in Chicago working for the Chicago Police Dept.

1883 letter from Patrick Daly to the Mayor and City Councilors of Wellington, New Zealand requesting compensation for a drowned horse owned by a Mr. Collier and used in Patrick's business. It reads in part, "Some time ago, a horse in my employ, working for the corporation, had the misfortune to go over the break mouth into the sea and as a consequence was drowned... trusting you will see your way to make him [Collier] some reasonable compensation..." Public domain.

Castlefarm, once the home of John and Agnes O'Connell Curtin and family, and site of the Moonlighter raid that resulted in the deaths of John O'Connell Curtin and Thady Sullivan. Credit: Carol Bengle Gilbert.

Patrick Daly, the forebear who might have been a racehorse but instead emigrated to New Zealand believed to be at far right. Margaret Green Daly is far left.

Genealogists at work, 2022: Batt Daly, right, author left. Credit: Andrew Bengle Gilbert.

Andrew Bengle Gilbert, Batt Daly, Carol Bengle Gilbert and Nellie Daly, Knockaderry, 2022. Credit: Andrew Bengle Gilbert

Faerie Sídhe at the Daly and Sullivan Farms in Knockaderry and Boolacullane

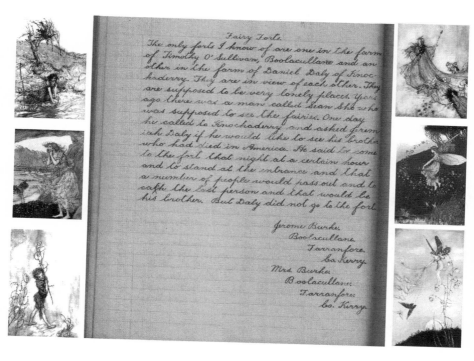

Fairy Torts.

The only forts I know of are one in the farm of Timothy O'Sullivan, Boolacullane and another in the farm of Daniel Daly of Knockaderry. They are in view of each other. They are supposed to be in very lonely places. Years ago there was a man called Sean Shō who was supposed to see the fairies. One day he called to Knockaderry and asked from Jeremiah Daly if he would like to see his brother who had died in America. He said to come to the fort that night at a certain hour and to stand at the entrance and that a number of people would pass out and to catch the last person and that would be his brother. But Daly did not go to the fort.

Jerome Burke
Boolacullane
Farranfore.
Co. Kerry

Mrs. Burke
Boolacullane
Farranfore
Co. Kerry

A magical genealogical find! Jerome Burke's 1930s school assignment describes fairy mounds (sídhe) on the Daly and Sullivan farms in Knockaderry and Boolacullane and a mysterious visitor of years ago calling himself Sean Sho who promised the author's great-granduncle Jeremiah Daly that a night visit to the sídhe would enable him to see his brother who had died in America. This paper illuminates the fanciful beliefs passed down by my great-grandmother Mary Daley O'Brien who lived alongside these faeries and their sídhe throughout her childhood. "The Schools' Collection, Volume 0460, Page 54" by Dúchas © National Folklore Collection, UCD is licensed under CC BY-NC 4.0. Used with permission. Midsummer Night's Dream faerie images are public domain.

ACKNOWLEDGEMENTS

A resounding thank you to EVERYONE contributing to the emergence of this book, especially my daughters Amy Gilbert (loyal reader and astute editor) and Cindy Gilbert (invaluable masking advice), my son Andy Gilbert (generously gifting the Ireland trip inspiring me to write the book and accompanying me in my travels), my sister Jan Ruidl (amplifying my recollections of childhood events), the late Jacques Bengle (sharing genealogy expertise and chiseling the bricks out of my wall of skepticism), the late Roberta Gasteyer and Sr. Julia Frances Killelea (cheerfully traipsing down Memory Lane to retrieve remembrances dating back more than a half century), the late Jeannette Alessi (gifting me the historic Bengle and Monat family photos), Pam Shoemaker, Gill Historical Commission, Peter H. Weis, Northfield Mount Hermon School archivist, and Edie Field, emeritus, Ann Tweedy, and Eva Gibavic, Leverett Historical Commission (going above and beyond in helping me sleuth out details of my family history and providing historical perspective), and to my old and new-found cousins who helped with anecdotes and photos, especially Kim Daly Crook (pulling together reams of records of Patrick Daly's life in New Zealand), Shaun Brosnan (whose decades of onsite investigation in consultation with our ancestor tracers in County Kerry helped rescue precious stories from history's dustbin), Mary Lessard Newburn (dusting off the old superstitions governing our Nannies' lives), and Christine Tetreault King (beta reading and cheerleading.) A particularly effusive shout of gratitude goes to Batt and Nellie Daly without whom this story would have no epilogue.

DIVERS DESCENDENTS OF DANIEL DALY
AND NORA CLIFFORD

Left to right and top to bottom, Row 1: Mary Daly Corcoran, Rose Dunn, Jerome Daly [non-descendent relative], Helen Clifford, Catherine Donovan Shea. Row 2: Evelyn Gaiser Bowler Andalina, Robert T. Daly, Mary "Minnie" Corcoran, Hon. Martin J. Dunn, Marie Hussey, Rev. William Killelea. Row 3: Cornelius H., Shea, Noreen Sullivan Besore, Elizabeth L. Hussey, , Mavis Daly Avello, Becca Ruidl. Row 4: Michael A. Hussey ,John J. Shea (above) John B. Daly (below), Mary Alta Sullivan, Marie Antoinette Sullican, and Virginia Marie Shea.

Mary Daly Corcoran>Timothy Daly>Daniel and Nora

Rose Dunn>Julia Daly Dunn>Jeremiah Daly>Daniel Daly>Daniel and Nora

Helen Clifford>Johannah "Hannah" Daly>Jeremiah>Daniel Daly>Daniel and Nora

Catherine Donovan Shea>Elizabeth Daly Donovan> Daniel and Nora

Evelyn Gaiser Bowler Andalina>Caroline Daley (with Herbert Gaiser)>Daniel J. Daley> Timothy D. Daley>Daniel Daly>Daniel and Nora

Robert T. Daley>Timothy E. Daley> Timothy D. Daley>Daniel Daly>Daniel and Nora

Mary "Minnie" Corcoran Sullivan>Mary Daly Corcoran>Timothy Daly>Daniel and Nora

Marty Dunn>John Dunn>Julia Daly Dunn>>Jeremiah Daly>Daniel Daly>Daniel and Nora

Marie Hussey Grace>Elizabeth Daly Hussey>Daniel Daly>Daniel and Nora

William Killelea>Lizzie O'Brien Killelea Gross (with William Killelea)>Mary Daley O'Brien>Daniel Daly>Daniel and Nora

Marie Antoinette "Nettie" Sullivan>Mary Marie Daly Sullivan>Daniel and Nora

Cornelius Shea>Catherine Donovan> Elizabeth Daly Donovan>Daniel and Nora

Noreen Sullivan Besore>Mary "Minnie" Corcoran Sullivan>Mary Daly Corcoran>Timothy Daly>Daniel and Nora

Elizabeth L. Hussey>Elizabeth Daly Hussey>Daniel Daly>Daniel and Nora

John B. Daly>Daniel D. Daly>Daniel Daly>Daniel and Nora

Virginia Marie Shea> George Raymond Shea>Catherine Donovan Shea> Elizabeth Daly Donovan>Daniel and Nora

Mavis Daly Avello>Daniel Daly> Patrick Daly> Daniel Daly> Daniel and Nora

Becca Ruidl>Jan Bengle Ruidl>Marie Bruce Bengle>Esther O'Brien Bruce> Mary Daley O'Brien> Daniel Daly> Daniel and Nora

Michael Aloysius Hussey>Elizabeth Daly Hussey>Daniel Daly>Daniel and Nora

Mary Alta Sullivan>Edward Ambrose Sullivan>Peter Sullivan>Mary Marie Daly Sullivan>Daniel and Nora

John Joseph Shea>Catherine Donovan> Elizabeth Daly Donovan>Daniel and Nora

Row 1: Andy Gilbert, Walter Wedow and Robert Wedow, Roger Daly, JoAnn Andalina Pio.
Row 2: Geraldine Shea, Mary Newburn, Michael Shea,. Row 3: Amy Gilbert, Cindy
Gilbert, Courtney Ruidl Krause, Grace H. Shea Weddow (above)/ James J. Dunn (below),
Tom Besore. Row 4; Jeff Ruidl,. Daniel P. Daly, Shelley Furkey, Robert G. Daly. Avis
Damon Lessard, Marie Agnes McGinty. Row 5: Liz Mather, Lisa Ruidl Nosbich, Rose
Marie Hussey Hooper, Margaret Sullivan.

Andy Gilbert>Carol Bengle Gilbert>Marie Bruce Bengle>Esther O'Brien Bruce>Mary Daley O'Brien>Daniel Daly> Daniel and Nora

Walter Wedow>Grace H. Shea Wedow>Michael Shea, Jr.>Elizabeth Sullivan Shea>Mary Marie Daly Sullivan>Daniel and Nora

Robert Wedow>Grace H. Shea Wedow>Michael Shea, Jr.>Elizabeth Sullivan Shea>Mary Marie Daly Sullivan>Daniel and Nora

Roger M. Daly>John B. Daly>Daniel D. Daly>Daniel Daly>Daniel and Nora

JoAnn Andalina Pio>Evelyn Gaiser Bowler Andalina >Caroline Daley (with Herbert Gaiser))>Daniel J. Daley>Timothy D. Daley> Daniel Daly>Daniel and Nora

Geraldine Shea> John Joseph Shea>Catherine Donovan> Elizabeth Daly Donovan>Daniel and Nora

Mary Lessard Furkey Mather Newburn> Avis Damon Lessard>Lulu O'Brien Schmidt (with Ralph Damon)>Mary Daley O'Brien>Daniel Daly>Daniel and Nora

Michael Shea>Elizabeth "Betsy" Sullivan>Mary Marie Daly Sullivan>Daniel and Nora

Amy Gilbert>Carol Bengle Gilbert>Marie Bruce Bengle>Esther O'Brien Bruce>Mary Daley O'Brien> Daniel Daly>Daniel and Nora

Grace H. Shea Weddow>Michael Shea, Jr.>Elizabeth Sullivan Shea>Mary Marie Daly Sullivan>Daniel and Nora

Tom Besore>Noreen Sullivan Besore>Mary "Minnie" Corcoran Sullivan>Mary Daly Corcoran>Timothy Daly>Daniel and Nora

Jeff Ruidl>Jan Bengle Ruidl>Marie Bruce Bengle>Esther O'Brien Bruce>Mary Daley O'Brien> Daniel Daly>Daniel and Nora

Cindy Gilbert>Carol Bengle Gilbert>Marie Bruce Bengle>Esther O'Brien Bruce>Mary Daley O'Brien> Daniel Daly>Daniel and Nora

Courtney Ruidl Krause>Jan Bengle Ruidl>Marie Bruce Bengle>Esther O'Brien Bruce>Mary Daley O'Brien> Daniel Daly>Daniel and Nora

James J. Dunn>Julia Daly Dunn>Jeremiah Daly>Daniel Daly>Daniel and Nora

Liz Mather>Mary Lessard Furkey Mather (with Mather)> Lulu O'Brien Schmidt (with Ralph Damon)> Mary Daley >Daniel Daly>Daniel and Nora

Daniel P. Daly>Patrick Daly> Daniel Daly> Daniel and Nora

Shelley Furkey>Mary Lessard Furkey Mather (with Furkey)> Lulu O'Brien Schmidt (with Ralph Damon)> Mary Daley O'Brien>Daniel Daly>Daniel and Nora

Robert G. Daly>Daniel P. Daly>Patrick Daly> Daniel Daly> Daniel and Nora

Margaret Sullivan>Patrick Sullivan>Mary Marie Daly Sullivan, Daniel and Nora

Lisa Ruidl Nosbich>Jan Bengle Ruidl>Marie Bruce Bengle>Esther O'Brien Bruce>Mary Daley O'Brien> Daniel Daly>Daniel and Nora

Rose Marie Hussey Hooper>Michael Aloysius Hussey>Elizabeth Daly Hussey>Daniel Daly>Daniel and Nora

Avis Damon Lessard>Lulu O'Brien Schmidt (with Ralph Damon)>Mary Daley O'Brien>Daniel Daly>Daniel and Nora

Marie Agnes McGinty>Daniel Daly> Patrick Daly> Daniel Daly> Daniel and Nora

DALY FAMILY GENERATION I

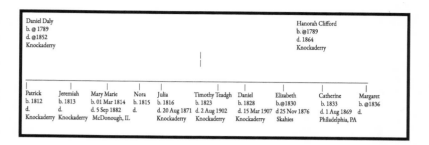

Daniel Daly								Hanorah Clifford	
b. @ 1789								b. @1789	
d. @1852								d. 1864	
Knockaderry								Knockaderry	

Patrick	Jeremiah	Mary Marie	Nora	Julia	Timothy Teadgh	Daniel	Elizabeth	Catherine	Margaret
b. 1812	b. 1813	b. 01 Mar 1814	b. 1815	b. 1816	b. 1823	b. 1828	b.@1830	b. 1833	b. @1836
d.	d.	d. 5 Sep 1882	d.	d. 20 Aug 1871	d. 2 Aug 1902	d. 15 Mar 1907	d 25 Nov 1876	d. 1 Aug 1869	d.
Knockaderry	Knockaderry	McDonough, IL		Knockaderry	Knockaderry	Knockaderry	Skahies	Philadelphia, PA	

DALY FAMILY GENERATION II

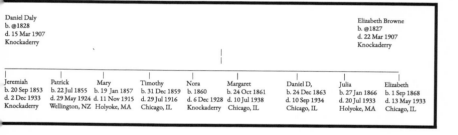

Daniel Daly								Elizabeth Browne	
b. @1828								b. @1827	
d. 15 Mar 1907								d. 22 Mar 1907	
Knockaderry								Knockaderry	

Jeremiah	Patrick	Mary	Timothy	Nora	Margaret	Daniel D,	Julia	Elizabeth
b. 20 Sep 1853	b. 22 Jul 1855	b. 19 Jan 1857	b. 31 Dec 1859	b. 1860	b. 24 Oct 1861	b. 24 Dec 1863	b. 27 Jan 1866	b. 1 Sep 1868
d. 2 Dec 1933	d. 29 May 1924	d. 11 Nov 1915	d. 29 Jul 1916	d. 6 Dec 1928	d. 10 Jul 1938	d. 10 Sep 1934	d. 20 Jul 1933	d. 13 May 1933
Knockaderry	Wellington, NZ	Holyoke, MA	Chicago, IL	Knockaderry	Chicago, IL	Chicago, IL	Holyoke, MA	Chicago, IL

DALY FAMILY GENERATION III

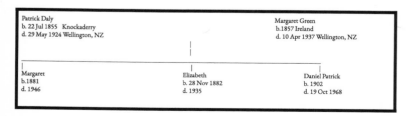

Patrick Daly		Margaret Green	
b. 22 Jul 1855 Knockaderry		b.1857 Ireland	
d. 29 May 1924 Wellington, NZ		d. 10 Apr 1937 Wellington, NZ	

Margaret	Elizabeth	Daniel Patrick
b.1881	b. 28 Nov 1882	b. 1902
d. 1946	d. 1935	d. 19 Oct 1968

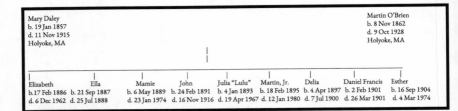

Mary Daley b. 19 Jan 1857 d. 11 Nov 1915 Holyoke, MA							Martin O'Brien b. 8 Nov 1862 d. 9 Oct 1928 Holyoke, MA

Elizabeth	Ella	Mamie	John	Julia "Lulu"	Martin, Jr.	Delia	Daniel Francis	Esther
b.17 Feb 1886	b. 21 Sep 1887	b. 6 May 1889	b. 24 Feb 1891	b. 4 Jan 1893	b. 18 Feb 1895	b. 4 Apr 1897	b. 2 Feb 1901	b. 16 Sep 1904
d. 6 Dec 1962	d. 25 Jul 1888	d. 23 Jan 1974	d. 16 Nov 1916	d. 19 Apr 1967	d. 12 Jan 1980	d. 7 Jul 1900	d. 26 Mar 1901	d. 4 Mar 1974

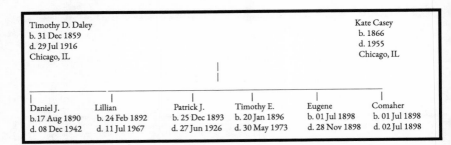

Timothy D. Daley b. 31 Dec 1859 d. 29 Jul 1916 Chicago, IL					Kate Casey b. 1866 d. 1955 Chicago, IL

Daniel J.	Lillian	Patrick J.	Timothy E.	Eugene	Comaher
b.17 Aug 1890	b. 24 Feb 1892	b. 25 Dec 1893	b. 20 Jan 1896	b. 01 Jul 1898	b. 01 Jul 1898
d. 08 Dec 1942	d. 11 Jul 1967	d. 27 Jun 1926	d. 30 May 1973	d. 28 Nov 1898	d. 02 Jul 1898

Norah Daly
b. 1860
d. 6 Dec 1928
Knockaderry

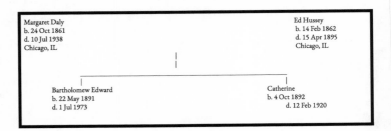

Margaret Daly b. 24 Oct 1861 d. 10 Jul 1938 Chicago, IL	Ed Hussey b. 14 Feb 1862 d. 15 Apr 1895 Chicago, IL

Bartholomew Edward b. 22 May 1891 d. 1 Jul 1973	Catherine b. 4 Oct 1892 d. 12 Feb 1920

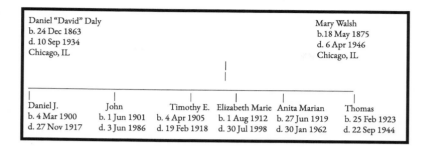

Daniel "David" Daly
b. 24 Dec 1863
d. 10 Sep 1934
Chicago, IL

Mary Walsh
b.18 May 1875
d. 6 Apr 1946
Chicago, IL

Daniel J.	John	Timothy E.	Elizabeth Marie	Anita Marian	Thomas
b. 4 Mar 1900	b. 1 Jun 1901	b. 4 Apr 1905	b. 1 Aug 1912	b. 27 Jun 1919	b. 25 Feb 1923
d. 27 Nov 1917	d. 3 Jun 1986	d. 19 Feb 1918	d. 30 Jul 1998	d. 30 Jan 1962	d. 22 Sep 1944

Julia Daley
7 Jan 1866
d. 20 Jul 1933
Holyoke, MA

John R. Fitzgerald
b. Dec 1867
d. 1940
Holyoke, MA

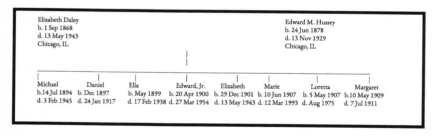

Elizabeth Daley
b. 1 Sep 1868
d. 13 May 1943
Chicago, IL

Edward M. Hussey
b. 24 Jun 1878
d. 13 Nov 1929
Chicago, IL

Michael	Daniel	Ella	Edward, Jr.	Elizabeth	Marie	Loretta	Margaret
b.14 Jul 1894	b. Dec 1897	b. May 1899	b. 20 Apr 1900	b. 29 Dec 1901	b. 10 Jun 1907	b. 5 May 1907	b.10 May 1909
d. 3 Feb 1945	d. 24 Jan 1917	d. 17 Feb 1938	d. 27 Mar 1954	d. 13 May 1943	d. 12 Mar 1993	d. Aug 1975	d. 7 Jul 1911

SOURCES

Sources Used Throughout

1.   Family accounts.

Additional Sources by Chapter

Chapter 2

2.   Beaudin, Pierre. *La Famille Lippé.* Montréal, 1975.

3.   Bordewich, Fergus M., "The Ambush that Changed History," *Smithsonian Magazine*, September 2006, retrieved from https://www.smithsonianmag.com/history/the-ambush-that-changed-hi story-72636736/.

4.   Scheffer, Ary, "Charlemagne at Paderborn," oil on canvas, 1835, Galerie des Batailles- Palace of Versailles, in Wikimedia Commons, December 31, 2021, https://commons.wikimedia.org/wiki/File:Ary_Scheffer,_Charlemagne_re%C3 %A7oit_la_soumission_de_Widukind_%C3%A0_Paderborn,_(1840).jpg.

Chapter 3

5.   Wilhelmy, Jean-Pierre. *Les mercenaires allemands au Québec du XVIIIe siècle et leur apport à la population.* Canada: Maison des mots, 1984, pp. 11, 13.

6.   Wilhelmy, Jean-Pierre. *Les mercenaires allemands au Québec.* Canada: Septentrion, 2009, p. 17.

7.   Watt, Gavin K. and Cruikshank, E.A., Brigadier-General. *The History and Master Roll of the King's Royal Regiment of New York*, rev. Ed. Milton: Global Heritage Press, 2006.

8.   Simms, Jeptha R. *The Frontiersmen of New York*, vol. II. Albany: zG.C. Riggs, 1883, pp. 517-519, retrieved from http://revwarpensions.com/lampmans.html.

9.   Ancestry.com, Genealogy of the Tucker Family from various authentic sources, North America Family Histories, 1500-2000, Provo, UT, 2016, Benjamin Tucker, Worcester, MA died 13 Sept 1806

10.   Theriault, Evelyn Yvonne. "Sprechen Sie Deutsche? The 'Secret' of Germans of Quebec and Their Part in Repelling the American Invasion of Canada." A Canadian Family, First Nations, French Canadians, & Acadians. September 19, 2009.https://acanadianfamily.wordpress.com/2009/09/19/sprechen-sie-deutsch e-the-secret-germans-of-quebec-and-the-american-invasion-pt-1/.

11.   Williams, Sherman, *Stories from Early New York History* (New York, Charles Scribner's Sons, 1906), retrieved from https://nyahgp.genealogyvillage.com/events-in-the-mohawk-valley.html.

12.   Greene, Nelson, ed. *The Story of Old Fort Plain and the Middle Mohawk Valley.* Fort Plain, NY: O'Connor Brothers Publishers, 1915), Ch. XXI, retrieved from http://threerivershms.com/greene21.htm.

13.   Greene, Nelson, ed. *History of the Mohawk Valley:Gateway to the West 1614-1925.* Chicago: The S. J. Clarke Publishing Co., 1925. Ch. 76, pp.

1127-1139, retrieved from
http://www.schenectadyhistory.org/resources/mvgw/history/076.html.

14. Merz, Johannes Helmut. Guide to Help You Find Your Hessian Soldier of the
American Revolution. Canada: J.H. Merz, 2001, retrieved from
AMREV-Hessian. 2006. Accessed 1/20/22,
http://freepages.rootsweb.com/~amrevhessians/military/a/amhessians3.htm.

15. "Participants in the Boston Tea Party." Boston Tea Party Ships & Museum.
2021, accessed 11/21/21,
https://www.bostonteapartyship.com/participants-in-the-boston-tea-party.

16. "The Boston Tea Party." Massachusetts Historical Society. 2021. Accessed
11/21/21, https://www.masshist.org/revolution/teaparty.php.

Chapter 5

17. Stoughton, Ralph M. *History of the Town of Gill, Massachusetts, 1793-1943.*
United States: R.M. Stoughton, 1950.

18. Bruce, Vivian M., 1930 United States Federal Census [database online]. Provo,
UT, US;, Ancestry.com Operations, Inc. 2012

19. Bruce, Vivien M., 1940 United States Federal Census [database online.] Provo,
UT, US: Ancestry.com Operations, Inc. 2012.

20. Bruce, Vivien M., obituary, *Ithaca Journal*, 3/21/84, p. 6.

21. Kyriakodies, Helen and King, Devon, transcribers, *10-1: Interviews with Leverett
Scholars* (Boston, Off the Common Books, 2021).

22. Amherst High School student enrollment card, "Vivian (sic) Bruce," 1941-42.

23. "A Brief History of Moore's Corner Church." Moore's Corner Church. 2022.
Accessed October 29, 2022, https://moorescornerchurch.com/p/18/History.

Chapter 6

24. Waterman, Edgar Francis. *The Waterman Family, vol. III.* Madison: University
of Wisconsin, 1942.

25. "Samuel Gorton (1593-1677). Warwick Rhode Island Digital History Project.
Accessed 11/21/21,
https://www.warwickhistory.com/index.php?option=com_content&view=artic
le&id=476:samuel-gorton-15931677&catid=57&Itemid=130.

26. "Massachusetts Bay 17: Samuel Gorton's Heresy." American History Podcast.
2018. Accessed 11/21/2021,
http://americanhistorypodcast.net/massachusetts-bay-17-samuel-gortons-heresy
/.

27. *"Samuel Gorton and his Gortonites Create a Church Among the Jack-an-Apes."*
New England Historical Society. 2014. Accessed 11/21/2021,
https://www.newenglandhistoricalsociety.com/samuel-gorton-and-his-gortonite
s-create-a-church-among-the-jack-an-apes/.

28. "The Attack on Shawomet." Warwick Rhode Island Digital History Project.
Accessed 11/21/21,
https://www.warwickhistory.com/index.php?option=com_content&view=artic

le&id=92:conimicut-village-and-its-environs-the-attack-on-shawomet&catid=42
&Itemid=95.

29. Gorton, Adelos, comp. *The Life and Times of Samuel Gorton*. Philadelphia: G.S.
    Ferguson Company, 1907, retrieved from
    https://www.google.com/books/edition/The_Life_and_Times_of_Samuel_Go
    rton/UnwZAQAAMAAJ?hl=en&gbpv=1.

30. "Organizing a Democracy." Rhode Island Genealogy. 2022,. Accessed
    1/29/2022,
    https://rhodeislandgenealogy.com/statewide/organizing-a-democracy.htm#the-p
    rovidence-compact.

31. Samuel Gorton person sheet, Fleming Family History, 2013, accessed
    1/29/22,http://freepages.rootsweb.com/~barbpretz/genealogy/ps03/ps03_265.
    htm.

32. Fuller, Oliver Payson, B.A. The History of Warwick, Rhode Island, Settlement
    in 1642 to the present time; including accounts of the early settlement and
    development of its several villages; sketches of the origin and progress of the
    different churches of the town, &c, &c. Providence: Angell, Burlingame& Co.,
    Printers 1875, retrieved from
    https://www.google.com/books/edition/The_History_of_Warwick_Rhode_Isl
    and_from/VcM-AAAAYAAJ?hl=en&gbpv=1

Chapter 9

33. "The Empire Theater Was Well Filled." *Palmer Journal*. May 1, 1919.
    https://archive.org/stream/palmerjournaljanjun1919/1919%28jan-jun%29_djvu
    .txt, accessed 1/29/2022.

34. "Dr. Everett P. Jewett Will Be Candidate." *Springfield Republican*. January 29,
    1927. Retrieved from Genealogybank.com.

35. "Frank Monat moved his confectionery..." *Palmer Evening Gazette*. May 24,
    1927. Retrieved from Genealogybank.com..

36. "Frank Monat and his daughters, Rose & Eleanor, have left for Detroit...."
    Palmer Evening Gazette. October 4, 1927. Retrieved from Genealogybank.com.

37. "Boy's Deportation Likely Because of 8 Days in Canada." *Battle Creek Enquirer*.
    November 28, 1940. Retrieved from Newspapers.com.

38. "Court Decree Banishes Boy from Life-Long Home." News clipping maintained
    by family members.

39. "Young Men Identified as Notorious 'Corktown Mob.'" *The Windsor Star*.
    September 15, 1928. Retrieved from Newspapers.com.

40. "Many Victims Recognize Gang..." *Detroit Free Press*. September 14, 1928.
    Retrieved from Newspapers.com.

41. "Suspects are Held." *The Windsor Star*. September 11, 1928. Retrieved from
    Newspapers.com.

42. "3 'Scarface Gang' Men are Spotted." *The Windsor Gazette*. September 14.,
    1928. Retrieved from Newspapers.com.

43. "Pile-on," Miriam-Webster Online Dictionary, 2022, accessed 1/29/22, https://www.merriam-webster.com/dictionary/pile%20on#:~:text=US%2C%20i nformal,other%20critics%20started%20piling%20on.

44. "'Good Boys Plea' Fails to Aid Scarface Gang." *Detroit Free Press.* October 7, 1928. Retrieved from Newspapers.com.

Chapter 10

45. Melish, Joanne Pope. "*Black Labor at Nightingale-Brown House.*" John Nicholas Brown Center for Public Humanities and Cultural Heritage. 2022. Accessed 1/30/22, https://www.brown.edu/academics/public-humanities/about/history/black-lab or-nightingale-brown-house.

46. Zilian, Fred, "Rhode Island Dominates American Slave Trade in 19th Century." Small State Big History. Accessed 1/2022, http://smallstatebighistory.com/rhode-island-dominates-north-american-slave-tr ade-in-18th-century/.

47. "Slavery and the Slave Trade in Rhode Island." John Carter Brown Library. Accessed 1/30/22, https://www.brown.edu/Facilities/John_Carter_Brown_Library/exhibitions/jc bexhibit/Pages/exhibSlavery.html.

48. Fisher, Linford D. "'Why shall wee have peace to bee made slaves' Indian Surrenders during and after King Philip's War." National Center for Biotechnology Information. 2017. Accessed 1/30/22, https://www.ncbi.nlm.nih.gov/pmc/articles/PMC5654607/.

49. Publications of the Rhode Island Historical Society, New Series, Providence, 1893.

50. "Revolutionary War Military Records." Rhode Island Historical Society, Manuscripts Division. 2000. Page 98. Accessed 1/30/22, https://www.rihs.org/mssinv/Mss673sg2.htm#unittitle.

51. "Abolitionists and Anti-Slavery Activists." American Abolitionists and Anti-Slavery Activists: Conscience of the Nation. April 4, 202. Accessed 1/30/2022, http://www.americanabolitionists.com/abolitionists-and-anti-slavery-activists.ht ml.

52. "Benoni and John Waterman Papers." Rhode Island Historical Society, Manuscripts Division. 2001. Accessed 1/31/22, https://www.rihs.org/mssinv/Mss787.htm.

53. Geake, Robert A. "Long Buried and Forgotten: Finding Traces of Slavery in Rhode Island."Small State Big History. Accessed 1/31/22, http://smallstatebighistory.com/long-buried-and-forgotten-finding-traces-of-sla very-in-rhode-island/.

54. "Historical Cemetery #: WK103 Slaves-Waterman Family." Warwick Rhode Island Digital History Project. Accessed 1/31/22, https://www.warwickhistory.com/index.php?option=com_content&view=artic

le&id=391:historical-cemetery-wk103-slaves-waterman-family&catid=62&Itemi
d=116.

55. Stattler, Rick, and Galpern, Jennifer. Guide to Manuscripts at the Rhode Island
Historical Society Relating to People of Color. August 1, 2018.Accessed
1/31/22, https://www.rihs.org/mssinv/PeopleofColorweb.htm.

56. Schipper, Martin., ed., Papers of the American Slave Trade, Part I: Brown Family
Collections. Bethesda, Maryland: University Publications of America,1998.
Accessed 1/31/22,
http://www.lexisnexis.com/documents/academic/upa_cis/1404_papamslavetrse
rapt1.pdf.

57. "Slavery and the University: Reclaiming a Difficult History in Providence."
Organization of American Historians, Process: a Blog for American History.
March 29, 2016. Accessed 4/8/22,
http://www.processhistory.org/slavery-providence/.

58. "Moses Brown Papers." Rhode Island Historical Society. 1996. Accessed
1/31/22, https://www.rihs.org/mssinv/Mss313.htm.

59. Davis, Paul. "Plantations in the North: the Narragansett Planters." Slavery in
Rhode Island. 2020. Accessed 1/31/22,
https://stories.usatodaynetwork.com/slaveryinrhodeisland/plantations-in-the-n
orth-the-narragansett-planters/site/providencejournal.com/.

60. Zilian, Fred, "In 1843, slavery was banned in Rhode Island," the Newport Daily
News, May 28, 2018, accessed 1/31/22,
https://www.newportri.com/story/lifestyle/columns/2018/05/28/looking-back-
at-our-history-in-1843-slavery-was-banned-in-rhode-island/12119944007/.

61. Zilian, Fred. "Rhode Island Dominates North American Slave Trade in 18th
Century." Small State Big History. Accessed 1/31/22,
http://smallstatebighistory.com/rhode-island-dominates-north-american-slave-tr
ade-in-18th-century/.

62. "Slavery and Justice." John Carter Brown Library. Accessed 1/31/22,
https://www.brown.edu/Facilities/John_Carter_Brown_Library/exhibitions/jc
bexhibit/Pages/exhibSlavery.html.

63. Woodson, Carter G., Free Negro heads of families in the United States together
with a brief treatment of the free Negro (Washington, D.C., The Association for
the Study of Negro Life and History, Inc., 1925), retrieved from
https://archive.org/stream/freenegroheadsof00wood/freenegroheadsof00wood
_djvu.txt.

64. "Abenaki." Wikipedia. Wikimedia Foundation, 5 November 2022. Accessed
11/24/ 2022, https://en.wikipedia.org/wiki/Abenaki.

Chapter 12

65. Sylvester, Herbert M. Indian Wars of New England, Vol. III. Boston: W.B.
Clarke & Company, 1910, pp.75-76, 361-362, retrieved from
https://archive.org/details/b24882045_0003/.

66. Rugg, Ellen R. The Descendents of John Rugg, p. 62.

67. "22 Sites of the Early Settlement." Lancaster Historical Society. 2020. Accessed 5/19/22, http://lancasterhistoricalsociety.org/historical-guides/.

68. Marvin, Rev. Abijah P. *History of the Town of Lancaster, Massachusetts.* New York: Frederick H. Hitchcock, 1879, pp. 52, 62, 110-115, 128, 133, 161-162, retrieved from

    https://archive.org/details/descendantsofjoh00rugg/page/n8/mode/2up?ref=ol &view=theater.

69. Family Card-Person Sheet, John Prescott, 2007, accessed 1/31/22, http://homepages.rpi.edu/~holmes/Hobbies/Genealogy2/ps14/ps14_087.htm.

70. Fairbanks History, *"Fairbanks and Prescotts, Friends and Neighbors who came to the New World in the Seventeenth Century,"* accessed 1/31/22, https://www.fairbankshistory.com/colonial-history/7oa040ah83lkr8hkuant228s vlb0xd.

71. Prescott, William. *The Prescott memorial, or, a genealogical memoir of the Prescott families in America, in two parts.* Boston: H.W. Dutton and Son, 1870, pp. 32-33, 46-47,

    https://www.google.com/books/edition/The_Prescott_Memorial/r-BLAQAAI AAJ?hl=en&gbpv=1.

72. Nourse, Henry S., A.M., ed. *"Early Town Clerk Records Excerpted from the Birth Marriage & Death Register Church Records and Epitaphs of Lancaster, Massachusetts 1643-1850,"* retrieved

    fromhttp://dunhamwilcox.net/ma/lancaster_ma_early_records.htm.

73. Reitwiesner, William Addams, comp., *"Ancestry of George W. Bush,"* accessed 1/31/22, http://www.wargs.com/political/bush.html.

74. Nourse, Henry S., A.M., ed. *The Early Records of Lancaster Massachusetts."* 1884.

    https://brittlebooks.library.illinois.edu/brittlebooks_open/Books2009-08/lanca s0001earrec/lancas0001earrec.pdf.

75. Mather, Cotton and Parkhurst, Thomas, *Magnalia Christi Americana* (1702). Book VII, retrieved from

    https://digitalcommons.usm.maine.edu/omi_rare_books/9.

76. Lincoln, Charles, H., Ph.D., ed., *Narratives of the Indian Wars 1675-1699* (New York, Charles Scribner's Sons,1913), pp. 80-166, retrieved from https://archive.org/details/narrativesindian00lincrich/.

77. *Representative Men and Old Families of Southeastern Massachusetts Containing Historical Sketches of Prominent and Representative Citizens and Genealogical Records of Many of the Old Families* (J.H. Beers & Co., 1912), p. 1642, retrieved from

    https://www.google.com/books/edition/Representative_Men_and_Old_Famili es_of_S/GHIWAAAAYAAJ?hl=en&gbpv=1.

78. Rowlandson, Mrs. Mary, *The Narrative of the Captivity and Restoration of Mrs. Mary Rowlandson,* (Cambridge, MA, 1682), pp. 94-99, retrieved from https://www.gutenberg.org/files/851/851-h/851-h.htm.

79. Theriault, J.R. *On John Prescott.* Historic Harvard Town. May 18, 2012. Accessed 5/2/22,

    https://historicharvard.wordpress.com/2012/05/18/a-blog-posting-on-john-pre scott/.

80. "The Heritage of the Grist Mill." Heritage Grains & Milling Co. 2019. Accessed 1/31/22, https://www.heritagegrainsco.com/grist-mill-heritage/.

81. Bell, Jay. "New England's Grist Mills: not run-of-the-mill historic buildings." Hidden New England. 2019. Accessed 1/31/22, https://www.newenglandgoodlife.com/hidden-new-england/new-englands-grist-mills-not-run-of-the-mill-historic-buildings.

82. Lovejoy, Evelyn M. W., *History of Royalton, Vermont, with family genealogies, 1769-1911* (Burlington, VT, Free Press Printing Co., 1911), pp. 398-399., retrieved from https://www.google.com/books/edition/History_of_Royalton_Vermont/XDQ TAAAAYAAJ?hl=en&gbpv=1.

83. "Stalag XII-A." Pegasus Archive. Accessed 1/31/22, https://www.pegasusarchive.org/pow/cSt_12A_History1.htm.

84. "Stalag XII-A." Indiana Military. November 28, 2005. Accessed 1/31/22, http://www.indianamilitary.org/German%20PW%20Camps/Prisoner%20of%2 0War/PW%20Camps/Stalag%20XII-A%20Limburg/History.htm.

85. " Guests of the Third Reich." National World War II Museum. Accessed 1/31/22, https://guestsofthethirdreich.org/home/.

86. "Forty-and-Eights." Fandom, Military History. Accessed 1/31/22, https://military-history.fandom.com/wiki/Forty-and-eights.

87. Norman, Calden R. , Marshall Foundation, "Whatever Happened to Company A?," 1991, pp. 84-101, accessed 1/31/22, https://www.marshallfoundation.org/100th-infantry/wp-content/uploads/sites /27/2014/06/Whatever_Happened_to_Company_A_003.pdf.

88. Bard, Mitchell G., Forgotten Victims: the Abandonment of Americans in Hitler's Camps, (CO: Westview Press, 1994), accessed excerpt 1/31/22 athttp://www.indianamilitary.org/German%20PW%20Camps/Prisoner%20of% 20War/PW%20Camps/Stalag%20IX-B%20Bad%20Orb/History.htm.

89. "Mannschafts-Stammlager (Stalag) IX-B." United States Holocaust Memorial Museum. Accessed 1/31/22, https://encyclopedia.ushmm.org/content/en/article/mannschafts-stammlager-st alag-ix-b.

90. "Photographs of Stalag IX-B in Bad Orb, Germany. "Lone Sentry. 2007. Accessed 1/31/22, http://www.lonesentry.com/badorb/.

91. .Memo to Secretary of State from Swiss Legation re: conditions in Stalag IX-B, April 7, 194. Accessed 1/31/22, http://www.lonesentry.com/badorb/document-images/stalag-ixb-document-1a. jpg.

92. Cablegram issued by International Committee of the Red Cross, April 19, 1945. Accessed 1/31/22,

http://www.lonesentry.com/badorb/document-images/stalag-ixb-document-1b.jpg.

93. *"Stalag IX-B,"* Wikipedia, Wikipedia Foundation, 21 December 2021, accessed 1/31/22, https://en.wikipedia.org/wiki/Stalag_IX-B.

94. "Fox Movietone Newsreels The War Years." University of South Carolina Libraries. Accessed 2/1/22, https://digital.library.sc.edu/collections/fox-movietone-news-the-war-years/.

95. Stewart, Phillip W., *"A Reel Story of World War II,"* *Prologue Magazine*, Fall 2015, retrieved from https://www.archives.gov/publications/prologue/2015/fall/united-newsreels.html.

96. "5807 Yanks Land at Boston Pier." *The Springfield Republican*. June 22, 1945. Retrieved from Genealogybank.com.

Chapter 15

97. "Sharon." *Vermont Watchman and State Journal*. December 27, 1882. Retrieved from Newspapers.com.

98. "Marriages." *Vermont Mercury*. September 30, 1842. Retrieved from Newspapers.com.

99. "Sharon." *Vermont Journal*. November 28, 1891. Retrieved from Newspapers.com.

100. "Sharon." *Vermont Journal*. September 15, 1883. Retrieved from Newspapers.com.

101. "West Hartford." *The Manchester Journal*. August 15, 1889. Retrieved from Newspapers.com.

102. West Hartford." *The Landmark*. August 23 Aug 1895. Retrieved from Newspapers.com.

103. "West Hartford." *The Landmark*. November 27, 1891. Retrieved from Newspapers.com.

104. "Sharon." *Spirit of the Age*. January 10, 1883. Retrieved from Newspapers.com.

105. "Sharon Screed." *Argus and Patriot*. August 21, 1895. Retrieved from Newspapers.com.

106. "Sharon Screeds." *Argus and Patriot*. June 18, 1890. Retrieved from Newspapers.com.

107. "Sharon Screeds." *Argus and Patriot*. November 12, 1884. Retrieved from Newspapers.com.

108. Joyce, Ira, 1880 United States Federal Census [database online.] Provo, UT, US: Ancestry.com Operations, Inc. 2012.

109. "Sharon Screeds." *Argus and Patriot*. July 11, 1888. Retrieved from Newspapers.com.

110. "Sharon Screeds." *Argus and Patriot*. August 16, 1893. Retrieved from Newspapers.com.

111. "Sharon Screeds." *Argus and Patriot*. September 20, 1893. Retrieved from Newspapers.com.

112. "Sharon Screeds." *Argus and Patriot.* April 6, 1892. Retrieved from Newspapers.com.
113. "West Hartford." *The Bethel Courier.* November 12, 1908. Retrieved from Newspapers.com.
114. "West Hartford." *The Bethel Courier.* October 15, 1903. Retrieved from Newspapers.com.
115. "West Hartford." *The Bethel Courier.* October 16, 1902. Retrieved from Newspapers.com.
116. "West Hartford." *The Bethel Courier.* May 20, 1909. Retrieved from Newspapers.com.
117. "West Hartford." *The Bethel Courier.* July 23, 1903. Retrieved from Newspapers.com.
118. "West Hartford." *The Bethel Courier.* June 23, 1904. Retrieved from Newspapers.com.
119. "West Hartford." *The Bethel Courier.* September 8, 1910. Retrieved from Newspapers.com.
120. "West Hartford." *The Landmark.* April 1, 1892. Retrieved from Newspapers.com.
121. "West Hartford." *The Landmark.* April12, 1895. Retrieved from Newspapers.com.
122. "West Hartford," *The Landmark.* April 17, 1896. Retrieved from Newspapers.com.
123. "West Hartford." *The Landmark.* February 17, 1893. Retrieved from Newspapers.com.
124. "West Hartford." *The Landmark.* December 2, 1882. Retrieved from Newspapers.com.
125. "West Hartford." *The Landmark.* September 20, 1895. Retrieved from Newspapers.com.
126. "West Hartford." *The Landmark.* November 27, 1891. Retrieved from Newspapers.com.
127. "State News." *The Manchester Journal.* August 15, 1889 Retrieved from Newspapers.com.
128. "Sharon." *The Landmark.* September 19, 1890. Retrieved from Newspapers.com.
129. "Sharon." *The Landmark.* December 27, 1884. Retrieved from Newspapers.com.

Chapter 16

130. Anderson, Mark D., Rees, Daniel I., and Wang, Tianyi, IZA Institute for Labor Economics, *"The Phenomenon of Summer Diarrhea and Its Waning, 1910-1930,"* March 2019, accessed 2/1/22, https://ftp.iza.org/dp12232.pdf.
131. University of Virginia, *"Early Research and Treatment of Tuberculosis in the 19th Century,"* 2007, accessed 2/1/22, http://exhibits.hsl.virginia.edu/alav/tuberculosis/#:~:text=%5B1%5D%20Very%

20few%20recovered.,hope%20for%20an%20active%20life.&text=It%20was%20e
stimated%20that%2C%20at,between%20ages%2015%20and%2044.

132. *A Tuberculosis Directory Containing a List of Institutions, Associations and Other Agencies Dealing with Tuberculosis in the United States and Canada* (United States, The Association, 1916), p. 31, retrieved from https://www.google.com/books/edition/A_Tuberculosis_Directory_Containin g_a_Li/9-4RAAAAYAAJ?hl=en&gbpv=1&dq=Bellevue+Isolation+Hospital+ %22chicopee%22+1910s&pg=PA31&printsec=frontcover.

133. Ponti, Crystal, When New Englanders Blamed Vampires for Tuberculosis Deaths, 28 Oct 2019, accessed 2/1/22, https://www.history.com/news/vampires-tuberculosis-consumption-new-engla nd.

134. "History of World TB Day," Centers for Disease Control and Prevention. December 12, 2016. Accessed 2/1/22, https://www.cdc.gov/tb/worldtbday/history.htm#:~:text=Tuberculosis%20(TB)%20was%20called%20%E2%80%9C,after%20Schonlein%20named%20it%20tub erculosis.

135. "Six Ways to Stop a Vampire," National Geographic, February 22, 2010, retrieved from https://blog.nationalgeographic.org/2010/02/22/six-ways-to-stop-a-vampire/#: ~:text=Decapitate%20and%20Burn%3A%20%E2%80%9CChop%20off,behead% 20and%20burn%20suspected%20vampires.

136. Tucker, Abigail, "The Great New England Vampire Panic," *Smithsonian Magazine*, October 2012, retrieved from https://www.smithsonianmag.com/history/the-great-new-england-vampire-pan ic-36482878/.

137. "History of Diphtheria." The History of Vaccines, an Educational Resource by The College of Physicians of Philadelphia. 2009,. Accessed 2/1/22, https://www.historyofvaccines.org/timeline/diphtheria.

138. "Diphtheria." Museum of Health Care at Kingston. 2022. Accessed 2/1/22, https://www.museumofhealthcare.ca/explore/exhibits/vaccinations/diphtheria. html.

139. Deaths. Vermont Journal. 22 Nov. 1861, p. 8.

140. Alsan, Marcella, and Goldin, Claudia, Watersheds in Infant Mortality: Massachusetts, 1880-1915, 20 Jan 2015, accessed 2/1/22, https://allucgroup.ucdavis.edu/uploads/5/6/8/7/56877229/alsangoldin_waters heds_cg_ma_20jan2015_final.pdf.

141. Manoli-Skocay, Constance, *"A Gentle Death: Tuberculosis in 19th Century Concord,"* 2015, accessed 2/1/22, https://concordlibrary.org/special-collections/essays-on-concord-history/a-gentle -death-tuberculosis-in-19th-century-concord.

142. Barberis, I., Bragazzi, N.L., Galluzzo, L., and Martini, M., "The History of Tuberculosis: from the first historical records to the isolation of Koch's bacillus," *Journal of Preventive Medicine and Hygiene*, March 2017, https://www.ncbi.nlm.nih.gov/pmc/articles/PMC5432783/.

143. Mullin, Emily, *"How Tuberculosis Shaped Victorian Fashion,"* *Smithsonian Magazine*, May 10, 2016, retrieved from

https://www.smithsonianmag.com/science-nature/how-tuberculosis-shaped-vic
torian-fashion-180959029/.

144. Brackemyre, Ted. "Immigrants, Cities, and Disease." U.S. History Scene.
Accessed 2/9/23, https://ushistoryscene.com/article/immigrants-cities-disease/.

Chapter 18

145. "Local and State Matters." *Vermont Journal*. May 21,1864. Retrieved from
Newspapers.com.

146. "Summary of News." *Vermont Phoenix*. January 27, 1865. Retrieved from
Newspapers.com.

147. "West Hartford." *The Landmark*. July 26, 1884. Retrieved from
Newspapers.com..

148. National Public Radio, "The Shipwreck that Led Confederate Soldiers to Risk
All for Union Lives," 27 Apr 2015, 2022, accessed 12/1/22,
https://www.npr.org/2015/04/27/402515205/the-shipwreck-that-led-confeder
ate-veterans-to-risk-all-for-union-lives#:~:text=The%20Sultana%20made%20it%
20only,boilers%20exploding%2C%22%20Potter%20says.&text=Many%20Sultan
a%20survivors%20ended%20up,Confederate%20control%20during%20the%20
war.

149. "News in Brief." *St. Johnsbury Caledonian*. May 5, 1865. Retrieved from
Newspapers.com..

150. "General News Items." *Vermont Journal*. May 20, 1865. Retrieved from
Newspapers.com..

151. "The Andersonville Prison." *Vermont Journal*. July 22, 1865. Retrieved from
Newspapers.com.

152. "The Horrors of Andersonville." *The St. Johnsbury Caledonian*. August 18,
1865. Retrieved from Newspapers.com.

153. "A Vermont Soldier's Recollection of Capt. Wertz." *The Daily Journal*. August
28, 1865. Retrieved from Newspapers.com.

154. "Wirz Trial." *Vermont Christian Messenger*. August 31, 1865. Retrieved from
Newspapers.com.

155. "Capt. Moore's Visit to Andersonville." *Vermont Chronicle*. September 2, 1865.
Retrieved from Newspapers.com.

156. The Trial of Capt. Wirz, Rutland Weekly Herald, 7 Sep 1865, p. 5, retrieved
from Newspapers.com.

157. "The Wirz Trial." *Orleans Independent Standard,*. September 22,1865.
Retrieved from Newspapers.com.

158. "Colonel Walker's Oration." *Vermont Watchman and State Journal*. July
12,1882. Retrieved from Newspapers.com.

159. "West Hartford." *The Landmark*. April 28,1893. Retrieved from
Newspapers.com.

160. "1st Heavy Artillery Stats." *Vermont Standard*. September 19, 1895. Retrieved
from Newspapers.com.

161. "White River Junction." *Burlington Weekly Free Press*. February 21, 1918.
Retrieved from Newspapers.com.

162. "American Civil War Prison Camps," Wikipedia, Wikimedia Foundation, 23 Jan 2022, https://en.wikipedia.org/wiki/American_Civil_War_prison_camps.
163. Hawks, Steve A. "1st Vermont Volunteer Heavy Artillery Regiment." The Civil War in the East. 2022. Accessed 2/1/22, http://civilwarintheeast.com/us-regiments-batteries/vermont/1st-vermont-heavy-artillery-regiment/.
164. Cunningham, Shawn. "The Charter Question: Wentworth, Chandler, and Chester's confounding founding history." The Chester Telegram. November 13, 2013. Retrieved 6/26/2022, https://www.chestertelegraph.org/2013/11/13/the-charter-question-wentworth-chandler-and-chesters-confounding-founding-history/.
165. Aldrich, Lewis C. and Holmes, Frank R. History of Windsor County (Princeton: D. Mason and Company, 1891).

Chapter 19

166. Johnstone, Ken, "Meet Quebec's Most Famous Family," Maclean's, February 1, 1955, retrieved from https://archive.macleans.ca/article/1955/2/1/meet-quebecs-most-famous-family.
167. "Julien Lippé Biography." IMBD. 2022, Accessed 2/1/22, https://www.imdb.com/name/nm0513707/bio?ref_=nm_ov_bio_sm.
168. "Julien Lippé." Binged. 2021. Accessed 2/1/22, https://www.binged.com/person/julien-lippe/.
169. "Julien Lippe." Festival de Cannes. Accessed 2/1/22, https://www.festival-cannes.com/es/artista/julien-lippe.
170. Newton, Hugh S., ed. Canadian Radio Yearbook 1946 Including Who's Who in Canadian Radio, p. 79. (Ottawa: North Miner Press, Ltd. 1945). Accessed 2/1/22, https://worldradiohistory.com/CANADA/Canada-Miscellaneous/Canada-Yearbook-1946.pdf.
171. Ramond, Charles-Henri. "Maudite Galette." La-Film de Denys Arcand. March 2, 2009. Accessed 2/1/22, https://www.filmsquebec.com/films/maudite-galette-denys-arcand/.
172. Nadeau, Daniel. "La maudite galette." Estrie Plus. December 4, 2013. Accessed 2/1/22, http://www.estrieplus.com/contenu--1844-28958.html.
173. "Gilles Carle and la Vrai Nature de Bernadette." Take One. Accessed 2/1/22, http://takeone.athabascau.ca/index.php/takeone/article/viewFile/1041/1028.
174. The Canadian Encyclopedia, La Vrai Nature de Bernadette, 2017, accessed 2/1/22, https://www.thecanadianencyclopedia.ca/en/article/la-vraie-nature-de-bernadette.
175. "Madeleine Carroll, Menjou Star in Final War Loan Show Tonight," The Gazette, March 6, 1942, p.6.
176. Billington, Dave. "There's No Easy Way to Get Films to the People," The Gazette, 25 Sep 1973, p. 22.

177. *"TV Show is Given in French, English,"* Battle Creek Enquirer, 27 Dec 1954, p. 9.

178. *"Meet the Plouffes"* advertisement, Calgary Herald, 20 Oct 1954, p. 16.

179. Skinner, R.J., *"Who's Your Favorite Canadian TV Dad?,"* CBC, 16 Jun 2017, accessed 2/1/22, https://www.cbc.ca/life/wellness/who-s-your-favourite-canadian-tv-dad-1.4164 446.

180. *"Guy Beaulne présente la famille Plouffe,"* Radio Canada Archives, accessed 2/1/22, https://images.radio-canada.ca/v1/ici-info/perso/radioroman-famille-plouffe-gu y-beaulne-archives.jpg.

181. *"Les débuts de La famille Plouffe au petit écran,"* Radio Canada Archives, November 2, 2018, accessed 2/1/22, https://ici.radio-canada.ca/nouvelle/1133293/teleroman-famille-plouffe-family-television-roger-lemelin-archives.

Chapter 20

182. "Laws in Ireland for the Suppression of Popery commonly known as the Penal Laws." Archival Moments. April 12, 2016. Accessed 2/1/22, http://archivalmoments.ca/tag/penal-laws/#:~:text=On%20April%2013%2C%2 01829%20a,a%20Catholic%20to%20do%20anything.

183. "The Existence of Irish Catholic Parish Registers: a Stroke of Luck." 'On a flesh and bone foundation': an Irish history. January 3, 2020. Accessed 2/1/22, http://thesearchforanneandmichael.blogspot.com/2020/01/the-existence-of-iris h-catholic-parish.html.

184. Keenan, Matt. History of Registration in Ireland. Accessed 2/1/22, http://www.mattkeenan.ie/pdf/GRO-History.pdf.

185. Paton, Chris, *Tracing Your Irish Family History on the Internet, A Guide for Family Historians* (United Kingdom, Pen & Sword Books, 2013), Chapter 2, retrieved from https://www.google.com/books/edition/Tracing_Your_Irish_Family_History_ on_the/mWLNDwAAQBAJ?hl=en&gbpv=0.

186. "Some old job titles from the textile industries." Weaste Cemetery Heritage Trail. 2022. Accessed 2/1/22, http://www.weasteheritagetrail.co.uk/Resources/some-old-job-titles-from-the-te xtile-industries/index.htm.

187. Bugbee, Ann, "Recollections of a Mill Worker," *Walloomsock Review*, Vol 12, https://benningtonmuseum.org/library/walloomsack/volume-12/mill-worker-r ecollections-of-a-mill-worker.pdf.

188. *"The* Journey to Ellis Land, New York." Irish Genealogy Toolkit. 2022. Accessed 2/1/22, https://www.irish-genealogy-toolkit.com/journey-to-Ellis-Island.html.

189. Inman Line advertisement, Liverpool Mercury, 27 Apr 1880, p. 4, retrieved from Newspapers.com.

190. Cunard Line advertisement, Liverpool Mercury, 27 Apr 1880, p.n4, retrieved from Newspapers.com.

191. "Latest Items," Sheffield and Rotherham Independent, South Yorkshire, England, 24 May 1880, p. 2, retrieved from Newspapers.com.

192. "Casualties." *Glasgow Herald*. May 27, 1880. Retrieved from Newspapers.com.

193. Lotspeich, Charlie, "Fear of Uniting: Labor Movements in Early Holyoke," *The Public Humanist*, Nov 18, 2009, https://www.hcc.edu/Documents/Library/Events/Union%20History%20in%20Holyoke%20MA.pdf.

194. Strahan, Derek. "Paper Mills, Holyoke, Mass." Lost New England. April 16, 2019. Accessed 2/1/22, https://lostnewengland.com/2019/04/paper-mills-holyoke-mass-2/.

195. "Unions." Creating Holyoke,. 2009. Accessed 2/1/22, http://www.creatingholyoke.org/exhibits/show/industry/unions.

196. Root, Joshua L., "'Something Will Drop': Socialists, Unions, and Trusts in Nineteenth Century Holyoke," *Historical Journal of Massachusetts*, Fall 2009, https://www.westfield.ma.edu/historical-journal/wp-content/uploads/2018/06/Something-Will-Drop-Holyoke-Socialists.pdf.

197. Greenlees, Janet, *"Workplace Health and Gender among Cotton Workers in America and Britain, c. 1880s to 1940s,"* Cambridge University Press, December 5, 2016, https://www.cambridge.org/core/journals/international-review-of-social-history/article/workplace-health-and-gender-among-cotton-workers-in-america-and-britain-c1880s1940s/83203AFE8FF2C75E13491D2DD6887434

198. Dupre, Deb, "Paper Mill Paper Maker Job Description," Chron., 2022, accessed 2/1/22, https://work.chron.com/paper-mill-paper-maker-job-description-25087.html.

199. American Writing Paper Company Records, Historical Note, University of Massachusetts Amherst, 2020, accessed 2/1/22, http://scua.library.umass.edu/american-writing-paper-company/.

200. American Writing Paper Company, Wikipedia, Wikimedia Foundation, 8 Dec 2021, accessed 2/1/22, https://en.wikipedia.org/wiki/American_Writing_Paper_Company.

201. Norway Heritage, "S/S City of Richmond, Inman Line," accessed 2/1/22, http://www.norwayheritage.com/p_ship.asp?sh=ciric.

202. Norway Heritage, "S/S Gallia, Cunard Line," accessed 2/1/22, http://www.norwayheritage.com/p_ship.asp?sh=galli".

203. Gribbon, H.D., *A New History of Ireland, Vol. VI, Ireland Under the Union, II*: 1870-1921 (Oxford, W.E. Vaughn, 2010), p. 271-276, retrieved from https://www.google.com/books/edition/A_New_History_of_Ireland_Volume_VI_Irela/eiiQDwAAQBAJ?hl=en&gbpv=1.

204. Flanagan, Mackenzie S., *"Irish Women's Immigration to the United States after the Potato Famine, 1860-1900,"* 2015, Senior Theses. 42, pp. 13-21, accessed 2/1/22, https://scholar.dominican.edu/cgi/viewcontent.cgi?article=1051&context=senior-theses.

205. Holyoake, George Jacobs. Among the Americans and a Stranger in America. Chicago:b Belford, Clark, & Co., 1881.

206. Santry, Claire. "An Irish Wake for the Living: American Wake." Ireland XO. May 11, 2022. Accessed 5/11/22, https://irelandxo.com/ireland-xo/news/irish-wake-living-american-wake?utm_medium=email&utm_source=emfluence&utm_campaign=American_wake.

207. LeLoudis, James and Walbert, Katherine. "Work in a Textile Mill." Anchor. November 13, 2018. Accessed 5/14/22, https://www.ncpedia.org/anchor/work-textile-mill.

208. O'Brien, Martin, 1920 United States Federal Census [database online.] Provo, UT, US: Ancestry.com Operations, Inc. 2012.

209. Voices of Holyoke's Past, Present, and Future. 2009. Accessed 6/17/2022, http://www.creatingholyoke.org/exhibits/show/industry/textile.

210. McGrath, Thomas. "Education: Primary Public Education-National Schools from 1831." Encyclopedia.com. Accessed 2/19/2023, https://www.encyclopedia.com/international/encyclopedias-almanacs-transcripts-and-maps/education-primary-public-education-national-schools-1831.

211. Education in Ireland in the 19th Century. Twinkl.com. Accessed 2/19/2023, https://www.twinkl.com/teaching-wiki/education-in-ireland-in-the-19th-century.

212. Educational History: the Hedge Schools of Ireland. Ragged University. 2022. https://raggeduniversity.co.uk/2017/01/02/history-hedge-schools-of-ireland/.

Chapter 22

213. Anne Hélène Ducharme Tetreau, "BMS 2000," database, \i www.bms2000.org\i0, Centre de généalogie francophone d'Amérique, www.bms2000.org : 2018).

214. Téreault, Josée, "Louis Tétreau, from Tessonière to Trous-Rivières" Association des descendants de Louis Tétreau, accessed 2/2/22, http://tetreaultgenealogie.com/louis-tetreau-from-tessonniere-to-trois-rivieres-by-josee-tetreault.html.

215. "Genealogy Louis Tétreau." Nos Origines. 2022, accessed 2/2/22, https://www.nosorigines.qc.ca/genealogieQuebec.aspx?name=Louis_Tetreault&pid=39275&lng=en.

216. Tetreault, Roland J., The Story of Louis Tetreau (Springfield, MA, 2000), pp. 3-4, 6-8, 15-21, 27-28, 45-49, 73, and 80-81.

217. Louis Tetreau History, accessed 2/2/22, 2002, https://cheysmom.tripod.com/louistetreau.html.

218. Tetreault, Roland J., A Tetreault Family History (10 Generations) (Springfield, MA, 2005), retrieved from https://www.google.com/books/edition/A_New_History_of_Ireland_Volume_VI_Irela/eiiQDwAAQBAJ?hl=en&gbpv=1.

219. "Acadian Colonists' Origins." Acadian-Cajun Genealogy & History. 1999. Accessed 2/2/22, https://www.acadian-cajun.com/colorig.htm.

220. "Louis XIV, Sun King." Very Beautiful. Accessed 2/2/22, https://vb.com/louisxiv/.

221. Popkin, Prof. Jeremy. "The Reign of Louis XIV (1643-1715): an Overview." University of Kentucky. *Accessed* 2/2/22, http://www.uky.edu/~popkin/540syl2007/540%20Louis%20XIV%20handout.htm.

222. Mieszkowski, Katherine, "The filthy stinking truth," *Salon*, Nov 30, 2007, https://www.salon.com/2007/11/30/dirt_on_clean/.

223. Major, Charles, *The Little King,: a Story of the Childhood of Louis XIV, King of France*, (Palala Press, 2015).

224. "Proteus and Hyacinth," Wikipedia. Wikimedia Foundation, 20 Jul 2022, https://en.wikipedia.org/wiki/Protus_and_Hyacinth.

225. "Hyacinth of Caesarea," Wikipedia, Wikimedia Foundation, 2 Aug 2022, https://en.wikipedia.org/wiki/Hyacinth_of_Caesarea.

Chapter 23

226. "Meet Dwight." Moody Bible Institute. 2021. Accessed 7/29/22, https://www.moody.edu/about/our-bold-legacy/d-l-moody/.

227. "History." NMH. 2021. Accessed 7/29/22, https://www.nmhschool.org/about/history#:~:text=Northfield%20Mount%20Hermon%20was%20founded,education%20because%20they%20were%20poor.

228. *"Northfield Mount Hermon School,"* Wikipedia, Wikipedia Foundation, 5 June 2022, accessed 7/29/22, https://en.wikipedia.org/wiki/Northfield_Mount_Hermon_School.

229. *"French King Bridge,"* Wikipedia, Wikipedia Foundation, 4 July 2022, accessed 7/29/22, https://en.wikipedia.org/wiki/French_King_Bridge.

230. "Ely Dedicates New Bridge Before Immense Gathering." *The North Adams Transcript*. September 15, 1932. Retrieved from Newspapers.com.

231. Gill: Town Meeting Grants Sum of $48.748." *Springfield Republican*. March 15, 1944. Retrieved from Genealogybank.com.

232. "Charles Otis Bruce Is Dead at Age of 70." *Springfield Republican*. November 21, 1940. Retrieved from Genealogybank.

233. "Town Meeting at Gill Praises Charles O. Bruce." *Springfield Republican*. March 12, 1939. Retrieved from Genealogybank.com.

234. "Gill." *Springfield Republican*. September 22, 1915. Retrieved from Genealogybank.com.

235. "Commonwealth of Massachusetts, Town of Gill, Notice to Contractors." *The Boston Globe*. July 25, 1925. Retrieved from Newspapers.com.

236. "Gill." *The North Adams Transcript*. September 23, 1933. Retrieved from Newspapers.com.

237. Stoughton, Ralph M. *History of the Town of Gill, Massachusetts, 1793-1943*. United States: R.M. Stoughton, 1950.

238. "Rigid Rules Removed." *The Plain Dealer*. October 14, 1898. Retrieved from Genealogybank.com.

239. "Representatives of 18 Towns at Highway Hearing." *Springfield Republican*. September 24, 1932. Retrieved from Genealogybank.com.

240. Mendoza, Julian. "Gill Historical Commission Looks to Ensure Severance House Preservation." *Greenfield Recorder*. February 1, 2023. Accessed 2/13/2023 https://www.recorder.com/Gill-Historical-Commission-looks-to-ensure-Severance-House-preservation-49741940.

Chapter 24

241. Landowski, Robert F. (2021, 5 Aug). Robert Landowski to Maria Acosta, August 5, 2021 [letter].
242. Obituary, Timothy D. Daley, *Chicago Tribune*, 31 Jul 1916, p. 11.
243. "Policeman is Shot to Death; Laid to Bandit." *Chicago Tribune*. June 27, 1926. Retrieved from Newspapers.com.
244. "Grill Six but Find No Clews in Police Killing." *Chicago Tribune*. June 28, 1926. Retrieved from Newspapers.com.
245. "Quiz Street Car Men in Death of Policeman." *Herald and Review*. June 28, 1926. Retrieved from Newspapers.com.
246. Homicide file for P Daley [redacted], Part I, Chicago Police Dept., Report #2344, 27 Jun 1926.
247. Homicide file for P Daley [redacted], Part II, Chicago Police Dept., Report #2344, 27 Jun 1926.
248. Police Department City of Chicago Annual Report, Year Ending December 31, 1926, p. 10.

Chapter 25

249. Thale, Christopher. "Railroad Workers." Encyclopedia of Chicago. 2004. Accessed 2/2/22, http://www.encyclopedia.chicagohistory.org/pages/1038.html.
250. Hudson, John C. "Railroads." Encyclopedia of Chicago. 2004. Accessed 2/2/22, http://www.encyclopedia.chicagohistory.org/pages/1039.html.
251. Smithsonian National Museum of American History, "Chicago, the Transit Metropolis," accessed 2/2/22, https://americanhistory.si.edu/america-on-the-move/essays/chicago-transit-metropolis#:~:text=By%201900%20there%20were%20at,stops%2C%20equipment%2C%20and%20fares.
252. Smithsonian National Museum of Locomotive History, "Locomotive Engineer," accessed 2/2/22, https://americanhistory.si.edu/america-on-the-move/lives-railroad.
253. "The Olympian," Wikipedia, Wikipedia Foundation, 20 Jan 22, accessed 2/2/22, https://en.wikipedia.org/wiki/The_Olympian.
254. "Milwaukee Road Employees Involved in ICC Reportable Accidents, 1911-1940," accessed 2/2/22, http://freepages.rootsweb.com/~sponholz/genealogy/iccpart01.html.

255. The Milwaukee Road Magazine, Vol 41, No. 11, February 1954, accessed 2/2/22, https://milwaukeeroadarchives.com/MilwaukeeRoadMagazine/1954February.pdf.

256. "Marion Zioncheck," Wikipedia, Wikimedia Foundation, 21 Jan 2022, accessed 2/2/22, https://en.wikipedia.org/wiki/Marion_Zioncheck.

257. "Race on the Rails." *Chicago Tribune*. March 11, 1895. Retrieved from Newspapers.com.

258. Milwaukee Road advertisement, Fayette County Leader, 20 Oct 1938, p. 4.

259. "Railroad Men Attend Final Rites for 100-Year-Old Veteran." *The Journal-Times*. February 8, 1938. Retrieved from Newspapers.com.

260. "Muscatine Man, Dragged from Beneath Wheels of Freight Train Three Times, Is Sent to Jail for Thirty Day Term." *The Daily Times*. March 4, 1938. Retrieved from Newspapers.com.

261. Kennealy death notice. *Chicago Tribune*. August 29, 1907. Retrieved from Newspapers.com.

262. "Crippled Children Go to Wisconsin Camp for Summer." *Chicago Tribune*. July 7, 1932. Retrieved from Newspapers.com.

263. "Man KKilled (sic) at Dells as He Jumps Before Train." *The Capital Times*. July 29, 1936. Retrieved from Newspapers.com.

264. "Executive Dies When Auto Hits Freight Train." *Chicago Tribune*. January 11, 1940. Retrieved from Newspapers.com.

265. "14-year olds from Kellogg and Hastings Taken off Freight Train Here." *La Crosse Tribune*. July 28, 1924. Retrieved from Newspapers.com.

266. "Killed Hitching Ride." *Kenosha News*. August 12, 1927. Retrieved from Newspapers.com.

267. "Man Is Killed in Fall from Train West of Buffalo." *The Daily Times*. September 30, 1937. Retrieved from Newspapers.com.

268. "Trouble Shooting Robot Car Spots Rail Flaws and Averts Accidents." *Chicago Tribune*. September 16, 1934. Retrieved from Newspapers.com.

269. Lionel toy train advertisement, "Chicago Tribune," 6 Dec 1931, p. 92, retrieved from Newspapers.com.

270. "He Gets Train West After a Dizzying Evening." *Chicago Tribune*. July 1, 1936. Retrieved from Newspapers.com.

271. "Berwyn Man Killed by Belt Line Freight." *Berwyn Life*. October 13, 1936. Retrieved from Newspapers.com.

272. "Roosevelt Due Tomorrow; Plan Demonstration." *Chicago Tribune*. September 29, 1932. Retrieved from Newspapers.com.

273. Photo. "Engineer Killed, 15 Injured, When Train Is Ditched." *Chicago Tribune*. July 7, 1932. Retrieved from Newspapers.com.

274. "City Welcomes Famous Flyers to Races Today." *Chicago Tribune*. August 21, 1930. Retrieved from Newspapers.com.

275. "3 Travel Events of Importance Set for Today." *Chicago Tribune*. May 29, 1935. Retrieved from Newspapers.com.

276. "Alaskan Bishop." *Chicago Tribune*. August 14, 1937. Retrieved from Newspapers.com.

277. "Race on the Rails." *Chicago Tribune*. March 11, 1895. Retrieved from Newspapers.com.
278. "Wreck on Milwaukee Road." *Davenport Morning Star*. August 7, 1902. Retrieved from Newspapers.com.
279. "Driver Is Killed in Summit When Train Hits Auto." *Chicago Tribune*. October 14, 1936. Retrieved from Newspapers.com.
280. "Milk Truck Hit by Fast Train; 1 Killed, 1 Hurt." *Chicago Tribune*. November 6, 1928. Retrieved from Newspapers.com.
281. "Body Found on Tracks." *Chicago Tribune*. January 31, 1930. Retrieved from Newspapers.com.
282. "Ceremonies Start New Florida Train on Its Maiden Trip." *Chicago Tribune*. January 3, 1935. Retrieved from Newspapers.com.
283. "Chicago Cool, as Heat Bakes Its Neighbors." *Chicago Tribune*. June 28, 1931. Retrieved from Newspapers.com.

Chapter 26

284. Stranahan, Susan Q., "The Eastland Disaster Killed More Passengers than the Titanic and the Lusitania. Why Has It Been Forgotten?" *Smithsonian Magazine*, October 27, 2014, https://www.smithsonianmag.com/history/eastland-disaster-killed-more-passengers-titanic-and-lusitania-why-has-it-been-forgotten-180953146/.
285. "The History Chicago Police Department." Eastland Disaster Historical Society. 2022. Accessed 2/2/22, https://eastlanddisaster.org/history/chicago-police-dept/#:~:text=The%20Chicago%20Police%20Department%20was,maintain%20control%20of%20the%20crowds.
286. Cooke, Judy. Iroquois Theatre. 2022. Accessed 2/2/22, http://www.iroquoistheater.com/chicago-police-chief-francis-oneill-iroquois-theater.php.
287. Survivors and Rescuers, *Lest We Forget, Chicago's Awful Theatre Horror* (Memorial Publishing Company), retrieved from http://moses.law.umn.edu/darrow/documents/Theater%20Horr%20ALL.pdf.
288. *Report of the General Superintendent of Police of the City of Chicago to the City Council for the Fiscal Year Ending December 31, 1903* (Chicago, Department of Police, 1904), retrieved from https://www.chicagocop.com/wp-content/uploads/Chicago-Police-Department-Annual-Report-1903.pdf.
289. Thale, Christopher. "Police." Encyclopedia of Chicago History. 2004. Accessed 2/2/22, http://www.encyclopedia.chicagohistory.org/pages/983.html.
290. "Ran into a Snow Bank." *The Chicago Chronicle*. November 28, 1895. Retrieved from Newspapers.com.
291. "Sentenced to Death." *Fitchburg Sentinel*. June 29, 1909. Retrieved from Genealogybank.com.
292. "Napoleon Monat Must Die." *Buffalo Evening News*. June 29, 1909. Retrieved from Genealogybank.com.

293. "Found Guilty of Murder." *Asbury Park Press.* January 29, 1909. Retrieved from Genealogybank.com.

294. "Napoleon Monat on Trial for His Life." *Poughkeepsie Daily Eagle.* January 24, 1909. Retrieved from Genealogybank.com.

295. "Monat Must Die in Fatal Chair," Star-Gazette, 29 Jan 1909, p. 1, retrieved from Genealogybank.com.

296. "Saved from Electric Chair." *New York Times.* February 15, 1911. Retrieved from Genealogybank.com.

297. "Gleanings in Local Fields." *Chicago Tribune.* August 28, 1889. Retrieved from Newspapers.com.

298. "A Policeman's Imagination." *The Inter Ocean.* August 28, 1889. Retrieved from Newspapers.com.

299. "History." Chicago Police Department. 2022. Accessed 2/2/22, https://home.chicagopolice.org/about/history/.

300. "Daley." *Chicago Daily News.* August 1, 1916. Retrieved from GenealogyBank.com.

301. "Say Foreigners Insulted Women." *Chicago Tribune.* August 25, 1910. Retrieved from Newspapers.com.

302. Skilling, Tim. "What is the Hottest Day on Record in Chicago?" WGN9 News. June 13, 2022. https://wgntv.com/weather/weather-blog/ask-tom-why/what-is-the-hottest-day-on-record-in-chicago/#:~:text=Using%20average%20daily%20temperatures%20a s,the%20full%2024%2Dhour%20period.

Chapter 28

303. "The Firies Disturbance." *Freeman's Journal.* February 1, 1886. Retrieved from Newspapers.com.

304. "Snowstorms through the centuries: A history of Irish cold snaps," the Irish Times, 26 Feb 2018, accessed 2/2/22, https://www.irishtimes.com/news/ireland/irish-news/snowstorms-through-the-centuries-a-history-of-irish-cold-snaps-1.3406525.

305. "Everything you ever wanted to know about snow in Ireland." *The Journal.* December 25, 2012, retrieved from https://www.thejournal.ie/snow-ireland-facts-723323-Dec2012/.

306. Diocese of Kerry, "History," accessed 2/4/22, https://www.dioceseofkerry.ie/our-diocese/genealogy/history/.

307. "Ku Klux Klan," Wikipedia, Wikimedia Foundation, 4 Feb 22, accessed 2/4/22, https://en.wikipedia.org/wiki/Ku_Klux_Klan.

308. "Fatal Affray with Moonlighters in Ireland." *The Lancaster Gazette.* November 21, 1885. Retrieved from Newspapers.com.

309. Thomas, Holly,. "The original rebels: Ireland's infamous whiteboys." Irish Central. July 5, 2016,. Accessed 2/5/22, https://www.irishcentral.com/roots/genealogy/the-original-rebels-irelands-infa mous-whiteboys?fbclid=IwAR2K9uzUVqF3XoLZMXAK_-BQ5eYSVFlHS3f T17qpUKHZJX0ZFFmpKxo21UE.

310. "Terrible Tragedy in Kerry." *The Freeman's Journal*. November 19, 1885. Retrieved from Newspapers.com.

311. "The Castlefarm Tragedy." *The Freeman's Journal*. December 22, 1885. Retrieved from Newspapers.com.

312. "The Castlefarm Tragedy, Important Statement by Judge O'Brien." *The Freeman's Journal*. December 24, 1885. Retrieved from Newspapers.com.

313. "The Curtin Family." *The Freeman's Journal*. January 25, 1886. Retrieved from Newspapers.com.

314. "The Firies Disturbances." *The Freeman's Journal*. February 3, 1886. Retrieved from Newspapers.com.

315. "The Curtin Family." *The Freeman's Journal*. March 13, 1886. Retrieved from Newspapers.com.

316. "Firies Chapel." *The Freeman's Journal*. March 26, 1886. Retrieved from Newspapers.com.

317. "Sale of Mrs. O'Connell Curtin's Holding at Castlefarm." *The Freeman's Journal*. January 25,1887. Retrieved from Newspapers.com.

318. "The Judicial Commission on the 'Times' Charges." *The Freeman's Journal*. November 22, 1888. Retrieved from Newspapers.com.

319. "The Boycotting of the Curtin Family." *The Freeman's Journal*. April 11, 1888. Retrieved from Newspapers.com.

320. "The Judicial Commission on the 'Times' Charges." *The Freeman's Journal*. November 30, 1888. Retrieved from Newspapers.com.

321. "The 'Times' Commission." *The Freeman's Journal*. April 11, 1889. Retrieved from Newspapers.com.

322. General Register of Prisoners, Cork Gaol, p. 754.

323. "Land Issues." Maggie Blanck. October 2015. Accessed 2/5/22, http://www.maggieblanck.com/Mayopages/LandIssues.html?fbclid=IwAR2yp wvaWPAzom_XU4xDAUNyisBqxBGUUlLNAQ5x2ntL26rUxjUamXCmjW U.

324. Dorney, John. "Today in Irish History: the Fenian Rebellion, March 5, 1867,. The Irish Story. Accessed 2/5/22, https://www.theirishstory.com/2011/03/05/today-in-irish-history-%E2%80%93 the-fenian-rebellion-march-5-1867/?fbclid=IwAR1dBjmmX69jvD8U5EWwnF GC1R65EKIYgZiVzRBJBdPcjSuQokpTBBUcKPg#.Yf7pq-7MJQJ.

325. Cusack, Margaret Anne, *White Boys, An Illustrated History of Ireland* (Ireland, 1868), Ch. XXXIV, retrieved from https://www.libraryireland.com/HistoryIreland/Whiteboys.php?fbclid=IwAR 0prO9nQAsuDY8H-_p4ZKdfSpM0Ibj1ec_yK6SPfa5D3oaGvXwrHOuC3ww .

326. "Land War," Wikipedia, Wikimedia Foundation, 31 Jan 2022, accessed 2/5/22, https://en.wikipedia.org/wiki/Land_War.

327. Joyce, R.B. Head Constable. "Moonlighting in Kerry in the Eighties– Murder of John O'Connell Curtin of Castlefarm– in Two Part's (sic)." The Royal Irish Constabulary Forum. February 1912. Posted April 23, 2014. https://irishconstabulary.com/moonlighting-in-kerry-in-the-eighties-murder-of-mr-t1735.html.

328. Fitzmaurice, George, *Five Plays by George Fitzmaurice: The Country Dressmaker, The Moonlighter, The Pie-dish, The Magic Glasses, The Dandy Dolls* (London and Dublin, 1914), p. 79.

329. Breathnach, Ciara and Geary, Laurence M., "Crime and Punishment: Whiteboyism and the Law in Late Nineteenth-Century Ireland," 2017, https://ulir.ul.ie/bitstream/handle/10344/9429/Breathnach_Geary_2017_Whiteboyism.pdf?sequence=1

330. "Daniel Daly, male prisoner number C-42." National Archives of Ireland. Accessed 2/5/22, https://www.nationalarchives.ie/search-the-online-catalogue/advanced-search/#!/details/111143009.

331. Parnellism and Crime: Evidence of Mr. E. Harrington, Mr. T.P. O'Connor, &c," reprinted from the Times, London, Harvard University, 1890, pp. 188-200.

332. "The system of penal servitude in Ireland." *The Sydney Morning Herald* July 30, 1856. Retrieved from Newspapers.com.

333. Howlin, Dr. Níamh, "Controlling Jury Composition in Nineteenth Century Ireland," *The Journal of Legal History*, December 2, 2009, pp. 227-261.

334. Zimmermann, Georges D., Songs of Irish Rebellion, pp. 278-288, via Feeley, Pat, "Moonlight Attack on Curtin's House," Songs of Agrarian Strife, pp. 10-11, accessed 2/5/22, http://fkancestry.com/wp-content/uploads/2016/08/SongsAgragrianStrife.pdf.

335. O'Donohoe, Michael. "Moonlighters in Castleisland." Retrieved from Castleisland District Heritage. 2015,. Accessed 2/5/22, http://www.odonohoearchive.com/the-moonlighters-in-castleisland/.

336. Lucey, Donnacha Sean. The Irish National League and Moonlighters. Land, Popular Politics, and Agrarian Violence in Ireland. Dublin: University College Dublin Press, 2015.

337. "The Kerry Moonlight Raid," *Dublin Daily Express*, December 22, 1885. Retrieved from Newspapers.com.

338. *Weekly Irish Times*, December 26, 1885. Retrieved from Newspapers.com.

339. "Moonlighters Sentenced to Penal Servitude." *The Leeds Mercury*. December 22, 1885. Retrieved from Newspapers.com.

340. "Evictions on Lord Kenmare's Estate." *The Irish Times*. January 8, 1886. Retrieved from Newspapers.com.

341. "Terrible Tragedy in County Kerry." *The Freeman's Journal*. November 16, 1885. Retrieved from Newspapers.com.

342. "Evictions in Kerry." *The Freeman's Journal*. March 19, 1886. Retrieved from Newspapers.com.

343. The National Archives of Ireland; Dublin, Ireland; CSPS 1/5318-5410. Ireland, Petty Session Court Registers, 1818-1819. Ancestry.com. Ancestry.com Operations, Inc. Lehi, Utah. 2020.

344. "Attempted Suicide in Courthouse." *The Devon and Exeter Daily Gazette*. December 17, 1885. Retrieved from Newspapers.com.

345. Daly, Daniel, 1910 United States Federal Census [database online.] Provo, UT, US: Ancestry.com Operations, Inc. 2012.

346. Ancestry.com, *Ireland, Catholic Parish Registers*, 1655-1915, Timothei Daly, Kerry, Molahiff, 1830-1872, [database on-line]. Provo, UT, USA: Ancestry.com Operations, Inc., 2016.

347. Daniel Daly, Ireland Census 1901, Ancestry.com Operations, Inc., 2013 Provo, UT

348. Timothy Daly, Ireland Census, 1901, Ancestry.com Operations, Inc. 2013, Provo, UT

349. Daniel Daley Death Record, https://civilrecords.irishgenealogy.ie/churchrecords/images/deaths_returns/deaths_1907/05535/4551616.pdf

350. Elizabeth Browne Daly Death Record, https://civilrecords.irishgenealogy.ie/churchrecords/images/deaths_returns/deaths_1907/05535/4551616.pdf.

351. "Around the Districts: Farranfore-Firies to Kenmare." *Independent.ie.* November 24, 2021. Accessed 6/30/2022, https://www.independent.ie/regionals/kerryman/south-kerry-news/local-notes/around-the-districts-farranfore-firies-to-kenmare-41082247.html.

352. "Knockaderry Townland, Co. Kerry." Townlands.ie. April 24, 2022. Accessed 6/30/2022, https://www.townlands.ie/kerry/magunihy/molahiffe/molahiffe/knockaderry/.

353. Letter from David C. Dunbar and James H. Wallis. Saints by the Sea. April 26, 1881. https://saintsbysea.lib.byu.edu/mii/account/1499. Accessed11/6/2022.

Chapter 30

354. Anxcestry.com, Ireland Catholic Parish Registers, 1655-1915, Honora Daly, Kerry, Molahiff, Ireland, 2016, Provo, UT

355. Nora Daly death certification, https://civilrecords.irishgenealogy.ie/churchrecords/images/deaths_returns/deaths_1928/04945/4344330.pdf

356. National Archives of Ireland, 1901 Census, Daniel Daly, House 18, http://www.census.nationalarchives.ie/pages/1901/Kerry/Molahiffe/Knockaderry/.

357. National Archives of Ireland, 1902 Census, Timothy Daly, House 17, http://www.census.nationalarchives.ie/pages/1901/Kerry/Molahiffe/Knockaderry/.

358. Caball, Kay. "Born in Kerry?" My Kerry Ancestors. July 20, 2920. Accessed 10/29/22, https://mykerryancestors.com/born-in-kerry/.

359. "The Bummer's Carnival." *The Chicago Tribune*. April 2, 1873. Retrieved from Newspapers.com.

360. "Fire and Explosion." *The Chicago Tribune*. July 5, 1893. Retrieved from Newspapers.com.

361. "The Drunken Assailant is Caught by the Police and Quickly Lodged in a Station House–Crime Takes Place in Hussey's Barroom, No. 140 North Sangamon Street–the Victim Is Removed to the Presbyterian Hospital, Where Physicians Pronounce the Injuries Mortal." *The Chicago Tribune*. January 26, 1894. Retrieved from Newspapers.com.

362. "To Come Before the Trial Board." *The Chicago Tribune*. January 4, 1893. Retrieved from Newspapers.com.

363. "Close Turf Contests." *The Inter Ocean*. March 31, 1887. Retrieved from Newspapers.com..

364. "The Turf." *The Inter Ocean*. July 23, 1886. Retrieved from Newspapers.com.

365. Melendy, Royal L., "The Saloon in Chicago." American Journal of Sociology. Vol. 6, No. 3. November 1900, pp. 289-306.

Chapter 33

366. "United States World War I Draft Registration Cards, 1917-1918," database with images, Family Search (https://familysearch.org/ark:/61093/3:1:33SQ-GB5LZ1K?cc=9FHC-2NL%3A928311301%2C928317401 : 24 August 2019), Massachusetts> Holyoke City no 2; H-Z > image 2253 of 4699; citing NARA microfilm publication M1509 (Washington, D.C.: National Archives and Records Administration, n.d.).

367. "Massachusetts Marriages, 1841-1915," database with images, *FamilySearch* (https://familysearch.org/ark:/61903/3:1:3Q9M-C9BD-9STW-L?cc=1469062 : 28 November 2018), > image 1 of 1; State Archives, Boston.

Epilogue

368. "Magistrate's Court." *New Zealand Times*. December 12, 1914. Page 11. Retrieved from Papers Past.

369. "Magistrate's Court." *New Zealand Times*. April 25, 1919. Page 8. Retrieved from Papers Past.

370. "Magistrate's Court." *New Zealand Times*. July 18,1896. Page 3. Retrieved from Papers Past.

371. "Magistrate's Court." *New Zealand Times*. April 19, 1911. Page 4. Retrieved from Papers Past.

372. *Dominion*. April 19 , 1911. Page 3. Retrieved from Papers Past.

373. "Magistrate's Court." *New Zealand Times*. February 18, 1885. Page 3. Retrieved from Papers Past.

374. "Magistrate's Court." *Evening Post*. October 28, 1885. Page 3. Retrieved from Papers Past.

375. "Magistrate's Court." *Evening Post*. January 12, 1900. Page 6. Retrieved from Papers Past.

376. *Dominion*. June 28, 1910. Page 9. Retrieved from Papers Past.

377. *New Zealand Mail*. January 3, 1891. Page 17. Retrieved from Papers Past.

378. "Magistrate's Court." *New Zealand Times*. June 2, 1904. Page 6. Retrieved from Papers Past..

379. "Magistrate's Court." *New Zealand Times*. September 25, 1914. Page 10. Retrieved from Papers Past.

380. *Evening Post*. January 9, 1889. Page 2. Retrieved from Papers Past.

381. "Magistrate's Court." *Evening Post*. April 24, 1919. Page 6. Retrieved from Papers Past.

382. Dominion. November 8, 1913. Page 7. Retrieved from Papers Past.

383. "Magistrate's Court." *Evening Post*. November 21, 1988. Page 2. Retrieved from Papers Past.

384. "Magistrate's Court." *New Zealand Times*. April 19, 1911. Page 4. Retrieved from Papers Past.

385. "Odds and Ends from Wellington." *Press*. November 8, 1913. Page 12. Retrieved from Papers Past.

386. "Magistrate's Court." *Evening Post*. May 14, 1887. Page 2. Retrieved from Papers Past.

387. "Coffin Ships: Death and Pestilence on the Atlantic." Irish Genealogy TOOLKIT. 2022. Accessed 11/11/22. https://www.irish-genealogy-toolkit.com/coffin-ships.html.

388. Irish American Journey. 2013. Accessed 11/11/22. http://www.irishamericanjourney.com/2011/10/irish-ships-to-america.html

389. "The Irish Emigrants' Guide to Surviving the Irish Famine Ships." New England Historical Society. 2021. Accessed 11/11/22. https://www.newenglandhistoricalsociety.com/irish-emigrants-guide-to-surviving-the-irish-famine-ships/.

390. Laxton, Edward. *The Famine Ships: the Irish Exodus to America*. (New York: Henry Holt and Co.) 1997.

391. George Rogers Taylor, *The Transportation Revolution, 1815-1860*, 110. (New York: Routledge.) 2015.

392. Advertisement. *Boston Pilot*. April 15, 185. Page 7.

393. Pedersen, Ellen-Marie. "Diseases and Conditions Aboard Coffin Ships." Star of the Sea: a Postcolonial/Postmodern Voyage into the Irish Famine. 4/15/2016. Accessed 11/11/22, https://scalar.usc.edu/works/star-of-the-sea-a-postcolonialpostmodern-voyage-into-the-irish-famine/conditions-on-coffin-ships.

394. The Irish Potato Famine. History.com. August 9, 2022. Accessed 11/12/2022, https://www.history.com/topics/immigration/irish-potato-famine.

395. Ireland's Great Famine. EH.net. Accessed 11/12/2022, https://eh.net/encyclopedia/irelands-great-famine/.

396. Famine and Emigration. County Kerry webpage. Accessed 11/12/2022, https://www.igp-web.com/Kerry/famemig.html.

397. Cooper, Pen. "Before There Was Plumbing, These Men Discreetly Got Rid of Human Waste." History Daily. 4/10/2016. Accessed 12/12/2022, https://historydaily.org/night-soil-men.

398. Pōneke, Me Heke Ki. Absolutely, Positively Wellington City Council. Accessed 1/1/2023,

https://wellington.govt.nz/wellington-city/about-wellington-city/history/histor y-of-wellington/1865-1890.

399. A History of New Zealand 1769-1914. New Zealand History. July 13, 2020. Accessed 1/1/2023, https://nzhistory.govt.nz/culture/history-of-new-zealand-1769-1914.

400. "Browne, Viscount Kenmare." Humphrys Genealogy. 2023. Accessed 1/6/2023, https://humphrysfamilytree.com/ORahilly/browne.viscount.html.

401. "Aodogan ó Rathaille." Humphrys Genealogy. 2023. Accessed 1/6/2023, https://humphrysfamilytree.com/ORahilly/poet.html#dineen.odonoghue.

402. Lalor, James F., "Mr. Lalor's Letter [to the Editor]." *The Irish Felon*. July 24, 1828, pages 9-10. Retrieved from Newspapers.com.

NAME INDEX

NAME

PAGE

Julia Daly Dunn, granddaughter of
Elizabeth Browne and Daniel Daly.

Batt Daly, right, and family members at the Daly residence in Knockaderry, 1969.

ABOUT THE AUTHOR

Carol is currently taking a course in Advanced Snark in preparation for her next writing adventure. A writer and attorney who has been solving genealogical puzzles for more than three decades, she often mentors less-experienced researchers. She's mom to three wonderful humans and four madcap felines. Some of her writing awards include Yahoo! Outstanding Contributor of the Year 2012 and Contributor Content of the Year 2013 and People's Media Award for Best Article 2008. Things she loves: Ireland, Broadway musicals, cats, ice cream, and travel. Things she isn't fond of: authoritarian governments and lumpy mashed potatoes whose choke-precipitating capacity is on par with that of the Boston Strangler.

www.carolbenglegilbert.com

Made in the USA
Middletown, DE
06 May 2023